Superheroes!

'Like a modern Gulliver, she brings back news of other worlds, of marvellous utopias and dystopias, in order to throw light on the one we live in – or think we live in. Roz Kaveney's knowledge is awesome, her analysis passionate: this is a work of eloquent advocacy, urging readers to pay more attention to a crucial arena where ideas about men, women, virtue, and power are discussed - and formed.' – **Marina Warner**

'Combines a command of literary theory with a hands-on grasp of how pop fiction gets built by producers and used by readers. Indispensable.' – **Geoff Ryman**

'Roz Kaveney writes about the superhero myths with intelligence and love, from the inside, without the lofty alienation that says these texts are interesting but too dumb to know it. This book should be on the shelf of every comics fan, and proves that everyone should be a comics fan.' – **Paul Cornell**

ROZ KAVENEY

Superheroes!

Capes and Crusaders in Comics and Films

I.B. TAURIS

LONDON · NEW YORK

Published in 2008 by I.B. Tauris & Co Ltd
6 Salem Road, London W2 4BU
175 Fifth Avenue, New York NY 10010
www.ibtauris.com

In the United States of America and Canada
distributed by Palgrave Macmillan, a division of St Martin's Press
175 Fifth Avenue, New York NY 10010

ISBN 978 1 84511 569 2

A full CIP record for this book is available from the British Library
A full CIP record is available from the Library of Congress

Library of Congress Catalog Card Number: available

Typeset by JCS Publishing Services, www.jcs-publishing.co.uk
Printed and bound in Great Britain by TJ International Ltd, Padstow, Cornwall.

This is for John M. Ford and for Jane

Contents

Acknowledgements

My special and particular thanks are due to Rob Hansen for spotting many factual errors in my various drafts, for pulling out vast numbers of individual comics that I needed to see in order to develop my arguments and for having me round once a week to go through a selection of the week's new comics. He bears no responsibility for those errors in which I persisted. It is no exaggeration to say that I could not have written this book without his constant help and advice; I also owe him and Avedon Carol endless amounts of hospitality in the shape of cups of coffee, mozzarella-and-tomato sandwiches and refried bean burritos.

My thanks are also due to Nick Lowe, whose almost casual remark, in the course of a train journey – that the DC and Marvel continuity universes were the largest narrative constructs of human culture – was the spark for this book, and to Graham Sleight, whose distinction, in conversation shortly before I finished, between terminable and interminable narrative helped me to think through some important points in revision.

Veronica Schanoes, Jennifer Stuller, Jennifer Stoy and Lesley Arnold all read sections of this book as work in progress and their comments were extraordinarily helpful.

Leyte Jefferson and Mary Borsellino and various of their friends provided me with many episodes of the animated shows *Gotham Knights* and *Justice League Unlimited*, and copies of the Toonverse comics, about which I would have written far more had I had more space, and to which I will devote due attention at a later stage. Lesley Arnold also provided me with access to many, many, issues of comics, as did Mehran Baluch.

Sierra Hahn and others in the publicity department of DC Comics were friendly and cooperative in the matter of complimentary copies of graphic novels, as were Nick Landau and Andrew James at Titan. The publicity department at Marvel were entirely polite in their response to my requests for assistance.

Various comics creators answered my questions and were generally helpful – among these were Neil Gaiman, Alan Moore, Peter Hogan and Mike Carey. Craig McGill, Grant Morrison's biographer, was also very helpful.

Adi Tantimedh gave me vast amounts of good advice, much of which I took.

Will Eaves at *The Times Literary Supplement* commissioned reviews of several of the films I discuss here.

My nephew Michael McCarthy turned out, over Christmas lunch, to be working on an undergraduate dissertation that overlapped with my discussion of many of the films here; our subsequent conversations were of significant help to me and, I hope, to him.

The staff of Forbidden Planet, Orbital, Gosh! and the late lamented Comics Showcase were extremely helpful.

My thanks are also due to the editorial staff at I.B.Tauris, particularly Philippa Brewster and Jessica Cuthbert-Smith.

Paule was, as always, deeply supportive while I was working on this project.

The chapter on Joss Whedon was written as a paper for the *Slayage* conference in Barnesville, Atlanta. My thanks are due to Rhonda Wilcox and David Lavery for inviting me to speak and for much hospitality while there.

The Freedom of Power

Some First Thoughts on Superhero Comics

Origin Story

Officially, I never read them as a child. They were gaudy trash and a waste of money, and I only got to read them round at the houses of friends. Later on, they were one of the things I bought with money I had earned, often by buying *National Geographic* and *Punch* cheap at jumble sales and selling them for slightly more at second-hand shops. Like most adolescent geeks, I had to find ingenious ways of subsidizing my habits.

Part of the appeal was that American superhero comics were forbidden. In newsagents in the 1950s and 1960s, if they were present at all, it was in the lower rungs of revolving wire racks whose higher rungs held pin-up and fetish magazines. You did not have to have read Frederick Wertham's *Seduction of the Innocent* (1954) to make a connection: beefcake poses and skin-tight clothing and queer intimacy.

Somehow it was less OK to read them than to read British comics, with patriotic heroes like Dan Dare, or the strips in the newspapers – and admittedly my childhood was a golden age for those, what with Jeff Hawke and 4-D Jones in the *Express*, which was my parents' newspaper of choice. The *Eagle* and the other comics in its group had lovely art; at one point, a sick friend was lent an entire back-run of both *Eagle* and *Girl*, and I got to sit and work my way through both. I still feel that Belle of the Ballet was almost as fine in its way as Dan Dare, and that Lettice Leef was significantly more amusing than her kinsman Harris Tweed.

Like pornography, superhero comics always teased, they always offered more than they could ever deliver, on splash covers where grinning villains played with our heroes and heroines as figures on a giant chessboard, or spun them on a wheel of death. Part of the thrill was always that, no matter how powerful superheroes were, they always managed to find themselves in a jeopardy commensurate with their strength. And yet, to deliver fully on that promise would always have been to make that jeopardy more real than the commercial medium could bear. Comics taught me that disappointed expectation of greatness that is part of the aesthetic experience: things are this good, but somehow, in one's mind, they might be better yet.

Yes, comics were strangely sexy, even when I was young enough not to be entirely clear what sexiness was. They offered fantasy and danger and risk and masks and skin-tight clothing. Wertham was a long way from being wrong about comics; he was just an uptight sexist prig who did not understand how complex and various human sexuality is. As a teenager, I was never quite sure what the Comics Code was, but I knew that every time I picked up a comic, it had passed some sort of censorship. I remember resenting this, inchoately, knowing that one of the reasons why comics so often disappointed me was that someone was leaning into my enjoyment, imposing limits on material whose whole point was that it should have none.

Yet, often, especially when I picked up Marvel comics rather than DC, I found material that blew my head off. Beings that ate worlds, like Galactus, or who simply had names as resonant as the Living Tribunal. They were creatures of dream and nightmare, available once a month for a shilling. Because comics had to avoid the specifically and overtly sexual, they often dealt in other kinds of ecstasy, and linked them with that pervading sexiness that nonetheless got through. This sense of the vast, oceanic and mildly perverse combined with my teenage religiosity to give me a taste for the sublime that has never deserted me.

At a more intimate level there were moments of psychological insight in the comics that I read that have haunted me ever since, no matter how corny they are, as when Mr Fear turned to Daredevil (the man without fear) and said that he had his own version of their story and in that version 'I'm the hero and you're the villain'. That was an important lesson for me to learn when I was 15 years old and a self-centred prig, and I learned it not from religion, nor political economy, nor from great literature, but from superhero comics.

To be fair to DC comics, which I read less frequently, they contained material that affected me as well. If, as a critic, I have been obsessed with shadow doubles, and with the nightmare self that is both threat and parody, it perhaps has something to do with Superman's freakish antagonist/other self Bizarro, or with the hideous Man Bat that Batman fought and conquered, yet whose hideous wings were capable of sky-borne flight where Batman could only ever swing or glide.

There is poetry in this material, both in the ideas and in the drawn images that embody those ideas. I used to own an issue of *Daredevil* in which, for page after page, the blind acrobat lawyer simply traversed rooftops and swung between skyscrapers, in total silence, without speech bubbles, thought bubbles or sound effects. It has stayed in my head as an image of pure athleticism and joy, as blissful as a Mozart rondo. Gene Colan was the artist for this, as for much else that I loved in the late 1960s and early 1970s.

Back then, if you liked comics, you liked superheroes, because they were most of what there was. There were still aviators, but I thought that the Blackhawks were big bores. There were mystic adventurers like Dr Strange, but he so clearly lived in the same world as Spider-Man and the Hulk that it was no surprise when he started teaming up with, or advising, Marvel's actual superheroes; his mystic powers were rather close to being superpowers, anyway.

There is a grey area between magic and impossible powers, to put it mildly. The original Green Lantern's ring was magic, and the later ones were given their rings by an intergalactic agency, the

Guardians of the Universe. (The original Green Lantern's magic ring was later explained away as indirectly deriving from the same technology, which involves magic as well as science, conveniently.) In both cases, they acted as a focus for will, and – as we all know – magic is a technology of will, and any technology sufficiently advanced is indistinguishable from magic.

Comics helped teach me to play with paradox, and with the complex and double-natured; they are one of the reasons why I enjoy the postmodern condition without needing to dignify it with elaborate structures of theory. If my work is 'theory anorexic' as has been claimed, comics are partly to blame, or thank.

Powers and Responsibilities

So, superheroes, male and female . . . what is a superhero?

A superhero is a man or woman with powers that are either massive extensions of human strengths and capabilities, or fundamentally different in kind, which she or he uses to fight for truth, justice and the protection of the innocent. A substantial minority of people without powers as such share a commitment to the superhero mission, so they are generally regarded as superheroes in spite of the absence of such powers. Prior to Siegel and Shuster's invention of Superman (1933–8), masked avengers of this kind were the default group and were only gradually largely superseded. The mission is an important defining characteristic, as much so as the powers – many of the opponents of the superhero are as powerful as the hero, or more so, but they either lack moral compass or have specifically chosen evil. Nor is it enough to do no harm; most superheroes are as obsessed with duty as are the central characters of Corneille's dramas.

Superman has powers of both kinds but has them of his nature, not by self-improvement: he has preternatural strength and preternaturally keen senses, but he is also able to fly, heat things with his gaze and bounce bullets off his chest. Daredevil, on the other hand, has keen senses, as a by-product of his blinding by radioactive material, and his developed senses include not merely the standard remaining four but other senses, such as balance and location, and an extra sense often called radar; he is also, by constant exercise, in superb but merely human physical condition. The Fantastic Four have ahuman abilities – stretching, invisibility, the capacity to become living flame, a stone-like skin coupled with immense strength – acquired by exposure to cosmic rays during an experimental space flight; they are also effectively the four elements.

In most cases, these powers are the result either of anomalous personal situations or of accidents. Superman is the survivor of an exploded planet and his powers derive in part from the difference between Krypton's sun and Earth's. Others have been bitten by spiders, or altered by cosmic or gamma rays, or given powers by beneficent aliens. It is the fate of the superhero to be set apart from the common run of humanity and to experience a degree of estrangement as a result.

Some figures normally classed as superheroes have no such powers in and of themselves, and thus regularly confuse the issue by being an exception to this rule. Batman is an extraordinary human being who has trained many standard human abilities to their limits and beyond, but has no special abilities. He is separate and estranged, however, as the result not of accident but of human malice – as a boy, he witnessed the deaths of his parents during a mugging and swore vengeance on all criminals.

What Batman does share with superheroes proper is this estrangement and the liminal status that is another of the superhero's defining characteristics. Superheroes are uncanny and exist at the threshold between states – it is the threshold that is important rather than the states it lies between, which is why liminality, of the most basic and literal kind, is a useful descriptive term here. There are many ways in which superheroes can be liminal – they can be socially dead, though alive, through the loss of their original family (Superman, Batman, Spider-Man), or exist as figures of the twilight (Batman). Many of them have an animal aspect, whether or not they literally metamorphose, others take on part of the nature of an alchemical elements, while remaining essentially human (the

Human Torch); to exist in two realms at once is also a way of being liminal. They can be the abstract embodiment of a quality – the various versions of the Flash, and Marvel's Quicksilver are both avatars of Speed.

They can, in a few cases, be literally both dead and alive; Superman has died and been reborn, as has Hal Jordan, one of several human Green Lanterns. They may be morally liminal, good and evil at once or at different times, or possess shadow doubles; Superman has been turned to evil by possession and by various sorts of Kryptonite, and he has a parodic surrealistic amoral double in Bizarro. Hal Jordan turned to the dark side – this was later explained away as his possession by Parallax, a powerful evil being – and then died, his spirit becoming the embodiment of the Spectre for a while, before being reborn free of the taint of Parallax.

Almost all superheroes are to some degree vigilantes: they do not work for the authorities, though at times they work alongside them, and they are sometimes accepted as a volunteer auxiliary of the police and other organs of the state. Superman, in particular, is deferential to elected officials to an extent that has sometimes led to his being portrayed negatively as the mere lackey of corrupt officials who exploit his goodwill – in Frank Miller's *The Dark Knight Returns* (1986), for example.

Some of them, and many of them some of the time, are at odds with the authorities. Batman periodically finds himself in conflict with new district attorneys who wish the police to dispense with the alliance. In the conclusion of Brian Michael Bendis' run on *Daredevil*, Matt Murdock has been imprisoned as the result of a long campaign by an FBI agent. In Alan Moore's *Watchmen*, (1986–7) masked vigilantism has been suppressed by law, and most of them have complied. In the Marvel *Civil War* storyline (2006–7), the superhero community is divided by an Act obliging them to register and reveal their identities, with internment as the punishment for non-compliance. (This is very clearly intended as a comment on the decline of civil liberties in Bush's America – Sue Storm, one of the moral centres of the Marvel Universe, says at one point that she thinks the USA went mad after 9/11.) Another of those moral centres, Captain America, is assassinated in the aftermath of *Civil War*, and this may be that rare thing in comics, a real and permanent death.

Most especially, the X-Men, as mutants, experience bigotry; as such, they have regularly operated as Marvel's stand-ins for ethnic and sexual minorities. To pick but one of many examples, in one storyline of Brian Michael Bendis' *Alias* (2002–4) – which has no connection with the television show of the same name – the misidentification of a lesbian teenager as mutant helps pinpoint the small-town bigotry from which she feels forced to flee.

In the Marvelverse, mutants are potential victims of hate crimes and of state-sponsored pogroms, and of the sort of bureaucratic prying that is often a prelude to the latter. The mutant community is shown as deeply politically divided between those who want to make an accommodation with standard-model humanity and those who either regard themselves as superior or regard genocide of so-called 'flat-scans' as the only way of saving mutant lives. Periodically, in side-bar alternate universes like the worlds of event[1] storylines like the *Age of Apocalypse* (1995) or the *House of M* (2005), we have been shown the boot on the other foot. As the character of the mutant supremacist Magneto evolved over years of continuity, we discover that he spent his childhood in a concentration camp, and that if you look into the abyss too long, the abyss will look into you.

There are also mutants who, as a result of social exclusion or because of poor morals, abuse their power to live outside the law: Gwen in the television show *Angel* is a good example of a criminal mutant and an odd outcropping of X-Men style mutants into the Whedonverse. Between the underworld of crime and the underworld of the hideously mutated or transformed living in sewers, the bright glossy world of comics has always had a dark side – one might almost say, a *noir* side.

Latterly, both in Joss Whedon's run of *Astonishing X-Men* (2004–7) and in the third film *X-Men: The Last Stand* (2006), mutants have

---

[1]   I have used the term 'event' generally throughout this book. For a full discussion of events, see Chapter 5.

to cope with the possibility of genetic therapy that would simply turn them back into ordinary humans. The analogy here is not merely with blue-sky theorizing about gene-therapy for sexual identity, but with the political project of gay absorption into the suburban mainstream preached by, for example, Andrew Sullivan. In the parallel Marvel continuity that has followed from the *House of M* storyline, most mutants have been turned back into normal humans by magic, and are still victims of persecution by other humans, now as ex-mutants.

In the *Civil War* and *Decimation* (2005) storylines (see Chapter 5), the small rump of mutants still extant are effectively being held as prisoners on what might as well be called reservations. Approached by the factions in the row about registration, they for the most part refuse to take sides. Approached by her former lover, Tony Stark, for support, Emma Frost, who survived the destruction of the mutant nation Genosha, simply asks him where he was, where were the Avengers, when millions died, 'when our babies were burning'. Mutancy in the Marvel Universe is a free-floating signifier, but a very powerful one, emotionally and polemically; the same is true of a number of other concepts, notably that of the superhero itself.

In many cases, this ambivalent relationship with the authorities is closely linked to areas of moral ambiguity. Particularly during the period when the Comics Code held sway, it is part of the mission statement of many superheroes that they do not kill, no matter what the provocation. Like many arbitrary artistic choices, this is an endless generator of story and the occasions when this rule is breached are always events – the execution of Maxwell Lord by Wonder Woman (to stop him using a hypnotically controlled Superman as his assassin) leads to an estrangement between her on the one hand and Batman and Superman on the other, which helps precipitate the *Infinite Crisis*, DC Comics' major 2005–6 rebranding exercise (for an extended discussion of this and its 1985 predecessor, see Chapter 5). However, as we shall see, long-established rules and characters are only broken or re-imagined with impunity some of the time, and mistakes are often made.

Because of this anomalous relationship with society, many superheroes have secret identities. Superman is the reporter Clark Kent, Batman the industrialist and socialite Bruce Wayne, Spider-Man the photographer Peter Parker. Sometimes the secret identity is merely a useful expedient, and sometimes it functions as the expression of a divided personality, most notably in the case of Bruce Banner, who turns into the Hulk under emotional stress, but rather more subtly in the case of Batman (where there often seems a profound disconnect between the playboy tycoon Wayne and the dour vigilante). The idea that the angst-ridden world of superheroes is straightforwardly a form of escapism is a misconception; the process of self-identification that is part of enjoying comics involves a far more complicated dialogue between one's own problems and those of the characters one enjoys. Part of the point of Matt Murdock for me, once Frank Miller took the character over in the early 1980s, was the heavy dose of Catholic guilt.

Many superheroes are either orphaned or otherwise estranged from their families of blood; many of them acquire families of the heart in groups of co-workers or support systems, or work together as groups. Batman has an entire family of assistants and associates – the various Robins being merely the most obvious – as well as Alfred, who is both Bruce Wayne's butler and Batman's technician and battlefield medic. Those of us isolated by temperament or sexuality in our teens need a literature that consoles with the possibility of finding friends of the heart, and comics provide it, but not in any simple wish-fulfilment form; the relationships between team-mates or mentor and pupil are almost always shown as works in progress, as prickly soap operas in which things can go wrong.

The long association of superheroes with each other in crossover groups like DC's Justice League of America (JLA) and Marvel's Avengers means that they and their broader support groups are caught up in each other's destinies. In Alan Davis' alternate world miniseries *The Nail* (1997–8), the non-involvement of Superman in the affairs of the world – he has been brought up by Amish parents instead of the Kents – means that his colleagues in the JLA are less effective and that some of Superman's closest associates, notably

Jimmy Olsen, have turned to evil. The playfulness of comics is often distinctly dark in its thought experiments with its own material.

Many superheroes are paradoxical beings: his blindness means that Matt Murdock can hide in plain sight, as it were, because he is the one person no one will ever suspect of being Daredevil. Most secret identities are of this kind – Bruce Wayne is frivolous and money-grubbing, as is Tony Stark, so that no one suspects them of being Batman or Iron Man. Both Superman and Spider-Man are news journalists, which gives them a perfect excuse for being near where the action is. The one natural thing that can harm Superman is a rock from his lost home. In his identity as the lawyer Matt Murdock, Daredevil sometimes defends men he handed over to the law in the first place, and latterly he has been accused of malpractice on this basis.

Iconographically, almost all superheroes are good-looking and muscular, and wear costumes that emphasize the fact. There are obvious exceptions – Ben Grimm of the Fantastic Four is not any the less a superhero for looking like a pile of orange rocks – but the same is true in the world of celebrity, for which the world of superheroes is, as Jennifer Stoy has pointed out, a fairly obvious metaphor. Both celebrities and superheroes are wish-fulfilment people, living complicated and glamorous lives that we envy in spite of the perpetual hard work and potential tragedy that goes with the glitz. 'When you've got it, flaunt it', says Max Bialystock in *The Producers* (1968) and that they certainly do, often given a particular assist by artists like Alex Ross and Alan Davis, both of whom sometimes draw characters so sinuous, sinewy and stylish that it hurts to look at them.

Of course, superheroes have supervillains to struggle against, though the lines are often drawn in an arbitrary way and there are a significant number of characters who have crossed the line in both directions. Hal Jordan, DC's best-known bearer of the Green Lantern uniform and ring, went to the dark side, and returned. Marvel has an entire team, the Thunderbolts, who were originally villains working a scam with new identities and variously sought redemption because they liked being good better. They were often

On the Artists – Briefly

If, in much of what follows, I talk far more about writers and editors than I do about the artists who give comics so much of their appeal, it is not, let us be clear, because I do not hugely admire the best of those artists. It is because they have been written about more, and because many of the writers in whom I am interested have been extraordinarily lucky in finding artists who were prepared to be servants of their vision. Sometimes I am writing about artists who were also writers, or managed to find writers to write what they wanted to draw – Alex Ross, for example, is the auteur of *Marvels* (1994) and *Kingdom Come* (1996) quite as much as the wonderful writer Kurt Busiek and the more ordinary Mark Waid. Let me here, though, record the names of artists like Bolland and Adams and Sienkewicz and Gibbons and Davis and Buscema and Romita and Colan and Vess and McKean and all of the others. Someone should write a book that properly celebrates the work of all these men, but that book is not this one, partly because it would cost so much to produce.

led by the current Baron Zemo, a figure more morally ambiguous than many of his team, since he may have laid aside his family's Nazi ideology, but he still regards himself as a man meant to rule. Post *Civil War*, as written by Warren Ellis, they are effectively a different group with different objectives, in spite of some continuity of personnel.

Some supervillains are career criminals; some are mad scientists using crime as an alternative to corporate or government funding; some are the rulers of rogue states; some are aliens or are time-travellers whose agenda are so caught up in paradoxes as to be almost incomprehensible. The Avengers' regular opponent, Kang, is at war with various other time-travellers and self-appointed or metaphysical guardians of chronological reality; he is also has problems with his younger and older selves, and with his clones. There are reasons why some supervillains decide that being good is an easier way to make a living.

Many superheroes have nemesis figures who are tragic, partly because they are the superhero's dark self. Superman has Lex Luthor, the millionaire and scientific genius whose quest for some way of damaging the being whose strength and integrity perpetually shames him regularly reduces him to ignominy. The television series *Smallville* (2001 onwards) places the origins of this feud in Luthor's young manhood and Superman's adolescence. This is not original, but rather a return to what was continuity before the *Crisis on Infinite Earths* reboot of the DC Universe in 1985 and the consequent reinvention of Superman continuity by John Byrne, and plays teasingly with the possibility that in this version of continuity things will work out differently. At one point, for example, Luthor has a vision of a world in which he becomes a completely ethical human being, and rejects it, without yet embracing evil, because it is a world in which he has no power and cannot escape the normal tragedies of the human condition. For a while, in main DC continuity, Luthor is President of the USA and abuses his office to attack Superman, risking the lives of everyone on Earth to do so; he ends up a deranged fugitive. In the aftermath of *Infinite Crisis*, however, he manages to blame his crimes on a genetically identical corpse (actually the son of his virtuous cognate in an alternate world). Such figures always find a way of coming back, but never really change, whereas Jean Grey and Elektra are at least chastened by tragic death and resurrection.

Very few, if any, of these arch-adversary figures are ever female – the relationship between the Batman and Catwoman has always been flirtatious as much as combative (and latterly she has largely rejected burglary for good works). His other significant female opponents are Poison Ivy – whose hatred for him is less personal than a question of his being a) male and b) not a plant – and Harley Quinn, whose feud with the Batman is mostly about attracting the attention of her main love object, the Joker, or Poison Ivy, with whom she has a relationship that is sometimes represented as being almost as romantic as the one she has with the Joker.

Generally speaking, the relationship between superhero and principal adversary is rarely seen as having a homoerotic component

– even now that the Comics Code no longer operates – and is more a matter of the motiveless malignity of an Iago towards an Othello: 'he hath a daily beauty in his life/ that makes me ugly'. One obvious exception to this is the relationship of Superman and Luthor in *Smallville*, where, because the show is as much a part of teen genre as superhero material, adolescent ambivalence is certainly a factor, along with their rivalry over various young women (see my extended discussion of homoeroticism in teen media in the first chapter of *Teen Dreams* (2006)).

Another such relationship is some portrayals of that between Batman and the Joker, explicitly in Frank Miller's *The Dark Knight Returns* (see below in Chapter 4), implicitly in his murderous attitude to Batman's young sidekicks, male and female. The Joker murders the second Robin, Jason Todd, and leaves Batgirl, Barbara Gordon, in a wheelchair for the rest of her life; in Alan Davis' *The Nail* he tortures both of them to death. Interestingly, the intensely perverse implications of this are comparatively rarely followed through even in 'slash' fan fiction, which has no particular problems about making use of the quasi-pederastic implications it is possible to impute to Batman's relationships with his male wards and assistants.

The other antagonist relationship that is sometimes given quasi-erotic implications is that between Charles Xavier (Professor X of *The X-Men*) and Magneto. It is a canonical given in continuity that the two mutant leaders used to work together and were friends; in the Ultimate[2] continuity, it is even canonical that Xavier neglected

---

[2]   In the 2000s, Marvel created various titles in what we must call the Ultimate continuity, some of which, but not all, differ radically from the main line of Marvel continuity. All set their origin stories at the time of publication. This affects *Ultimate Spider-Man* comparatively little, save that Aunt May is a contemporary active woman in her late fifties rather than the standard near-crone. The *Ultimate X-Men* storylines tend to be grittier and use parallels with contemporary terrorism. *The Ultimates*, the equivalent of *The Avengers*, is very gritty indeed, with several of the team being near-psychopaths and the Hulk a monster who eats at least some of his victims. Earlier they created the M2 continuity that

his heterosexual partner, Moira McTaggart, and son David because of the intensity of the relationship with Magneto. As portrayed by Patrick Stewart and Ian McKellen in the Bryan Singer and Brett Ratner films, the implications of this are strongly played up to, especially in the flashback to some 20 years earlier in *X-Men: The Last Stand*, where the two men – still friends – are shown bickering like an old married couple. Since McKellen is apparently aware of the existence of the slashfic culture, in which this pairing is common, this may be a decision of the actors rather than the director.

The struggle between good and evil tends, of course, to take the form of violent struggle, because that is the way that, since the beginning, comics have chosen to stylize moral contention. It is not the only way – insidious corruption or inventive outwitting of cunning schemes are also reasonably common – but it is the predominant mode. Some editors, Marvel's Jim Shooter, for example, have regarded fights as so important that plot and character could be largely discarded in their favour.

There are superhero comics that manage to avoid this almost entirely – Neil Gaiman's Black Orchid (1988–9) is that rare thing, an almost entirely pacifist superhero, most of whose enemies give up in self-contempt when shown her moral and physical beauty – but they are rare. Punch-'em-ups are as standard a feature of superhero comics as they are of chivalric romances, and that is just how things are, a rule of the genre.

Powerful Adversaries

Parents disapprove of comics, and so do teachers. In 1974, I was brought face to face in the most telling way possible with the sheer dislike that superhero comics engender in some other people, as well as with a version of one of the criticisms of them that any study is going to have to engage with. I had been living and working

---

deals, rather charmingly, with the next generation of various Marvel characters' families, notably Peter and Mary-Jane Parker's daughter, who becomes Spider-Girl in her teens.

in Leeds, and renting a room from a young feminist woman I knew through the nascent Leeds Gay Liberation Front and because she went to the same consciousness-raising group as my best friend and my assistant at Yorkshire Television. When I lost my job and returned to London I could not shift all of my possessions at once, and got her permission to store, in her attic, a refrigerator box that contained the comics I had collected between the ages of 15 and 25. When, a few weeks later, I returned to Leeds to collect them, she informed me, through a closed door, that she and some of her friends had had a discussion about the sexism explicit in and implied by superhero comics, and had taken my collection from the attic and burned it.

I always tell this story when explaining my commitment to anti-censorship politics, but it raises other questions as well. I have never been under the impression that their decision was motivated by a serious examination of the implications of particular storylines; the point was that they felt the imagery of superhero comics to be objectionable in and of itself, so objectionable that it could not be recuperated or merely critiqued, and had to be burned. I find the sheer visceral quality of that position intriguing in itself.

Yet, they had a point. In some of what follows, I discuss the often-unthinking male-centredness of both of the comics industry and its products, the occasional misogyny towards, and regular marginalization of, women characters. Though there have been significant women comics writers in the superhero field, and occasionally artists, women have tended to be most important to the industry in editorial roles.

It is no coincidence that some of the finest storylines that comics have ever produced, the runs in which they have come closest to real tragedy, as well as many of the most tiresome, have dealt, quite specifically, with women who overreach themselves. Both Jean Grey and Elektra, in their classic storylines in *X-Men* and *Daredevil* respectively, arrogated to themselves a level of power that they could not combine with firm adherence to a moral compass, and fell. I cannot think, off-hand, of storylines involving sympathetic male characters in which there was such a fall, partly because male characters tend to be treated with greater indulgence. The male characters who overreach, and fall, are always supervillains, either the cosmic powers like DC's Darkseid and Marvel's Thanos, or that small group of supervillains who are more than career criminals.

The avoidance of homoeroticism at least means that, in general, the superhero comic has dispensed with that common trope of mainstream media, the antagonism between men in which the heroine is the field of conflict, or only there to make homoeroticism deniable. It is not that female characters are never placed in jeopardy in superhero comics, so much as that this happens to them no more often than it does with male characters. This is partly a matter of the increasing number of tough female characters in comics since the 1970s, partly a matter of the law of diminishing returns. After Spider-Man's first sweetheart, Gwen Stacey, died from a fall from which he failed to save her, killed by the Green Goblin, there was little point in trying to duplicate that particular sensational moment. One of the very few examples in recent years of woman as hostage came in the Jeph Loeb/Jim Lee *Hush*, where the Batman and Catwoman put Lois Lane in danger in order to snap Superman out of the besotted trance in which Poison Ivy has placed him.

One of the few other exceptions is one of the most unpleasant and egregious ones, and has been the source of much righteous feminist protest among comics fans. During the thoroughly inferior *War Games* event (2004–5) in which the Batman's contingency plan to set Gotham's gangs against each other gets used in an attempt to impress him by Stephanie, a supernumerary female Robin figure, who is captured and tortured to near-death by the hideously disfigured Black Mask with an electric drill. She subsequently dies, because Dr Lesley Tompkins decides she has had enough of patching up young people the Batman has involved in his world. Not only is a young woman hideously penetrated and broken by a male monster; her actual death is partly caused by her stepping out of a subordinate role and is reconfigured as the responsibility of an older woman who, let us be clear, is one of the people who helped parent Bruce Wayne after his death, and whom he now rejects, specifically punishing her by making it impossible for her to practice medicine, even in the Third World, where she goes to seek redemption. There is a complex of misogynistic ideas here – Stephanie is a manipulative adolescent who overreaches through good intentions – that leave a very nasty taste. Nor is the situation helped by the death in the middle of all of this by one of the Batman storyline's few African-American characters, Orpheus. (The question of race issues in superhero comics is a complex one that has been addressed so cogently in Jeffrey A. Brown's *Black Superheroes, Milestone Comics and their Fans* (2001) that I feel unqualified to address it here.)

Let us be further clear that it is not the fact of physical vulnerability that is the issue here. This is not the first time that characters in Batman's circle have been badly hurt. Batman had his back broken by Bane, and, as already mentioned, the Joker beat the second Robin to death and shot Batgirl in the spine, leaving her paraplegic. In none of these cases, though, was there such a strong sexual implication in the violence, and in none of these cases was the guilt spread around from a male villain to a second, female character. The point, though, is less that comics are capable of ill-thought-through sadistic woman-blaming material than that this was a rare case that sparked the coming together of feminist fans to protest.

It is not as if the tendency of comics to occasional misogyny were no worse than those of any other art form. The not-always positive reaction of comics to the revival of feminism in the 1960s and 1970s – the Hulk was attacked by the Valkyrie with the cry 'every male chauvinist pig will tremble!' – was short-lived. However inadequately, comics often depicted women who were strong and also nurturing, and it is a matter of historical fact that the influence of writers like Chris Claremont, working on *X-Men* in the 1980s, was to have an effect on the rise of the strong woman character in films and television in the 1990s and 2000s. We would know this even if Joss Whedon had not said so in, for example, interviews surrounding his own work on *Astonishing X-Men*. The rise of such characters in television and film has had a knock-on effect in comics. One of the most interesting comics of the early 21st century has been Brian Michael Bendis' *Alias*, even if, as I argue at length in Chapter 2, it is far more about general issues of personal growth and autonomy than it is a specifically feminist parable of those issues.

Long before second-wave feminism, long before a serious if intermittent attempt by the comics industry to clean up its act, comics also gave us, back in the Golden Age,[3] two of the strongest and most active women in popular media. Wonder Woman was so very obviously a feminist icon that she was condemned by Wertham as a possible lesbian role model from a post-Second World War perspective in which any woman who stepped outside the home and pursued a career was seen as suspect, and the idea of a woman who might be dominant in her emotional relationships was especially so. Various attempts to tame her have never taken in the long term, even the period in the late 1960s and early 1970s when she was stripped of her powers and connection to the Amazons' island was an attempt to modernize her as a heroine in the Emma Peel mould; Diana is and always will be a proud Amazon.

It also needs pointing out that Lois Lane, though sometimes the butt of crude practical jokes by Superman that play on her vanity and pettiness, is also a career woman and good at what she does. Inasmuch as she fails to notice what is in front of her face – that her klutzy colleague Clark is actually the demigod of her dreams – it is signalled as a paradox, because normally Lois is a woman whose ingenuity and perspicacity cut through complex deceits.

---

[3]   There is a convention in fan and critical discourse about comics, whereby the period from the invention of Superman and Batman in the 1930s, through the Second World War, and on to the Kefauver Hearings and the introduction of the Comics Code is seen and referred to as the Golden Age. The subsequent two decades are referred to as the Silver Age, which is generally held to end with the liberalization of the Comics Code in the early 1970s. The subsequent decade is sometimes referred to as the Bronze Age, and the decade and a half that started in 1985 with *Watchmen* and *The Dark Knight Returns* is rather more acceptedly referred to as the Dark Age. Some critics have tried to popularize the idea that the rise of writers like Busiek and Bendis in the late 1990s and the early 21st century has inaugurated a neo-Silver Age.

Sometimes she puts herself in danger as part of an elaborate flirtation; more often the dangers in which she finds herself are the result of her being so good at her job. This was also the case back in the early days of the newspaper strips and comic books: Lois was always a smart sassy career girl, in contrast to the other women in Superman's life. The period during which she was often demeaned was the 1950s, in which women were being driven out of work and into the home, and the whole point about Lois was that she stuck with her career. Compare Lois Lane with the protagonists of Doris Day's films and those of her imitators, and the point is clear.

More recently, since John Byrne's reboot of Superman continuity in 1986, Lois has been a knowing partner and wife to Superman, while assisting in the pretence that she is married to Clark Kent, but without abandoning her career for a second. It is more or less a given that she is a more gifted reporter than her husband, partly because he spends so much time disappearing to change into his other persona. When Superman seems to disparage her career in any way, it is usually solid evidence that he is temporarily on a wrong path. It is because the comics continuity, after enjoying the game of keeping Lois in the dark for so long that the 1940s sex-war comedy aspect of it started to get stale, moved on to an equal partnership between them, that it is sad that not only the 1970s Richard Donner films, but also the 2006 Bryan Singer *Superman Returns* went back to the old assumption that Lois does not know. At least in the Donner cut of *Superman 2* (as opposed to the commercially released Dick Lester cut) she was shown as intelligent enough to have worked it out and only re-deceived because Superman turns back time.

There is also, of course, the question of the art, and the ways in which women are represented, especially on covers. All superheroic characters are presented in a sexually objectifying manner, but women characters are especially so, with breasts and buttocks constantly exaggerated. There is even a fannish term — Good Girl Art — for the most cheesecakey kind of pose, with the term Bad Girl Art being reserved not for work of a low standard, but for work that most approaches the pin-up. This is something that has worsened over the decades — the people who burned my comics had comparatively little to complain about by the standards of what was to come. It is certainly an aspect of comics that reflects a predominantly heterosexual male world of writers, artists and readers and is often alienating to everyone else.

Part of what some of my sisters and comrades have tended to find offensive about superhero comics has been that very sense of the possibilities of extraordinary human beings on which comics are intrinsically built. Our lives, it is argued, will be changed by mass movements of solidarity, not by single extraordinary individuals, whether or not they wear masks and capes. This critique is, it seems to me, rather beside the point. It was never the case that the superheroes of either the DC or Marvel universes were pure vigilantes; they always deferred to legitimate authority to at least some extent, rather more so than most pulp heroes had. The relationship between Batman and Commissioner Gordon is complex and problematic, certainly, but it is far more collegiate than confrontational – as demonstrated by the Batsignal.[4] The point of the *Civil War* storyline is a discussion of whether superheroes serve society best as agents of the state or as independent responsible individuals, and the point is made that Bush's America, with its easy abandonment of civil liberties, is not a state anyone should feel comfortable serving.

Nor is reliance on superheroes ever shown as a substitute for collective action; at the most patriotic times of the Second World War, superheroes were shown as participating in the war effort, not as replacing it. It is not just for practical reasons that you do not have, in the middle of a war, Superman settling things once and for all; it is because it would feel wrong. Superheroes lead a life of selfless public service for the most part – glory-hounds like DC's Guy Gardner (one of the secondary Green Lanterns) or Booster Gold, or Crackerjack in Kurt Busiek's *Astro City* (1995 onwards) are mocked. It was by trying to profit from his powers and sulking

---

[4]   The searchlight with a Batman symbol stencilled onto it with which Gordon and other police alert Batman to the fact that he is needed.

when he could not, that Spider-Man got his Uncle Ben killed, the sin that haunts him ever afterwards.

More recently, as we shall see below, the extent of the problem of superheroes is one that the comics themselves have considered far more thoroughly than almost any other medium. 'Unhappy the land that has no heroes', someone says in Brecht's *Galileo*, receiving the riposte 'unhappy the land that needs them'. For the last two and a half decades, one of the great themes of comics, as we shall see below, is the question of whether superheroes, and by extension other extraordinary people, can be trusted with their powers. Alan Moore's *Watchmen* deals with this theme, but so, in different ways, do Ross and Waid's *Kingdom Come*, Brian Bendis' *Powers* and many particular runs of longer-lasting titles (see Chapter 3 for a more extended discussion of this).

Spine-Tingling Sagas

Because, however intermittently, I was reading comics in the 1960s and 1970s, in my teens and twenties, I never had the difficulty some people have in reading comics, which is that of not knowing quite how to look at a page and decipher which way the narrative line goes from frame to frame, especially given the post-1960s greater freedom of artists and writers to make use of splash pages – a single powerful image dominating a double spread – or the extension of the standard grid across a whole spread, or the subversion of that grid. The best thing one can do is to treat grid like the idea of metre, something that is always there in a sense, even if it defines its presence by absence, and expect to read left to right, left to right, in several rows heading downwards, even when this is not necessarily what is going to happen in this instance. Scott McCloud, in his *Understanding Comics* (1993), tackles this far better than I ever could, and I strongly commend his work to the attention of those with this problem.

Another problem, less often cited but nonetheless real, is the distinctly cavalier handling of time within comics continuity.

Referred to as the sliding or floating timescale, this means that things that happened in comics of the 1960s and were shown as happening in the then present – the Fantastic Four's flight, Spider-Man's being bitten – are at any given point things that happened at an unspecified point in the past considerably less than four decades ago. When he got his powers, Spider-Man was a teenager; when, in 2006, with G.W. Bush or someone very like him in the White House, he outs himself (in *Civil War*) as Peter Parker as part of his support for the Superheroes Registration programme, he is at most in his early thirties, and more probably his late twenties. Time happens in superhero comics, but it happens slowly in some respects, rather more briskly in others.

There have been various attempts to rationalize this, particularly by DC – re-imaginings of origin stories in time periods less long in the past, the revelation that certain characters age slowly as a result of whatever gave them their powers – but it is simply one of those areas in which the commercial need to keep certain characters going forever is more important than any even vague attempt at realism, which, after all, in worlds where men and women can fly, is hardly a consideration. Like the tight clothing and overly lush diction, this was something I learned to live with.

Another reason why I had comparatively little problem with comics was that, during the same years, I was developing my passionate love of opera, an art form of infinite respectability with which comics have a surprising amount in common. Both are radically impure forms based on some fundamentally absurd conventions; both are irritating if one does not develop a taste for preposterous rodomontade and brightly coloured costumes. Both of them can do certain things that other art forms can only do with great difficulty; comics and opera can slow narrative time down while moving it forward at a steady pulse, without having necessarily to indulge in the dreamy floatiness of slow-motion photography. Both forms can give you, effectively and without implicit comedy, the thought processes of both parties in a dialogue, or a clear sense of what everyone is saying at the same time in a complex scene. Both are also concerned to show us gods and heroes and monsters, male and female, in all their power and dignity, but also with all their passionate emotional human intensity. Both, accordingly, have a tendency to inflate language into something that can become bombast, or can be more charitably seen as a necessary, if sometimes loopy, grandiloquence commensurate with the scale of what is sometimes being portrayed. At their best, both can portray immense emotions played out on vast canvases, and yet be capable of dropping to pianissimo in a second when it is needed.

Both opera and superhero comics often need length as well as scale to tell their stories. Wagner's *Das Ring Des Nibelungen* runs for many hours over four nights to take us from Alberich's original theft of the Rhinegold to his son Hagen's eventual drowning as the Rhinemaidens take it back and Valhalla burns in the sky. The Dark Phoenix saga played out over many months, from Jean Grey's original awakening to the Phoenix's power when she self-sacrificingly piloted a spacecraft from orbit to save her friends, assuming she would die, to her eventual acceptance of the necessity of her death.[5] In between these two sacrificial 'deaths', we have her in the politics of the Shi'ar, one of the Marvel Universe's several galactic empires. We have her slow corruption in dreams by the mental manipulations of the Hellfire Club, and we have her eventual metamorphosis into the Dark Phoenix, a being that rends star systems for its prey and regards her friends as amusing trivia. One of the many reasons why the versions of the Dark Phoenix plotline in *Ultimate X-Men*, *X-Men: The Last Stand* and, more loosely and with Willow rather than Jean Grey, in Season Six of *Buffy the Vampire Slayer*, failed to work is that the process of corruption and

---

[5] When the assumed past of a comic or some other franchise is changed in order to make sense of current continuity, this retroactive continuity is standardly referred to as a retcon (retroactive continuity). The subsequent retconning of this particular storyline – the Phoenix produced a duplicate Jean while the original slept in a cocoon under the sea – is something that needs to be ignored when considering the original impact of this storyline. It was, very clearly, an afterthought, and not an entirely welcome one.

redemption was never given time to breathe, and the scale on which an evil Jean can be effective never shown.

When I talk more generally of thick texts – texts that we learn to read as collective, contingent compromises – both operas and superhero comics are significant parts of the template I have in mind. Both are collective works of art, in which the librettist and composer, or writer and penciller, are crucial to each other's input and others, like the conductor or the inker, almost as important. Both are commercial works of art that are always based on the compromises that that involves; there is always a crucial sense of how things might have been productively other, and sometimes we get to see how that might have worked. We get to listen to the early draft *Leonora* as well as to *Fidelio*, and learn a lot about the latter from the former; Alan Moore tells us in detail, in the notes to the hardback and Absolute[6] editions, how *Watchmen* in its final form evolved from a distinctly different project; the Absolute edition of Neil Gaiman's *Sandman* shows us how radically different were the original colour schemes from what we have got to know.

Both comics and opera are minority art forms in which it is possible and desirable to develop areas of expertise, an expertise that marked one out as slightly weird, slightly obsessive. To know one's way around the operas of Verdi or Wagner or Mozart may be very much more respectable than to understand the arcana of Marvel Comics' continuity, but it still means that, sooner or later, you are going to find yourself expounding far too much detail for your hearers, when someone expresses a mild taste for the Queen of the Night's second aria, or Sam Raimi's *Spider-Man* films. They are also fields in which there is always going to be someone who knows more than you. Both comics and opera have a significant following of the anti-social and awkward; a taste for them can also teach you the hard way to be sensitive to other people's lack of interest.

---

[6]   The Absolute editions of DC comics are glossy hardbacks with very high production values.

Both are art forms that teach you to cope with disappointment. In the case of opera, the issue is sometimes the particular problems of performance – the soprano's sore throat, the conductor's perversity – and sometimes more particular problems of the canon: if you love Verdi, you may not be as fond of Donizetti; if you love *Aida*, you may not be so taken with the early works of Verdi like *I Masnadieri*. In the case of comics, there are disappointments intrinsic to the mode of production – the need to produce to a planned release date means that some months, artists or writers may not perform at their best – as well as the fact that some writers and artists are persuaded to take on titles for which they have no especial fondness or compatibility. It is always worth bearing in mind that the best way to think about comics is in terms of a particular run of a title or a particular storyline; few titles manage to retain consistent excellence over the decades.

Learning to read comics is also a matter of coming to understand not only the specifics of continuity, but of its importance in the abstract. Narrative universes as vast as those of the Marvel and DC continuities are not the product of any one person, even of an editor-in-chief as creative and innovative as Stan Lee of Marvel, but rather the process of slow accretion and of the desire to make sense of what were once quite random narrative choices as they came to impinge on each other. No one artist or writer is responsible for these continuities – they are collective works of art.

One of the sources of this book was the casual remark by Nick Lowe in the course of a train journey that, by now, these two continuities were the largest narrative constructions in human culture (exceeding, for example, the vast body of myth, legend and story that underlies Latin and Greek literature), and that learning to navigate them was a skill-set all of its own. That conversation helped me to formulate the ideas that I spell out at greater length in the first chapter of *From Alien to the Matrix* (2005) about competence cascades, thick texts and the geek aesthetic; it also made me realize that I had, as part of my loose intellectual project of engaging with aspects of popular culture as difficult, to deal with the comics mainstream. I have mentioned above the relevance of comics to my concept of the thick text; the entire history of the frequent evolution of comics fans into comics creators of real ability is a good example of what I mean by competence cascades.

Another applies more generally to all comics readers. Like most comics fans, I discovered, I am still learning the finer points of continuity by reading and re-reading, and by asking friends to explain things, and by paying attention to the small footnotes that Marvel sometimes put in the corner of the frame. Understanding continuity is one of the pleasures of serial works of art; another is the realization that, if you don't understand quite everything that is going on, nonetheless the texture of referentiality that you are experiencing at the same time as your incomprehension is something that you can both trust and be comforted by. There is the sense that this is a creation you can trust; there is the sense that you will understand more on later readings.

When he was working on *Sandman*, Neil Gaiman remarked to me that he was putting in the level of reference, both to comics and to other material, that he loved in work he admired as a teenager; after all, he said, 'one of the most valuable lessons I learned from books and comics was that, if I did not understand something, I had better go and look it up'. If the non-comics reader is sceptical about this being an issue, I refer them to Walt Simonson's *Thor* in the 1980s, where an extended run during which Thor leads the struggle against an invasion of Earth and Asgard by frost giants is followed by a shorter run in which, transformed into a frog, he leads the frogs of Central Park against the local rats. Is this a reference to the lost *Batrachomythia* in which Homer is supposed to have parodied his own heroic gestures? Given Simonson's academic background before he became a comics writer, it is at least plausible. (It also signals that at least one major writer in the field is conscious of the sense that what is being created is a version of epic.) One trusts that the use of continuity and of other knowledge will give one an entertaining ride. And there is also the possibility, thrilling as a tight-rope walk until it actually happens, that that trust will be betrayed.

The continuities of comics universes are also valuable commercial properties and, as is usually the case when art and commerce mix, not every decision that gets made is in the long-term interests of either shareholders or the Muses. Comics are as prone as any other art form to latching onto short-term fashions while missing out on important long-term trends. The two major comics houses have often made decisions with an eye on their rival instead of on what they do best. Sometimes, decisions have been made at an editorial level that were bad in terms of the developments that followed, but which also retrospectively compromised previous material, which it no longer became quite as possible to view with nostalgia. For example, as part of the 2006 reboot of DC and the plot of *Project OMAC*, a part of the *Countdown to Infinite Crisis* (2005–6) storyline, the decision was made to have the minor superhero Blue Beetle Ted Kord murdered in cold blood by the tycoon Maxwell Lord, previously his friend. This had the positive result of freeing up the costume and name of Blue Beetle to be attached to a young Chicano superhero, but at the cost of retrospectively trashing the extended friendship of Kord and Lord as we had seen it in the long 1980s run of *Justice League of America* written by Keith Giffen and J.M. DeMatteis.

This run is itself a good example of how superhero comics are not always what you would expect; it largely consisted of a situation comedy in which a number of costumed men and women sat around in rooms, waiting for crises and bitching at each other, very amusingly. If we are now to read this with the later murder of one of these characters by another in mind, our enjoyment is compromised. This would be forgivable if the actual material in which it happened were better, but, alas, it was part of the *Countdown to Infinite Crisis* . . . Because of the long-term damage to past and future it involves, I have referred to this sort of corporate editorial decision below as 'strip-mining the continuity'.

Another good example, also from DC, is the death of Sue Dibney, wife and partner in detection of the Elongated Man, in *Identity Crisis* (2004). If you have gone to the trouble, over many years, of creating a Nick and Nora Charles pairing whom your audience loves and laughs with, it is never a good idea to kill one of them off for the sake of a cheaply gimmicky mystery. Sue's 'murder' turns out to be an accidental death caused by another superhero wife's experiments with her husband's equipment, the Atom's shrinking gadgetry – things that the mind of woman is not meant to know. The crucial clue is footprints on the surface of Sue's brain; there is a level of what is at once silly and unpleasant that does not gel with tragedy. In the Marvel Universe, there is the trashing of the long-term character Wanda Maximoff, the Scarlet Witch, in order to facilitate the reboot of the Avengers and set up the *House of M* and *Decimation* storylines.

One of the major driving forces of the creation of these universes was the commercial imperative to create brand loyalty to more titles within a single publishing house's products. Crossovers, in which a character from one comic produced by a house visited the story of another, meant that there was a chance that readers who were not buying the first comic would start to buy it in addition to the second. Team-up comics like the *Justice League of America* were even more likely to interest readers in characters they had not previously bothered with.

Though there have always been other rival houses, the domination of the field since the 1960s by DC and Marvel has meant that there were two very clear and distinct brands; the point about a continuity is that, generally speaking, its characters inhabit the same universe and no other. If you were reading the various *Superman* titles, you might expect him to be visited by Batman, Green Lantern or the Martian ManHunter; you would not expect him to have to deal with Spider-Man, Thor or the Incredible Hulk. The distinction between these universes is crucial: the reader who is not comics-literate needs to keep it clear in her mind from the start.

What may have started as a commercial decision has become a distinct difference of philosophy and style, even though there are many writers and artists who have worked for both houses at one time or another. Broadly speaking, DC is all about heroes and Marvel is all about heroes and their feet of clay; generally, DC is unfailingly, one might say glibly, optimistic about human nature, and Marvel rather more sceptical. And the moment one says such things, one thinks of a million ways in which they are untrue while continuing in the knowledge that the two universes have a radically different feel.

A crude way of putting this would be to take DC's Superman and Marvel's Spider-Man as representatives of the two houses. Superman is, essentially, a god; his alien origins have given him powers that make him one of the most powerful players in his universe and his moral virtues and wisdom make it hard for him to make mistakes. He is ruled by a sense of duty. His secret identity as Clark Kent is in many ways a mask behind which he hides to protect those he cares about. He knows, and cares, that his entire planet and people died soon after his birth and after his father sent him to Earth, but he does not agonize about this the whole time.

Spider-Man, by contrast, is deeply fallible, human and young, and dominated by a sense of guilt towards those whom he failed to save. His Uncle Ben, who taught him that 'with great power comes great responsibility', died because Spider-Man stood by and let a man who had cheated him be robbed; Gwen, his first love, died because there are limits to his powers – he caught her falling, but could not stop simple inertia breaking her neck. Most importantly, Spider-Man, gallant, constantly quipping, is the mask behind which the shy working stiff photographer Peter Parker hides; all that they have in common is neurosis. Superman is idolized by almost everyone except the deeply evil; Spider-Man is endlessly traduced by the media. DC heroes are on the brink of being gods and Marvel heroes are always at risk of being regarded as monsters. The period when Lex Luthor is President is one of the few points at which Superman has trouble with the authorities; in the Marvel Universe, even the Avengers regularly have problems with bureaucrats who, for example, object to organizing security clearance for all their supernumerary members.

On the few occasions when both houses have licensed crossovers, the results have been mixed. The best of them is undoubtedly Kurt Busiek's *Avengers/JLA* (2004–5), which was drawn by George Perez, who has been a stalwart of both houses for years. This is partly because it acknowledges the radical differences of tone between the universes: the Avengers regard the spick and span DC Universe as proof that the JLA are fascist control freaks, whereas the JLA regard the messiness of the Marvel Universe with disdain – and partly because Busiek and Perez get to produce imagery that draws on the accumulated iconic power of both worlds. The sight of Superman in torn costume making a last stand clutching Captain America's shield and Thor's hammer is genuinely iconic because so deeply wrong at important levels. It is magnificent and it is also in a real sense contrary to nature.

Crossover narrative threads, which start in one of a house's titles and continue over the months in several others, are an effective way of compelling readers to spend more money. Inevitably, for any of this to work, and not seem entirely and transparently a matter of tricking readers into spending more money, the crossovers and the team-ups have to be done at the same level of creativity as the primary material. Such crossovers are sometimes ways of rebooting the entire universe, or significant aspects of it – this will be dealt with in greater detail below. Of course, one reason for events is to compete on equal terms with the other house.

For example, because in 2005–7 DC were running the *Countdown to Infinite Crisis* event and *Infinite Crisis* title and the subsequent *52* title and *One Year Later* event as major reboots both of the universe and individual characters, Marvel ran the mediocre *House of M* event, and its sequels, the intergalactic event *Annihilation* and the rather superior *Civil War* event, all of which significantly rebooted some aspects of the Marvel Universe and the relationships between characters. This is not to disparage the Marvel events – on the contrary, I think *Civil War* rather more interesting than the DC material, fine as some of that is, partly because of its real-world political commentary. The company's commercial masters saw the need for an event, the editors and writers came up with a particularly good idea; we do not complain that Bach's cantatas were commissioned for specific liturgical or political purposes.

Individual superheroes are shown as having back-story; the obvious examples of this are Superman's birth on the doomed planet Krypton and his father's decision to send him away from certain death, or Batman's witnessing the murder of his parents. Either a title will start with an origin story or will sooner or later go back and fill it in; occasionally, as with DC's Donna Troy, the back-story will be changed, but this will never be a simple matter of 'pressing the reset button'. It will be a new origin story that includes an explaining away of what was previously claimed to be the case, whether through amnesia, time paradox or whatever.

A team presented as a team from the beginning, with characters that had not previously existed, like the original X-Men line-up, will have an origin story as a team, but will also have back-stories for each of the members of that team, which we may not learn for some time and which will be a source for more story. Generally speaking, these back-stories will not be revised so much as subjected to endless elaboration, sometimes creating entire new characters in the process. For example, Scott Summers (Cyclops of the X-Men) was originally an orphan who subsequently acquired a brother Alex (Havoc). Later on, Chris Claremont told how they were parachuted together when the plane carrying their parents went out of control. Subsequently, he decided that their parents were kidnapped by aliens, that their mother was raped and murdered by the Shi'ar Emperor D'Kenn and that their father Christopher Summers became the interstellar buccaneer and freedom-fighter Corsair (for complex reasons, he did not reveal his actual identity to his sons and persuaded the telepaths in their lives to keep the matter quiet).

Later still, in Ed Brubaker's 2006 miniseries *Deadly Genesis*, it emerged that their mother was pregnant with her husband's child at the time of her death, that the child Gabriel was born by caesarian, enslaved by the Shi'ar and found his way to Earth in late childhood, where he was recruited by Charles Xavier from Moira McTaggart's research group. Gabriel Summers (Vulcan) was one of several X-Men sent by Xavier in a doomed rescue attempt when the original group were captured, assumed dead, at the hands of Krakoa, the Island that Walks Like a Man; this took place during the Len Wein run that preceded Claremont in the late 1970s after the revival of the title that had lapsed during the 1960s. The team were killed, save for Gabriel and one other, Darwin, who were carried into space, comatose, when the second rescue team, the one containing what we had hitherto considered the canonical secondary group, defeated Krakoa. The only inconsistency – that the new first rescue party save Scott, as did what is now the second group – is ironed out by the fact that his mind and memory had been suppressed by Krakoa and not restored by Xavier, not that this cuts much ice with his newly discovered brother.

This is a radical revision of canon, but it is done with enough attention to what has gone before, and opens up enough of what is implied by canon, that it is to be distinguished from strip-mining. We have always, for example, known that Charles Xavier, however benevolent, is capable of real ruthlessness and of expending the lives of his young protégés for what he regards as the greater good. It does not compromise the tone of what has preceded it.

That fidelity to tone is important: Brubaker's *Winter Soldier* run on *Captain America* took one of the basic premises of the character's continuity and changed it, but in the process not only remained faithful to that continuity's emotional weight, but actually deepened it. Captain America, it needs to be remembered, emerged into the Marvel Universe in 'modern times' (see above for a consideration of time in superhero comics) with an extended back-story as the artificially created super-soldier of the Second World War. In this role he had a teen sidekick, Bucky, whose death in an explosion, just before Captain America was frozen for decades, has constantly haunted him. It affected, for example, his relationship with serial sidekick Rick Jones back in the 1960s; in the early 2000s, it is a plot point in his refusal to give approval to teen superhero groups like the Runaways and the Young Avengers, who subsequently are among his supporters during *Civil War*, to his mild embarrassment.

What Brubaker did was at once to darken the Bucky of the 1940s by showing him as the Young Turk trained to do the back-stabbing and throat-cutting part of commando work, which Captain America was too honourable to cope with, and by announcing that he did not exactly die. Frozen like Captain America, he was captured, defrosted and brainwashed by the Soviet Union. He is, in fact, the Winter Soldier of the title, an assassin decanted as necessary by his controller, now, after the fall of Communism, a freelance.

In one sense, this changes everything and in another it changes nothing. Captain America gives Bucky his memories back and it is unclear whether Bucky can live with them; Captain America has exchanged one set of guilty feelings for another. A motivating wound in danger of becoming a cliché has been effectively renewed; drastic revision of continuity is sometimes a good idea. One cannot know for certain, but it seems likely that this exemplary resurrection of Bucky is intended as a rebuke to DC, whom Brubaker had left for Marvel, for the botched resurrection of Jason Todd, the dead Robin in the *Red Hood* storyline.

It certainly contains a rebuke to another Marvel handling of Captain America. Mark Millar in *The Ultimates* portrays Captain America as a gung-ho fanatic, a necessary man whom it is dangerous to cross or even disagree with. The left-wing Millar dislikes Captain America, but is fascinated by what he has created to the extent that he has him say things too brilliant for a real right-winger to come up with. When Brubaker has his quiet, democratic version of Captain America talk eloquently about the sacrifices made by the French Resistance, it can, I think, be taken as a gentle rebuke to Millar for the moment where he has Captain America say, to a Nazi alien 'Surrender!! You think this letter on my forehead stands for France!?!'

When previously established characters come together as a team, there needs to be an origin story for the team, a particular emergency that they have to handle together. In the case of the Avengers, it was a series of incidents involving the likes of the god Loki and the temporal invader Kang the Conqueror. One of the problems with such teams is that most of the villains and emergencies individual superheroes tackle are not such that they need a group. Inevitably, the existence of teams demands a constant escalation of the scale of menaces, either in terms of the particular cunning of individual villains or in terms of the introduction of problems on a cosmic scale, such as the various wars between interstellar empires in which Marvel heroes in particular are prone to involve themselves – the Kree–Skrull War, and the rather crassly titled *Operation Galactic Storm*, or even vaster conflicts between quasi-abstract principles of existence such as the so-called Infinity War and Infinity Crusade that Jim Starlin wrote for Marvel. Major events and reboots (see below) tend in this direction, as does the most successful crossover between the two houses' continuities, the Kurt Busiek/George Perez *Avengers/JLA* in which two cosmic entities engineer a collision between the two multiverses in order to outwit a third entity, recruiting the two teams for the purpose.

Both houses' continuities embody – Marvel cheerfully, DC rather more ambivalently – the idea of a multiverse, in which there are a number of alternate worlds in which the standard characters may be radically different or non-existent. (One of Marvel's superhero teams, the eXiles, consists of alternate versions of various X-Men, who travel between timelines fixing anomalies, like a world in which the Avengers have become vampires.) The DC Universe has the anti-matter Earth 2, which is ruled by a Crime Syndicate who are radically different versions of Superman, Batman and so on, who are opposed by a virtuous Luthor and others (pre-*Crisis* these existed in an alternate world). Generally speaking, DC has tried to prune these outcroppings to a minimum; the point of the *Crisis on Infinite Earths* of the mid-1980s, the *Zero Hour* of the 1990s and the *Infinite Crisis* of the mid-2000s was not merely to sell extra comics but to render manageable potentially over-proliferating material. Ironically, the lasting effect of 2006's *Infinite Crisis* is gradually revealed (in the weekly comics *52* and its sequel *Countdown* (2006–8) to have been the return of the DC Multiverse.

Unfortunately, one of the side effects of *Crisis on Infinite Earths* – which killed some characters off and changed the back-stories of others – was that some authors felt justified in entirely arbitrary additional revisions of back-story. As I argue elsewhere, this is the sort of thing that is only justified by results, and in some cases was not: the character and career of Hawkman has endlessly been made unclear as a result of this. Part of the pleasure of reading in continuity is watching the slow unfolding of a career and the spins that different writers put on a character within the parameters that have been collectively created; radical alterations to the facts of such a career are often a falsification of the emotional content that has attached itself to that career across time.

The Marvel Universe, by contrast, has always gloried in the proliferation of timelines to an extent that it sometimes becomes almost impossible to keep straight in one's mind, yet somehow it remains accessible to most readers. To give two examples: Rachel Grey is the daughter of Scott Summers and Jean Grey but was born into a timeline, came to the present from a dystopian future that never happened. Cable, her half-brother, Summers' son by Madeleine, the woman he married when Jean was supposedly dead, was sent into the future to have a disease cured and came back when he was significantly older than his father. Marvel material is explicitly set in a multiverse; when they were working for Marvel's short-lived UK line, Dave Thorpe created and Alan Moore developed, as part of the story of Captain Britain, a powerful empire that rules across many timelines and polices, in its own interests rather than altruistically, such matters as waves of probability sweeping out destructively from individual timelines.

This empire was added to the mainstream Marvel Universe along with Captain Britain, like him, mostly occurring in the various X-titles as written by Chris Claremont and by Alan Davis (who was Thorpe and Moore's artist on this material in the first place). Captain Britain's erstwhile girlfriend Courtney Ross, his world's analogue of the inter-universe empress Saturnyne, has become a recurring character in the continuity, sometimes as Emma Frost's rival as White Queen of the Hellfire Club. The run of *Uncanny X-Men* during the *House of M* event dealt in part with the ramifications of so sudden an alteration of reality when viewed from the perspective of Saturnyne's empire. Neil Gaiman's re-imagining of the Marvel Universe in terms of the Jacobethan period *1602* (Nick Fury as Walsingham, Magneto as Torquemada) is explicitly positioned as a timeline created by time paradox caused by scientific meddling in one of the dystopian alternate futures that Marvel's heroes constantly fight to prevent.

If, as is the case with both houses, your heroes have powers that enable them to move entire worlds by acts of will, as well as to stop quite trivial stick-ups by the judicious application of minimum force, you are going to need storylines set on a vast canvas. There are only so many times that a figure as titanic as Superman can content himself with the local and petty. Accordingly, the backdrop of both continuities is vast in scope and scale, time and space and levels of power – the multiverse is only one aspect of this question of scale.

Both continuities contain horizontal layers of reality as well as these lateral ones, the nature of these embodying the rather different implied theological assumptions of the two houses. Much of DC's theology is to some extent optional, given that much of it is contained in the various 'adult' comics of DC's Vertigo line, but at least some of the characters and assumptions of the Vertigo titles remain consistent with material in the DC mainline. Neil Gaiman's

The Identity of Captain Marvel

DC, Marvel and various other US and UK publishers have at different times claimed rights in Captain Marvel, into whom, originally, Billy Batson turns by saying 'Shazam!' (The original Fawcett title closed after DC sued for plagiarism, alleging similarities to Superman, but the British reprint, under different laws, continued with new material, closed and was later revived.) Threatened with a suit by Marvel, the UK publisher of the magazine *Warrior* changed their version's name to Marvelman, under which title both Alan Moore and Neil Gaiman did impressive runs early in their careers. As reprinted and completed in the USA by Eclipse as *Miracleman*, the Moore run and its Gaiman sequel is one of the most impressive meditations on superheroes as quasi-deities and redeemers, but remains incomplete as the result of lawsuits and other issues.

Meanwhile, Marvel felt entitled to create a character called Captain Marvel, or more correctly Mar-vell, a captain in the Kree space navy, who defected to the USA on which

The Books of Magic was commissioned to be a summary of all the material about magic and the supernatural across the whole of the continuity as well as with material from his own work and that of Alan Moore. Inevitably, he created a viewpoint character for the occasion, Tim Hunter, who became a figure in continuity, as well as being an interesting precursor of Harry Potter with his untidy hair and spectacles.

Supernatural and Godlike Beings

In the DC Universe, then, magic and the supernatural exist alongside the wonders of mutation, aliens and super-science. Superman is vulnerable to magic as well as to Kryptonite; other heroes, notably DC's version of Captain Marvel, owe their powers to magic rather than to that sort of highly developed, or fictional, science which is indistinguishable from magic

he was spying and became an Earth superhero and defender of righteousness throughout the galaxy. He even acquired a human alter-ego in the shape of Rick Jones, who changed places with him, in exile in the Negative Zone, by clashing wristbands. Later on, Mar-vell died; his powers were inherited by his son Genis, an occasional member of the Thunderbolts, who does not use his father's name. For a while the name Captain Marvel was appropriated by a black superheroine, who subsequently adopted the sobriquet Photon, a name briefly adopted by Genis. Mar-vell's opponent – as spy – and occasional lover subsequently, Carol Danvers, goes by the name Ms Marvel in tribute to him. It is also worth noticing that in the Marvel Universe, Captain Marvel's powers are conferred by alien super-science and breeding – Carol Danvers got in the way of a Kree super-weapon and gained her powers by surviving, whereas in the DC Universe the powers of the various members of the Marvel family – including the morally ambiguous tyrant Black Adam – are conferred by magic.

Though the Marvel Universe has its magicians – notably Doctor Strange – the DC universe is perhaps happier with magic than its rival. Some occasional members of the Justice League and the Justice Society are magicians, such as Zatanna and Doctor Fate; during Grant Morrison's run on the *Justice League of America* another member of the team was an angel, Zauriel, who had taken a prolonged sabbatical from Heaven in order to stay out of the way of a more powerful angel he suspected of plotting rebellion.

Angels, then, in the DC Universe, are roughly as they are in Judaeo-Christo-Islamic mythology, only with less damned nonsense about merit; they are the police writ large, with the standard copper's arrogance towards civilians, or the Feds, with the standard sense of a big picture to which individuals may need to be sacrificed. Heaven is the Silver City where angels live – where God is mentioned, he is either indirect or literally, in Mike Carey's *Lucifer* series, *deus absconditus*. This sort of thing has only affected the mainline of DC continuity through the presence of Zauriel and his enemies in the Grant Morrison-era *Justice League of America*, and through the Spectre – originally a spirit that helped the unjustly dead work for justice, who has gradually been revised so that he is the literal Wrath of God – given moderation and humanity by a dead human anchor. He is rather more than an angel in his powers and, when not moderated by a human partner, quite terrifying. For a while the fallen Green Lantern Hal Jordan worked his passage to redemption by being the spirit through whom the Spectre manifested. This in turn meant that the Spectre was, like Jordan, corrupted for a while by the demonic Parallax, one of several occasions when the Spectre has ceased for a while to be a force for good.

Devils and demons are rather more common players in the DC Universe, participants in Faustian pacts on occasion, sometimes possessors of human bodies and souls. Jack Kirby created Etrigan, who was summoned by Merlin to influence the outcome of Arthur's final battle, and Etrigan, turned into (or possessing – continuity is contradictory on this point) a human called Jason Blood, fights evil less out of virtue than for sport. Later, Alan Moore reinvented

Etrigan as a rhyming demon, who talks in verse. Occasionally a character will continue to be involved in the storyline even though dead and damned, as Arcane did in Alan Moore's period of *Swamp Thing*. (*Swamp Thing* also included, in Moore's 'American Gothic' storyline, one of the few occasions where the DC Universe has seemed less monotheist and more gnostic; apparently opposing forces of good and evil turn out to be hands, one dark and one light, reaching out for a handclasp.)

There are other supernatural layers to the DC Universe. It has a version of Faerie, though this most usually occurs in Neil Gaiman's work and work spun off from it; it has the realms of the Endless, Gaiman's personifications of abstractions like Dream, Death, Despair and Desire. Beyond Gaiman's own work, the Dreaming has been the ultimate destination of the starfish-like mind-controlling invaders that periodically bedevil the JLA. There is the home dimension of the magic-working imp Bat Mite and Mr Mxyzptlk (not apparently magic, but having multi-dimensional powers that indicate he might as well be), who bedevil Batman and Superman respectively. There is the Green, the continuum of plant life that underlies our reality; various once-human beings, all of whom once studied biology together, are to a varying extent participants in the Green. Among these are the Swamp Thing as reinvented by Alan Moore – a plant elemental with the memories of the dead Alec Holland – Black Orchid, as reinvented by Neil Gaiman – a constantly re-blooming flower with the memories of a dead woman who fights crime – and the Batman villainess Poison Ivy, aka Pamela Isley.

There are also quasi-eschatological beings that operate in the world of DC continuity. Jack Kirby created the New Gods, a race of superbeings led by the Highfather, and his opponent Darkseid, a monstrous being in search of the Anti-Life equation that will enable him to rule the universe. Though these are called gods, they are properly conceived of as mortal entities of immense power and longevity; Superman has stood up to Darkseid in battle in *Justice League Unlimited*, the television cartoon series, and even defeated him in Jeph Loeb's *Batman/Superman* in the 'Supergirl' storyline where Darkseid had apparently destroyed Kara, Superman's cousin. Both Darkseid and the Highfather have sons, and exchanged them as hostages to the intermittent truce between them. Darkseid's son Orion, who hides his disfigured facial legacy behind a mask, has become a paladin of good, his heritage occasionally manifesting in ill-temper and intolerance; the Highfather's son escaped the orphanage into which Darkseid cast him and became the escape artist Mr Miracle, aka Scott Free (Kirby is an intense creator, but never a subtle one). The Mr Miracle who features in Grant Morrison's *Seven Soldiers of Victory* is a different character, one of Free's acolytes. Though the Jack Kirby titles featuring the denizens of Apokolips and New Genesis included the title *The New Gods*, there has never been a sense in which Darkseid and All-Father have ever been seen, particularly once formally adopted into mainstream DC continuity, as more than powerful beings living in a universe created by Another.

The Marvel Universe, by contrast, has far more in common with the world of the Gnostics than it does with that of standard Judaeo-Christian mythology. It has, notionally, a single ultimate deity, very occasionally referred to as the One Above All, to whom the Living Tribunal answers, but, on the only occasion that purported to show this entity, what we got was Jack Kirby at his drawing board. Most of the time, the Marvel Universe is a field of contention between powerful beings in constantly shifting alliances.

The most important entity we have seen regularly in the Marvel Universe is Eternity, a quasi-personified embodiment of everything that is. For a while it seemed that Eternity had a peer, perhaps a consort, in the shape of Infinity, but it became apparent that they were aspects of the same androgyne. Possibly as important are Death, sometimes a hooded skeleton and sometimes a beautiful silent woman (quite unlike the teen Goth Death that Gaiman created, and who has become the default version of Death in the DC Universe ever since), and her male aspect Oblivion.

Though one thinks of him as a star-travelling menace, the world-eater Galactus is regarded by all/both of these as their peer;

interestingly, given that he was once a mortal man. Galactus, a being who eats worlds, and devours the life energy of their inhabitants, is a survivor from the cosmos that preceded the Big Bang, a creature whose intelligence has become subsumed into vast appetite. He is in some sense an embodiment of entropy, to some degree a threat that subjects peoples and their planets to trial; though powerful, he can be defeated by intelligence rather than brute force.

There are other figures of eschatological importance, like the Living Tribunal, who arbitrates disputes at this level, and the quasi-gods who rule various magical realms – of these the most important are the opponents of the magician Dr Strange, Dormammu and his sister Umar. Marvel has its own equivalent of Darkseid in Thanos, originally part of a family of dissident gods who fled Olympus for the moon Titan. Thanos is erotically obsessed with Death, commits endless murders, and tries to make himself a player on her level in order that she notice him; at times he becomes godlike, but always overreaches himself, is always dragged back to the level of flesh by the less-powerful heroes who oppose him, and by the potentially godlike Adam Warlock. Warlock resists godhood because he knows its temptations; divinity is one of several sites in the Marvel Universe where the righteousness of great power is constantly interrogated.

To complicate matters, Warlock has a time-travelling future self, the Magus, keen to ensure that Warlock be corrupted and become him, the emperor of a vast realm in space and the metaphysical. Warlock is at one point Thanos' pawn against the Magus; on another occasion they are allies when the Magus returns from non-existence. The morality of these alliances is often an interestingly grey area; the Marvel Universe is one in which moral sides are not always neatly drawn and as below, so above.

The pantheons of Greek and Norse mythology have objective existence in the Marvel Universe – Thor and Hercules are superheroes as well as gods – but they are purely local phenomena of comparatively little cosmic importance. It is sometimes argued, as in Jim Kreuger's *Earth X*, that they are shapeshifting aliens locked into their current forms by human worship and imagination.

Asgard and Olympus are locations within the Marvel Universe, and characters with no particular connection with them are liable to end up there when caught up in the schemes of its enemies, notably the X-Men and the New Mutants. The villains of these mythologies – the God Loki in particular – are liable to turn up and act as supervillains; Loki's schemes are part of what brought the original Avengers together. Though Thor is a god and hero, the occasion when he brought Asgard into close proximity to Earth was a disaster for both worlds; his disastrous reign as god-king of Earth, undone by time paradox, is a good example of the nightmares created by power out of control, which I discuss futher below.

The Marvel Universe also has a variety of Hells and Devils, only some of which are finessed as alternate dimensions. The Silver Surfer and the Scarlet Witch are both manipulated by a tempter called Mephisto; the X-Man Ilyana Rasputin is kidnapped to, and grows to maturity in, a dimension ruled by the demonic Belasco (named, obscurely, after the actor-manager who wrote *Madame Butterfly*).

Another layer of quasi-supernatural material was added to the Marvel Universe by Jack Kirby. The Celestials are space gods along the lines of Erich von Däniken's claims, vast demiurgish beings who intervened in human evolution at various points. Their principal creations, the immensely powerful and immortal Eternals, and the monstrous Deviants, have had roles in human history. This material is currently being revisited and re-imagined by Neil Gaiman in what is only his second outing in Marvel material and the first in main continuity. Kirby and Stan Lee also created in the purely temporal world beings so powerful that they might as well be supernatural. The Watchers are a corps of alien observers who sit around not intervening in the lives and deaths of entire species, but every so often one of them cheats in a good cause.

One of the most impressive things about the Marvel Universe is that it has managed, on occasion, to build on the sheer mythopaeia involved in Kirby's original creation of Galactus with his vast purple armoured head-dress; in *Avengers/JLA* Busiek has his characters solemnly intone as they arrive at the site of their conflict with the villain, 'His stronghold . . . It's Galactus. He built it from the remains of Galactus'. When comics are at their best, the art is as monumental as this sort of dialogue; George Perez represents the stronghold as a vast jumble, crowned off-centre with the head-dress. The teams' ship, which a few pages earlier dominated an entire double-spread splash page, is reduced to the size of an insect by comparison.

Both DC and Marvel's superhero continuities have a large space-opera element. Green Lantern is only one of a corps of such recruited by the benevolent Guardians of the Universe (currently four Green Lanterns are from Earth, not counting the JSA Green Lantern, whose powers derive from magic and only indirectly from the Guardians). In DC continuity, Earth has been invaded by a variety of species, sometimes operating as an alliance, and one of the events of the *Infinite Crisis* was a war between two powerful alien planets, Rann and Thanagar. Though the quasi-avian inhabitants of Thanagar are generally malevolent, two of them, Hawkman and Hawkgirl, have been active as superheroes on Earth, albeit with conflicting loyalties. An Earthman, Adam Strange, regularly saves the inhabitants of Rann, though lacking superpowers. These details aside, there is a tendency for the space-opera elements in the DC Universe to be ad hoc.

The space-opera elements in the Marvel Universe are somewhat more thought out. Essentially, there used to be three significant interstellar empires: the blue humanoid Kree, the green shapeshifting Skrull and the quasi-avian humanoid Shi'ar. The Kree Empire fell apart, something largely engineered by its ruler, the Intelligence Supreme (a brain in a tank containing the minds of many significant Kree), as a eugenic measure – he wanted the Kree to experience adversity and start evolving again. The Skrull were crippled when Galactus ate their homeworld and have declined into squabbling fiefdoms looking for a royal claimant to give them legitimacy (this latter struggle is a plot point in both of Marvel's comics aimed at younger readers, *Runaways* and *Young Avengers*). The Shi'ar have become a dominant power by default, but clearly not for long, since a current (at writing) storyline in X-Men continuity is called 'The Fall of the Shi'ar Empire'. The Shi'ar have a long and complicated involvement with the X-Men: their current empress, Lilandra, was for a while Charles Xavier's lover, but they were badly damaged by his twin, Cassandra, when she took over his body. More recently, they wiped out all of Jean and Rachel Gray's relatives in an attempt to prevent any recurrence of the Phoenix in human shape. Lilandra is a despot, only benevolent by comparison with her entirely monstrous brother and sister, who in turn have been betrayed at the height of their seizure of power by Gabriel Summers, Scott Summers' evil younger brother, the murderer of their father Corsair and now self-crowned emperor of the Shi'ar.

I have gone into some detail about the backdrop of these two continuities, simply to give an idea of their scale and complexity, a scale and complexity achieved less by design than slow accretion of plot conveniences and periodic attempts to rationalize the result systematically. They are vast and gaudy, and as nothing in complexity to the personal stories that the comics produced by the two houses tell.

In the 1950s, DC comics re-imagined a number of pre-existing superhero titles that they owned, or had acquired, and fitted them into the same universe; Green Lantern is a good example of this, with the ring being changed from a magical device to one provided by alien super-science, but retaining the need to be recharged regularly, and its operation as the embodiment of the wearer's will. The point about Marvel's superheroes is that most of the crucial ones were invented, in a string of brilliant ideas, by Stan Lee, Jack Kirby and Steve Ditko over a period of a couple of years. The others were inherited from the various companies out of which Marvel had grown – both Submariner and Captain America were Golden Age characters who were re-imagined and reintroduced in the early days of Marvel, with an explanation for their long disappearances (Captain America was frozen in an iceberg; Submariner became an amnesiac bum).

As has, I think, been demonstrated without need for extended further summary, the interlocking story arcs of the characters of the DC and Marvel universes are endlessly fascinating both as soap opera and myth cycle. These are stories that constantly generate new characters, and any character, no matter how seemingly ad hoc their creation and sketchy their original creation, may become the focus of a particular writer's attention and start to be dealt with inventively and in detail. To pick two examples, Renée Montoya, a Gotham City detective who originally appeared in the animated *Batman* TV shows, has gradually become a significant figure in DC comics, partly as the focus of storylines in Ed Brubaker's police procedural comic *Gotham Central*, and more recently as the ex-lover of the new Batwoman and as a replacement for the dead vigilante, the Question. Cassie Lang was periodically mentioned as the object of custody suits between her mother and her father, Scott Lang, the Ant-Man murdered by Wanda Maximoff; she is now one of the Young Avengers, as Stature, having inherited her father's powers.

This is even without the sort of radical invention that periodically occurs. The next chapter will deal at length with Jessica Jones, a character created by Brian Bendis in *Alias* and inserted into Marvel continuity as if she had always been there. When Neil Gaiman was first invited to work for DC he took on a comparatively obscure heroine, Black Orchid, and reinvented her as one of a group of plant beings all connected with the same research programme. Again, he took a crime-fighter with a sleep gun, the Sandman, and made him a mere shadow of the real Sandman, the Lord of Dreams. Many comics creators rightly complain about working for hire, and that the products of their imagination can be endlessly recycled by the company; the up-side of this is that some of what later writers do with characters created by someone else is fascinating work in its own right.

Particular events in continuity may be revisited and sometimes revised endlessly. This will sometimes take the form of flashbacks – the murder of Bruce Wayne's parents during a casual mugging is something that almost every significant *Batman* writer has shown us replaying in his head sooner or later – and sometimes take the form of visits through travel back through, or across, time. When it originally happened in an episode of *The Fantastic Four*, the destruction of the Skrull homeworld by Galactus was an impressive enough event; it was even more so when, during the Alan Davis run on *The X-Men*, Xavier and a selection of his pupils found themselves, via time travel, caught up in this event. Xavier, no great believer in Prime or Temporal Directives, tries and fails to dissuade the Eater of Worlds from his course of action; the X-Men fight copies of themselves and other superheroes created by a Skrull spy school (aided by copies of dead heroes who resent being regarded as surplus to requirements). The eXiles find themselves at one point in a universe running a few years late, where the Dark Phoenix saga is playing out with a potentially different outcome.

What I want to suggest is that much of what is best in superhero comics comes from the sheer size of the body of lore that comes as part of the package, that one of the things that makes for good work in this field is letting the wisdom of continuity work for you. This idea is less hideously Jungian than it sounds; to work consciously in a shared universe, and to go with the grain of that universe as most comics writers do most of the time in their best work, is to demonstrate that particular sort of competence that comes in what I have elsewhere called 'competence cascades'. This may be an example of what Steven Johnson calls emergent phenomena in his book *Emergence* and elsewhere, and may be an example of what James Sarowiecki in his 2004 book of that name calls 'the wisdom of crowds', without being nearly as determinist as even those models that I am describing.

If you are guided by the internal logic of the artistic form or corpus you have put yourself in the way of working with, and so produce something that can be called an emergent phenomenon, it is, as I would describe it, rather more the result of conscious choice than either Johnson or Sarowiecki has suggested. There is, after all, a reason why poets wrote sonnets for several centuries and why composers write symphonies, and that reason is not only to do with the demands of the cultural market place. There is at once challenge and comfort in writing something that may surprise an audience, but will do so in a context of structure that they find familiar and congenial. No one forced those poets and composers, and they would not necessarily have starved if they had done otherwise, yet they chose to work inside a cultural context that gave them access to constant metonymy of other poems and music. We often do our best work when working with what we know.

All genres have rules. Works within a genre often echo each other, sometimes polemically, sometimes as a game and sometimes because there are particular extraordinary examples of a form that later creators can only with difficulty get around. The second subject of the finale of Brahms First Symphony echoes the choral finale of Beethoven's Ninth; asked about this, Brahms merely responded that any fool could see that. What I am suggesting is something further: in part, one of the particular genre rules of the superhero comic is successful navigation of, and negotiation with, the vast body of lore and continuity that the form has built up.

It is perhaps because it represents such a withdrawal from the possibilities of writing with continuity as well as a betrayal of the conspiracy between writer and audience to believe that continuity makes entire sense, that strip-mining of the kind involved in the deaths of Stephanie and Sue Dibney, and the madness of Wanda Maximoff, comes across as so deeply irritating. For the sake of brief sensation or plot convenience, things are unpicked that worked and had further life in them. When, as is always the case – at least by default – the company and its editors make or allow the decisions involved, it is usually a piece of short-termism that does not make entire commercial sense in the long run. At just the point when the Batman comics had started to acquire a significant online female fandom, *War Games* alienated that fandom with the gratuitous torture and death of Stephanie, and was not good enough in objective artistic terms, or successful enough in financial ones, to justify this.

This, above all, is one of the standard indictments of comics writing, that it takes place within a cash nexus, that it is work for hire and almost by definition unoriginal. Certainly the failure of the comics companies to recognize any moral right on the part of their writers and artists in the products of their hands and brains has led on many occasions in the past to quite signal injustices, most notably in the case of the long struggle of Siegel and Shuster to profit from their original creation of Superman, particularly when the character spun off from comics into television, film and other properties. The question of economic injustice and contractual inequality has to do with a particular model of copyright that exists under late capitalism, and is not necessarily to be linked to the broader question of whether originality in the arts is necessarily a precondition for high quality.

The assumption that the great artist necessarily makes up new things is both something that has never been fully true and something that was always a product of a particular moment in history. Much of Western literature, art and dramatic music has concerned itself with the Greco-Roman or Judaeo-Christian myths, or with such lesser bodies of narrative accumulation as the matter of Britain. The realism of the 19th and 20th centuries concerns itself with the representation of a consensual set of assumptions about what society is, which has left many texts stranded when cultural attitudes to class, gender, race and sexuality have changed, and the unreality of some of those assumptions is exposed. This is not to judge the quality of work on the basis of its adherence to later views that were not available to it at the time, but it is to throw into question the realist project and its implicit assumption of moral superiority over material based on myth, fancy or whimsy.

The law of copyright means that the only way to work publicly with the material of the DC and Marvel universes is to work for hire for those companies, or for the associated television and film franchises. There is, of course, one exception, which is symphonic music; the American composer Michael Daugherty (who also wrote the opera *Jackie O.* and the piano concerto *Le Tombeau de Liberace*) produced a *Metropolis Symphony* portraying, inter alia, Lois Lane in perpetual danger and Superman's (temporary) death at the hands of the rampaging monster Doomsday (portrayed through a tango that rises to a crescendo). He is also the composer of a linked orchestral piece representing Bizarro. Camp as Daugherty's composition often is, his work based on the Superman mythos is as serious as he is capable of being; his project is as much to recruit popular culture as material on which high art can be based as to mock it.

The two best literary novels to come out of our obsession with superheroes avoid the problem of campness. The two adolescent protagonists of Jonathan Lethem's *Fortress of Solitude* (its very title an allusion to Superman's retreat) are comics fans, and the novel's sense of period is as closely tied to the month-by-month issue of comics in the period it covers as it is to developments in pop and rock music. When they discover and use a ring that makes it possible for the wearer to fly, and play with it in the way that makes most sense to them, by acting as masked vigilantes, it is a thing that bonds them together and yet not enough to prevent issues of class and race and educational attainment driving them apart. Lethem writes, here and in his essays, out of deep affection for the superhero trope; he also does so without illusions.

Michael Chabon's *The Adventures of Kavalier and Clay* alludes constantly to the comics of the Golden Age in its portrayal of the industry in its 1930s and 1940s first heyday. Rather than slot his two protagonists into the careers of known figures, Chabon invents an entire career for them; their creation of their first character, the Escapist, leads to their getting the opportunity to create others. Chabon plays an inventive game here, whereby Kavalier and Clay anachronistically play with some of the themes and artistic experiments of considerably later periods in their 1940s work; this is a game that only means anything to people who know what he is talking about, of course, and is only possible because he is clearly a deeply committed fan himself.

Not only do Lethem and Chabon demonstrate that comics are a valid theme for fiction to discuss, they also make it clear that comics creators and fans are too. Where various screenwriters have moved into comics with varying degrees of success – Kevin Smith's *Daredevil* run, Joss Whedon's period on *Astonishing X-Men* (which I discuss in Chapter 6) – and comics have recruited various genre writers like Brad Meltzer and Orson Scott Card, as yet no mainstream novelist has moonlighted in the industry. Given that Chabon did work on the script of the second Spider-Man film, it is clearly only a matter of time. As I write, the thriller writer Ian Rankin has just been recruited to write a run of the John Constantine comic *Hellblazer*.

I should at least mention in passing the ongoing *Wild Cards* shared world anthology series (1987 onwards) produced by George R.R. Martin and various friends and associates. This had its origins in a role-playing game improvised by Martin's circle, in which superpowers were the positive outcome of an experimental alien virus that more usually caused grotesque deformity or death. The *Wild Cards* continuity allowed its writers to deal with AIDS, urban squalor, the McCarthy era and the rise of demagogic politicians, and was the source of a few quite extraordinary stories like Howard Waldrop's 'Sixty Minutes Over Broadway'.

Interests have to be declared – I contributed superhero stories of my own to *Temps* (1991) and *Eurotemps* (1992) devised and edited by Alex Stewart and Neil Gaiman, part of a series of shared world anthologies that they, I and Mary Gentle produced in the early 1990s. All that is relevant to mention here is that the first of these stories – 'A Lonely Impulse' – used the superhero motif primarily to make some sarcastic points about government bureaucracy and the tall poppy syndrome, and secondarily to be lyrical about dreams of flying. By the time of the second anthology and my story for it, 'Totally Trashed' (texts of both stories can be found on my website),[7] the world we had collectively built had already acquired enough story complexity that I found myself writing something where the main point was to make sense of other people's continuity glitches. In the process of doing that, though, I found myself with a well-dovetailed farce plot in which even a typo that we had let slip in the first volume could be made use of as a central plot point. When I talk about 'the wisdom of continuity', I

---

[7]   www.glamourousrags.dymphna.net

have some experience of how that works, even in a continuity that consisted of twenty or so stories.

One subject I have generally not addressed in this book is that of superheroes on television (but see the box on *Heroes* for an exception), simply because the sheer scale of the subject would have unbalanced my discussion of other issues. Superman has been the subject of several shows – most notably *The New Adventures of Superman/Lois and Clark* and the current *Smallville*, while the Batman featured in the campy 1960s show and in various rather superior animated series, currently *Gotham Knights*. *Justice League*

Heroes

There is also *Heroes*, whose first season was aired in 2006–7, but is clearly work of a standard that radically revises one's view of what is possible with superheroes on television. One of the crucial things is how slowly it moves. We are used to stories of superheroes moving fast enough that five significant things can happen in the 20-something pages of the average comic. *Heroes*, though, is gently paced even by the standards of episodic television; by the half-way mark of the first season, we were little closer to understanding what is going on and a very long way from forming a superhero team or dealing with the atomic explosion that will soon destroy New York. Several of the characters didn't even have a proper handle on what their powers are yet, and were even further from accepting that they have them and are stuck with them. Several characters' powers were still evolving by the series finale.

Heroes is a genuine serial in that it deals with the slow accumulation of knowledge among the characters and in the audience, episode by episode. We remember individual shows as much for what we find out as for what happens – there was, after all, a time when we thought that the preternaturally persuasive Eden was just a helpful neighbour or that Sylar was simply an ordinary brain-eating serial killer. *Heroes* is also a show that takes the time to see its characters in the round, with all their moral ambiguity and mixed values; a decision that Eden makes in the last seconds of her life turns around everything we have thought about her, and leaves us with an indelible impression of someone smart and resourceful enough to make a right choice when she seems to have no choices left.

Episodic television is at one level all about making the audience watch next week, partly for the thrills and spills, and partly for the characters. Making us fall in love with characters is hardly something original to *Heroes*. One might argue, indeed, that the real originality rests in a show like the new *Battlestar Galactica*, where it is fairly hard to like any of the variously deranged religious fanatics that populate it, yet we remain fascinated. What *Heroes* does, though, is create several characters whom we start off liking, and love more the more we see them, while allowing them to be largely ineffectual, at least for the moment

The closest thing to a central focus to the show is in the end the Petrelli brothers, Peter and Nathan, an unlikely pair of saviours. Peter is a neurotic New Yorker, trapped in the shadow of his corrupt politician brother and a father badly in hock to the Mob; he is a competent male nurse who over-invests in his dying patients and has fallen in love inappropriately with the daughter of one of them. He is only just starting to understand what his powers are, and misunderstanding them has taken him closer to self-destruction than is quite sane or comfortable. What he has, though, is a sense that it is important to try to do the right thing, and it is this sense of right action, without the safety net of clear knowledge, that is a significant part of the show's mission statement. The fact that, in the end, it is the corrupt older Nathan who has to save the day and, moveover, save it from Peter's inability to control his powers.

Even more than in Peter, though, this ethos is embodied in the show's most attractive character, the chubby Japanese nerd Hiro, of course. Peter, though, has had to work it out for himself, whereas Hiro has a long-standing fascination with comic books to provide him with a moral compass once he learns that he can bend time and space around himself. When he uses his powers to cheat at cards, he expects it to go wrong because he knows from comics that personal gain should form no part of the hero's journey; he feels guilt when he tries and fails to save people as much as joy when he succeeds. He has a gift for friendship; part of the attraction of Hiro is his utter and reciprocated devotion to his best friend Ando, but another part is the way that he manages to charm everyone he meets, even Peter's cynical brother Nathan. If in the end Nathan does the right thing, and (presumably) dies in the attempt, it is because he cannot bear the disapproval of Hiro and of Claire.

Hiro is also the focus for much of the show's sheerly fannish pleasures: when, at the end of the first episode, he finds that he has teleported himself from a Japanese commuter train to the middle of Times Square, we feel a surge of utter joy as he waves his hands in the air and shouts 'Hello New York', a surge that we feel all over again when he finds the scene duplicated in a comic book that he has to steal when he realizes he has come to the USA without dollars.

One of the reasons that *Heroes* works is that it never neglects the pragmatically real; Hiro and Ando cheat at roulette and cards because they are trying to survive in a foreign country without money, and Nathan is worried about the effect on the electorate should they ever believe that a candidate can fly. Part of learning to be heroes is acting in completely non-heroic ways. The geneticist Mohinder gets fed up trying to prove his murdered father's belief in mutants true and goes back to India for several episodes. This is also, we may as well point out, a mainstream American show, several of whose characters are not white, or American.

What then is there not to like? Blandly menacing as Mr Bennett – the man who is trying to put a lid on all this – is, he is too much a default setting for this sort of plot: his reaction to the fact that his adopted cheerleader daughter is self-regenerating is to try to steal her memories as a way of keeping her safe, right up to the point where he demonstrates his redemption by sacrificing his memories of paternal love for her for the same reason. The cheerleader Claire is one of too many women in peril, only one of whom, the bad girl Niki/Jessica, sex worker with a super-strong murderess for split personality, has much chance of doing things for themselves. *Heroes* is glorious, touching, fun and we can hope that in these respects as in others, the creators have thought of ways for it to be better.

Unlimited exploits continuity intelligently, while various earlier JLA animations like *Superfriends* and most Marvel-based animations have not. There are a plethora of non-continuity superhero shows – *Mutant X* is dull and *The 4400* interesting in concept but mediocre in execution.

Death, Rebirth and Other Plot Devices

I am, as is reasonably clear from everything I have written so far, not only intellectually fascinated by superhero comics and what they have to tell us about creativity, originality and attractive people in tight-fitting clothing, but also a fan. I have read superhero comics on and off for 40 years and more and am unlikely ever to stop doing so permanently. The current book was originally to some extent intended to be primarily a study of the superhero films, which treated the comics as crucial background material, rather than what it has become: a study of comics that treats the films based on them as essentially second-hand material and only occasionally of merit in their own right.

However, one of the things that informs what follows is the period during which I became largely alienated from superhero comics from the late 1980s to the late 1990s, for a variety of reasons. Part of the issue was time and part was money – either one buys comics as they come out or, increasingly, waits for the trade paperback collections – and part was the uneasy awareness that somewhere else in the continuities might be material by interesting new writers and artists that one had never heard of and that would turn out to be crucial both to one's appreciation and to making sense of continuity. A friend was so outraged by the poor quality of *Avengers Disassembled* that he did not bother with Bendis' subsequent work for Marvel, thus missing out not only on his best work, *Alias*, but also on plot elements in *New Avengers* that may yet turn out to be crucial to *Civil War*. It is possible to resent quite deeply the extent to which the comics companies are keen to part one from one's money.

This became so nakedly the case during the period when I largely stopped reading superhero comics, as to be entirely repellent. The so-called Dark Age was also the age of laminated covers, of multiple editions of the same issue carefully bagged by collectors for the different cover art, of people buying comics to collect and not to read. At the time, this felt like a betrayal of the promise some of us had felt at the time of *Watchmen* and even of *The Dark Knight Returns*, the promise that comics were going to grow up, and the feeling that part of that growing up might be setting superheroes aside.

This was also the period of a lot of rather wonderful non-superhero comics, of the lives of Mexican villagers and hip young Chicano dykelets in the work of the Hernandez brothers – whose work is still gorgeous, but who long ago stopped saying anything that struck me as especially new – of the satiric picaresque adventures of the barbarian warlord Cerebus the Aardvark (before Cerebus' creator Dave Sim became so caught up in deep misogyny as to make his still-brilliant work almost unreadable in its anger and pain). It was the time of serious graphic novels in what was almost the literary mainstream, of which perhaps the most lasting example is Art Spiegelman's *Maus*, which manages the almost inconceivable feat of writing about the Holocaust in terms of cartoon animals. It was the period when Alan Moore moved on from *Watchmen* to the abortive *Big Numbers* project with Bill Sienkewicz, which, had it ever consisted of more than two issues, might conceivably have changed things forever.

It was a time when DC and to a lesser extent Marvel were hedging their bets with Vertigo and other subsidiary houses and playing around with eschatological comics as a substitute for superheroes. This is as good a point as any to discuss *Sandman*. Asked by DC's Vertigo editor to pick a character to re-imagine, Neil Gaiman took the name of a Golden Age crime fighter and almost nothing else. His Sandman is Morpheus, the Lord of Dreams, and in his company Gaiman takes the reader on a voyage through Heaven, Hell and the human heart (see Neil Gaiman and *Sandman* box).

What attention I was paying to comics tended to go towards Neil's work and that of his stablemates rather than to superhero comics that seemed to me to have taken a step back from plot and character into endlessly proliferating combat scenes. Nor was I

Neil Gaiman and Sandman

As a critic, I am in an odd position about Neil Gaiman's work in general and *Sandman* in particular, not merely because we have been friends for two decades, but because we were particularly close during the years when he was writing it. I can remember, perhaps even better than Neil himself, various plotlines that he never got round to but discussed over drinks; I am my own best source for various crucial pieces of information about how totally the central story arc was planned from an early stage. At least one character in one Sandman volume has been widely and erroneously supposed to have been based on me; the truth is more complex and the character is based in part on one of my ex-flatmates whom Gaiman met, in part on the idiolect of characters in an unpublished novel of mine. I mention this to indicate the difficulty of trying to unpack the roots of so complex a creation. This makes objectivity hard, which is why I have taken so long to get around to discussing this work in print.

In *Sandman*, Dream is, and for a while we are not clear what this means, one of the Endless. We know that Death is his sister, because he has been imprisoned by the magus Burgess as the result of a ritual that went wrong and summoned him in her place. Even so, it is not for a while that we meet Death, who turns out to be a sparky Goth punkette, a perfect foil to Morpheus' dour gloombucket. And yet, we are told from the beginning, she is quite specifically his elder sister, the oldest but one of his siblings.

These are, as we eventually discover, Destiny, Death, Dream, Desire, Destruction, Despair and Delirium (who used to be Delight). They are not gods – they are rather more important than that – so much as embodiments of crucial aspects of the universe's nature, that came into being as soon as the universe produced life; we learn from one of the side-bar tales (this one included in *Endless Nights*, a collection produced several years after the body of the text) that life in this context includes the beings we know as stars as well as the angels and demons of popular mythology. In *The Books of Magic* Gaiman shows us the very end of the cosmos, with Destiny finally closing his book and dying, and his sister ending all things. They are a family, and bicker and have favourites and feuds; Gaiman is touching about the brother/sister relationship of Death and Dream, and of Destruction and his two younger sisters, while the antipathy between Dream and Desire becomes the driving force of what we gradually realise to be the most tragic of plots.

This plot proves to be the story of how Dream, weary of his own existence, especially after his long imprisonment by Burgess, settles his affairs and, without consciously setting out to do so, creates a set of circumstances in which he will cease to be. There are certain laws that even the Endless are forced to obey, and among these is a prohibition on kin-slaying, which Desire tries to manipulate Dream into breaking unconsciously. In the end, however, and as part of a set of circumstances that Desire set in train many years earlier, without intending this consequence at the time, Dream kills, or more precisely mercy-kills, the immortal severed head of his son Orpheus. As a result, he becomes the prey of the Furies, and dies.

The Furies are set on Dream by Lyta Hall, widow of Hector Hall (one of several men in continuity who bore the name, though not necessarily the gasmask and sleep gun of the original Golden Age Sandman), whose son was born in Dream, Morpheus' realm, and was therefore taken from Lyta by Dream to be his successor. Morpheus never acknowledges to himself that he is pursuing his own destruction, but his every act is consistent with it. He is a being of immense power, but he is a prisoner of limitations and of the nature of the universe. The version of the DC Universe that Gaiman creates is vast in its scope in space and time, and yet it is still bounded by necessity.

Sandman is an incredibly rich text, full of interpolated tales, many of them meditations on aspects of story, like the condign punishment of the author who rapes and imprisons a Muse and is afflicted with a plague of story ideas. It is typical of Gaiman that the ideas are good ones and that he was inventive and profligate enough to throw them away on this particular narrative point. *Sandman* is also the story of various humans in whose lives Morpheus ends up intervening; there is Rose, the heroine of *A Doll's House*, whom he rescues with her brother from a serial killer's convention, one of the most chillingly funny things Gaiman has ever written, and which he originally improvised in conversation over dinner with Alan

Moore; there is Barbie, Rose's ex-flatmate and the heroine of her own story, in ways that she and we never quite imagined were possible; and Hob and William Shakespeare. It is a work of huge linguistic and imaginative invention; it is also quite profoundly humane.

entirely wrong, though in the process I missed some fascinating work that I have had to catch up with since.

On the other hand, not all of Vertigo's product was as good as *Sandman* with its constant inventiveness of myth and story. Some of the best Vertigo comics were those that spun off from the sub-universe created by Gaiman. The work done by Peter Hogan and Caitlin Kiernan in *The Dreaming* took some of Gaiman's characters and setting and made them more intensely Gothic, or simply Goth. And Mike Carey's 75-issue run on *Lucifer* took the sardonic spin that Gaiman had added to the figure in Judaeo-Christian mythology and made something very rich and strange from the story of how he and Michael, and their various human children, cope with the realization that the Creator has plans of his own and has manipulated them endlessly, even in their loyalty or rebellion.

Hellblazer was never as good in other hands as it had been in its early days under Jamie Delano; the scruffy trench-coated magus John Constantine is not a character around whom an infinite number of stories can usefully be told, which is why, when Alan Moore invented him, he was a foil to Swamp Thing, his Virgil through the Gothic world of the real America and through his own powers. Grant Morrison's *The Invisibles* was a little too determinedly hip in its take on magic for my taste; a similarly scary hipness characterized *Transmetropolitan,* Warren Ellis' homage to Hunter S. Thompson.

People whose judgement I respect are fonder of Garth Ennis' *Preacher* than I am, and some of its conceits – the John Waynesque assassin who eventually takes his six-shooters up against the Lord God, the untrustworthy Irish vampire – were indeed powerful and sometimes amusing. On the other hand, I got very tired of jokes about bodily mutilation and male rape, though the nadir of that particular trope was reached in an episode of the de- and re-constructed superhero comic *The Authority*, when a particularly unpleasant assassin is turned into a number of chickens and will spend eternity being anally penetrated by his own yokel relatives.

One of the odder phenomena of the Vertigo years was the way that British writers, working with American material, were capable of a degree of social snobbery about the American poor that they would have considered unacceptable when applied to other British people. Does it really have to be spelled out that rape is no laughing matter even when its victim is a psychopathic mass murderer working for the Priory of Zion? It did not take especially long for the new adult comic to become bogged down in laddish clichés of its own, ones rather less innocent than those of most superhero comics. By the turn of the millennium, I had ceased to expect very much from the comics I had had hopes for in the late 1980s and superhero comics started to interest me again (see box on Alan Moore).

In thinking superhero comics a form that had burned out, I had been a victim of the Whiggish theory of pop cultural history in which things move forwards in an endless progress of excellence and forms that have reached their use-by date are discarded. Joanna Russ' concept of the wearing out of genre materials was one that appealed to me, because, at the time, I was also (wrongly) inclined to think that the big glossy space opera[8] had had its day in the novel, and we would not see much more of that . . . I have, people tell me, some strengths as a critic, but an ability to foresee the future is clearly

---

[8] Space opera is the standard term for the subgenre of science fiction which is less concerned with original perceptions about science and society and the ways in which they impinge on each other than it is in drawing on the body of SF for gaudy backdrops and swashbuckling adventure plots. It has at times been used in a derogatory sense, but is more generally accepted as one of the things that SF does well.

Alan Moore

One of the reasons for the reawakening of my interest was the (temporary) return of Alan Moore to the form in a number of titles for America's Best Comics. Moore had spent much of his time since *Watchmen* writing a novel, and on his vast Jack the Ripper tapestry *From Hell* and on the pornography project *Lost Girls* with Melinda Gebbie – both of these are monuments to just how fine non-superhero comics can be as works of serious art. However, Moore found that there were still stories about superheroes that he wanted to tell, however vast his irritation with the partial failure of the revolution he had started in the 1980s. *Supreme*, which completely destroys the fourth wall between comic and reader and shows his hero dealing with different versions of himself, including abortive drafts by other hands, was a piece of blasphemy against the Golden Age only possible to someone who was still deeply in love with the material.

This is how it always seems to be with Moore's radical critiques of the form he has revolutionized and constantly turned against and constantly turned back to. He writes *The League of Extraordinary Gentlemen* with its late Victorian team-up – Mina Harker, Alan Quartermain, Hyde, Nemo and the Invisible Man – and he displays the imperialist racist sexist corrupt warmongering of the time. Yet he also enjoys the idea of what he is doing as a ripping yarn, and the monstrous rapist Hyde dies bravely holding the Thames bridges against Martian tripods. *Tom Strong*, Moore's tribute to all those brilliant scientific adventurers who built electric cars and lived in towers and travelled to the farthest reaches of the Earth and beyond, is genuinely charming and innocent. Part of the point is, of course, that Moore uses Strong to demonstrate that this sort of hero did not in fact have to be as racist and sexist as they actually were; the result, though, transcends any satirical point. The sheer power of the Tom Strong universe is demonstrated not least by the fact that it became a continuity that generated other material – most notably Peter Hogan's slick and pacy *Terra Oscura*.

Promethea combined Moore's desire to create an iconic female superhero with a meditation on the power of story. Promethea is an identity that suffuses creators who make use of it – a portrayal of magical initiation; Moore is fascinated by ritual magic as a mode of performance that changes consciousness the way art is supposed to, and by a consideration of what it is to end the world – or should that merely be 'the world as we know it', the mundane world of pragmatism and sexist racist classist things as they are? *Promethea* succeeds in all these things, partly because of J.H. Williams' wonderful art; I once read the entire run through in an afternoon, and spent the next hour walking in parks in a state of bliss previously only encountered through religion, chemical means and the late quartets of Beethoven.

Then there is *Top Ten* and its pendants *Smax* and *The Forty-Niners*. The easy description of *Top Ten* is the pitch '*Hill Street Blues* in Superhero City' but, as always with such things, this simplification misses the glorious farce of some of its plots, the inventiveness of the world and the characters' bizarre powers and the deep compassion of Moore's characterization: an alien superheroine whose life cycle means that, some of the time, she needs to eat a lot of people, but is not otherwise a bad person, and the laddish butch dyke cop she vamps telepathically. *Smax* takes two characters to generic fantasy land and lets Moore do his take on all those tropes, including killing a dragon that really, really deserves it, while *The Forty-Niners* is the coming-of-age story for the elderly Precinct Captain of *Top Ten* and how he found himself after a good Second World War as a pre-teen fighter ace. Moore always manages to take the whimsical and make it deeply and poignantly humane; his tales of superheroes constantly raise and redefine the standard.

not one of them. The various critiques and parodies that seemed to herald the final decadence and departure of the superhero comic turned out, in the long term, to demonstrate that it had strengths that made it viable, and tested those strengths to destruction. Also, the particularly dull period that superhero comics went through in the 1990s proved to be a historical phenomenon rather than a permanent thing – characters started having conversations again, and even going several pages without hitting anyone.

What also became clear to me was that this material interlaced imaginatively with everything else I was interested in and working on. Joss Whedon, creator of *Buffy*, was a man whose creativity was informed at a deep emotional level by his adolescent reading of comics; in due course he has become a comics creator in his own right. The same is true of all the screenwriters and others whom Jennifer Stoy has usefully christened the 'fanboy creators' – Kevin Smith, Alan Heinberg, Guillermo Del Toro and so on.

The audience for the teen movies I was working on overlapped significantly with one of the main markets for superhero comics, and the audience for the science-fiction movies I was writing about with the audience for superhero-based blockbusters. And, as I developed my ideas about thick texts and the universalization of the geek aesthetic, it became clear to me that superhero comics were a crucial part of my ongoing argument about ways of looking seriously at popular culture.

Hence the present book, and hence also a rediscovered love in advanced middle age of what I loved when I was a teenager, and loved again in my thirties. I should have known, when I felt disillusioned with the whole subject for a while, that the thing about superheroes is this: they always come back from the dead sooner or later.

2

The Heroism of Jessica Jones

Brian Bendis' *Alias* as Thick Text

There is, in a sense, no such thing as a typical superhero comic, simply because there are, in the end, only the very popular and the doomed, two categories that do not particularly or reliably reflect merit, even inversely. There are, as I have said, particular runs of certain long-lived titles that are worthy of critical consideration. On the other hand, some of the best short-lived titles were never designed to be anything else, resulting from the need to plug a particular gap in continuity or from the availability for a comparatively short time of an artist and a writer who had a particular project in mind.

I shall consider runs of long-standing comics that are both typical of that comic and superior to its general level, and runs that were particularly designed to be innovative, to break the mould of that comic as it had been up to that point in Chapters 4 and 5. For the moment, though, I shall deal with *Alias*, a short-lived, though much-admired, title from the early 2000s, which Brian Michael Bendis added to his already considerable body of work for Marvel and various independents. Simply because it manages to be remarkably thoughtful about the nature of the superhero even after half a century of consideration, it demonstrates the capacity of such a title to be a rich, thick text.

It is often asserted by those who disapprove of paying serious attention to popular art that popular art is incapable of being complex and sophisticated in its structure and its appeal. Many of the false friends of popular culture admire it precisely because they assume it is never complex and sophisticated – and, let us be clear, some popular culture, like some high culture, works at a simple and naive level. In both cases, the simple and the naive are choices taken in the context of sophistication's being available as an option; even the naive is never an innocent choice, and has not been for several centuries.

It is also far too common among the defenders of the less commercial kind of graphic novel to create a false dichotomy between their work and that produced for the major houses. Lazy journalism is often a part of the mix here: it is far too easy for someone who has just discovered Art Spiegelman or the Hernandez brothers to praise them by disparaging superhero comics and saying that they are not like them. One of the reasons why this book is necessary is because of too many lazy comments about underwear worn outside tights, or about the useful convention of sound effects.

This chapter will accordingly demonstrate, at some length, that *Alias* responds to a close reading as a thick text, a reading that pays attention to its relationship to the rest of its writer's work, that deals with the book's relationship with the broader issues of Marvel continuity and that gives some weight to the collaboration of writer and artist. *Alias* is a particularly fine superhero comic, but its merits differ from the standard run of such things in degree, not in kind; one of the reasons why I have selected a piece of work by Brian Michael Bendis for this extended discussion is that he is not one of the best-known stars of the field, but a well-respected professional who is currently doing a lot of work for Marvel. I might equally have written at this kind of length on Kurt Busiek or Peter David, for example.

Brian Michael Bendis, a Career in Comics

Much of Bendis' early work in comics does not deal with superheroes at all: *Goldfish* and *Jinx* (late 1990s) deal with the lives of petty criminals at the point when they find themselves pulled into rather more seriously criminal events, and *Torso* (1999) is a fictionalized documentary about the little-known serial killer case in which Elliot Ness was factually involved in after his successful pursuit of Al Capone. *Fortune and Glory* (2000) is a satirical account of Bendis' own adventures in Hollywood when there was some possibility of his work being optioned; rather closer to being a superhero comic, *Sam and Twitch* is a supernatural police procedural about two detectives caught up in the bleakly sardonic world of Todd McFarlane's Grand Guignol comic *Spawn*.

Bendis is currently producing *Powers* (2000 onwards) for Top Cow Comics (a quasi-independent comics company in a close working relationship with Marvel), a police procedural set in a world of superheroes. It is thematically linked to *Alias* in that it deals with two homicide cops, one of whom is a superhero who has lost his powers and become mortal after millennia of life, the other an aggressive and brutal young woman who develops lethal power after being taken hostage and tortured. Her powers first manifested at the expense of an ex-boyfriend who attacked her, but Deena has used her police skills to conceal the manslaughter and may be on her way down a very dark path indeed. *Powers* demonstrates the richness and complexity of Bendis' thoughts on the subject of superheroes.

When Bendis started working for Marvel in 2000, he threw himself into it with great brio and some considerable success. His run on *Daredevil* (2001–6) was an exemplary re-imagining of what has always been one of my personal favourites among Marvel's titles, but only became a comic of real stature during Frank Miller's run in the early 1980s. In Miller's and again in Bendis' hands it became a wonderfully dark piece of cinematic noir. Bendis' run on *Ultimate Spider-Man*, (2000 onwards), where his brief was to tell the early years of Spider-Man's exploits as if they were contemporary, managed to be both thrilling and charming.

At his best, Bendis brings to comics writing a delicious pseudo-realistic terseness that is highly cinematic. He is very fond of the pregnant pause in dialogue – in comics this tends to mean the shift to a panel or two of silent close-up of the person who is communicating more by their silence than they would by speech. His characters often have a default dry wit, but he is not so obsessed with this as to abandon the stock idiolects we have grown up loving; as written by Bendis, Spider-Man is still the same bantering neurotic as in any other hands.

Not all of Bendis' work was of the highest standard. His brief run on *Ultimate X-Men* was no more than competent, and the part of it that dealt with Wolverine on the run in New York and involved with Spider-Man and Daredevil rather than his usual team was significantly better than the section that re-imagined Emma Frost as a mildly hostile schoolmarm and killed off Hank McCoy. The nadir of his work for hire was *Avengers Disassembled* (2004), where he carried out editorial decisions to break up the long-standing team and in the process made sexist nonsense out of the character of the Scarlet Witch, Wanda Maximoff, having her go insane and kill several of her team-mates. This was one of the prime examples of what I call above 'strip-mining the continuity'. It might not have been so bad, had the actual story-telling not been wretched, surprisingly so for Bendis.[1]

The traducing of Wanda Maximoff continued in the central story of the *House of M* event, in which the deranged Wanda changes the whole of reality so that her father Magneto won his war with the humans years before. However, without being exemplary, the actual writing here is competent and there are some neat conceptual twists and powerful emotions deriving from them. In a world in which there are far more mutants than ever before, the statistics of wild probability have produced one, a young girl, whose power it is

---

[1]   However, see below for an account of 'What if Jessica Jones had Joined the Avengers?'.

to see that this reality is a fever dream created by a sick woman, and to communicate the truth to all she talks to. However, Peter David writes the character significantly better in the run of *X-Factor* (2005 onwards) in which she later appeared. Bendis does a fine job of showing the effect of this revelation on those whom she disenchants – they realize what the life they should have been leading would have been, and in many cases are appalled by the crimes that the illusion has made them complicit in. In the end, Bendis' *House of M* is no more than a structure on which other comics in the event – of distinctly varying merit – could be hung, but it is not shameful.

Nor, surprisingly, are the early parts of Bendis' work on a re-imagined *New Avengers*, with a grittier team taking up the slack left by the collapse of the earlier one. In the gifted hands of Kurt Busiek, for example, who is accomplished in this sort of game with continuity, the basic team of seven allowed for in the group's charter was constantly being extended with associates, probationers and visiting past members to a point where it was sometimes hard to keep track of the fact that the group was supposed to be small and lean. A case can be made that a radical break was needed – what was actually done was crude and unpleasant and, it needs to be pointed out, has since been undone in respect of the death of Hawkeye – Clint Barton is apparently back from the dead, even if his *nom de guerre* has been reassigned to Katie Bishop of the Young Avengers. Both current versions of the team – Bendis' and the far darker incarnation Mark Millar has produced in *The Ultimates* – are small lean teams.

Like the original team, back in the 1960s, Bendis' Avengers are brought together by a particular emergency in which they find themselves fighting alongside each other. Originally it was the machinations of the god Loki; here it is a prison break on the high-security supervillain facility attached to Riker's Island, the Raft. Some of the team are visiting the Raft – Daredevil in his civilian identity as Matt Murdock, Jessica Drew (Spider-Woman) in her capacity as a SHIELD officer – when Electro mounts his raid. Others, like Captain America and Spider-Man, head out there the moment they realize that there is a problem.

Bendis' handling of this material is psychologically acute and inventive. Faced with the outnumbered superheroes who put them away, many criminals defer any attempt actually to escape in favour of mayhem and the quest to find out precisely who, say, Spider-Man is – the answer being someone they have never noticed. Spider-Man and Captain America work together effectively, but the older man is intensely irritated by the younger one's incessant neurotic bantering prattle. Bendis makes the rather routine criminal Electro credibly individual with his decision to do the job in his old costume simply because he can, and his subsequent attempt to escape frustrated by his efforts to persuade a waitress he has a crush on to go with him. This sort of thing is why we read Bendis' work, but it is not, or at least not yet, the best of his work with superheroes.

The best is his work on *Daredevil* and his quite remarkable work on the comparatively short-lived comic *Alias*. *Alias* was followed by a linked comic of considerable merit, *The Pulse*, also scripted by Bendis, which continues the adventures of Jessica Jones, now a celebrity columnist on the *Daily Bugle* and in a relationship with Luke Cage. Since Luke Cage is now a member of the new Avengers, Jessica also appears in *New Avengers*, where one issue deals with their marriage; she is clearly a creation of whom Bendis and his audience have become very fond. *The Pulse* overlaps with another short-lived event, *Secret War*, also written by Bendis, in the course of which Luke is injured. A segment of *The Pulse* deals with the progressively desperate attempts of the pregnant Jessica to find where he has been taken for safety. I shall, however, in what follows, restrict myself to Jessica's arc in *Alias*, only mentioning later material about her by Bendis and others when it is directly relevant.

Alias

Alias was the flagship for MAXX, a Marvel line of comics aimed at a non-adolescent market. What this meant in practice was that its heroine was at liberty to be foul-mouthed and drunken, and to sleep around, none of which was, for once, gratuitous, and all of which helped contribute to the book's intelligent meditation on what it is to be a woman superhero. *Alias* is, though, the first mainstream comic in history whose first line is 'Fuck!'; although on this occasion it is one of her clients who swears, Jessica's swearing is an intrinsic part of her character and within a few panels she begins as she means to go on.

The events of *Alias* happen concurrently with some of the events of Bendis' run on *Daredevil*, most especially the outing of the blind lawyer Matt Murdock as the crime-fighting superhero and his decision to maintain the deception for the greater public good. If he acknowledges the truth, he will be prosecuted, jailed and disbarred, and criminals he has helped put to away will be back on the streets. The runaway Rebecca's obsession with Daredevil in *Alias'* second volume, *Come Home*, relates to this revelation: 'What I mean is that I love him for representing something morally ambiguous . . . this beautiful man who so clearly defines something undefinable'. Jessica and Luke's stint as Murdock's bodyguards overlaps entirely with incidents in *Daredevil* where we see the moment when a disguised Black Widow is allowed past them from her point of view instead of theirs; Bendis established his own sub-continuity within the Marvel world.

The overlap is in part thematic: in both comics, the theme being dealt with is the complexity of truth, the necessity of lies to survival and the need to make things real again. I mentioned above Electro's decision to wear his costume to commit a crime he is hired for, in which he has no personal investment save his fee; for Bendis, masks and the reality they both obscure and make manifest are one of the reasons for his fascination with costumed crime-fighters.

The titles, both of the comic as a whole, and of the individual volumes in which it has been bound prior to its collection in a single hardback, are rather more significant in their details than is sometimes the case; thought has gone into this. *Alias* as a title for the series as a whole indicates that it is a book about all the people Jessica has been – daughter, orphan, mother, lover, sister, hero, drunk, slut, detective and moral agent; it is a title linked to our discovery of who Jessica actually is. As the title of the first volume, it indicates that she is not who she thinks she is, that she can be

Jessica Jones

To summarize briefly, as written by Brian Michael Bendis, Jessica Jones, who used to be the superheroine Jewel, until something bad happened, is a burnt-out case, a hard-drinking private detective whose cases, during the run of the book, increasingly pull her away from divorce work and the like and into a renewed interaction with the world of superheroes and supervillains from which she walked away some years earlier. She still has her powers – flight, strength and a degree of invulnerability – but most of the time she chooses not to use them; indeed, they make worse the standard tension between the police and the private sector. Jessica thinks of herself as someone who is deeply unlovable and unworthy of love, even though she has friends and lovers who care deeply about her. She acquires a sidekick, in the shape of a young man who insists on running her office for her, whether she wants him to or not. (More recently, in Alan Heinberg's *Young Avengers* comic, we discover that there is a whole generation of wannabe superheroes who think of her as their role model.)

As presented in the early stages of the comic's arc, Jessica is the antithesis of the Good Girl Art superheroine. She wears baggy clothing instead of a tight revealing costume, and presents herself as almost shapeless; her hair is unkempt and her language foul. She is refusing not only to be a superheroine, but also to present herself in ways that might be consistent with that role. Where most superheroes have a secret identity, she is plain Jessica Jones, and unadorned; one of the more ironic meanings of the title is that where most characters in a superhero comic present themselves under secret and assumed identities, she is the simple thing, unmasked. She refuses glamour along with everything else: my view is that this is a point about autonomy in general rather than a specifically feminist one.

more. She can not only return to the person she used to be; she can be better.

The title of the second volume, *Come Home*, relates in part to Jessica's attempt to find the runaway Rebecca; it also relates to her growing reinvolvement with the world of superheroing, which she left and to which she is having gradually to return. Volume three, *The Underneath*, refers to the sordid underworld in which Jessica searches for Mattie Franklin; it also refers to the repressed secrets that Madame Web forces her to confront. And *The Secret Origin of Jessica Jones*, the title of the fourth and last volume, is not merely a reference to that volume's flashbacks and explanations of past trauma; it is an indication that this entire four-volume arc has been an 'origin story', that everything so far in these volumes and the flashbacks is the story of who Jessica came to be, not Jewel, but Jessica Jones, the better, stronger, version.

Part of Jessica Jones' problem, we gradually realize, was that she came of age and into her powers in a time that expected her to be a superheroine, always pretty and always bright and cheerful. The very name she took, Jewel, and her costume of virginal white, sky blue and pastel pink, were part of a more innocent age, or – more to the point – part of a more innocent way of looking at things, a way of looking at things that ignored much of reality. Jewel was in love with the idea of being a superhero; *Alias* is a book that punctures that particular romanticism to replace it with something equally romantic, but harsher.

A superhero is, very clearly, what Jessica is, no matter what she says or does. She has the powers and the mission to perform righteous acts; she also has the liminality. I have been criticized for seeing liminality wherever I look and need it, but let us confront the evidence. Jessica has risen from not one, but two comas, and if there was any question of the extent to which her comas are metonymic deaths, they should be answered by the scene in which one of the more obnoxious of her and Peter Parker's schoolfellows, Flash Thompson, precipitates her discovery of her powers by mocking her as 'freaky coma girl' while doing a zombie impression. She has lost her original family; the death of relatives is for heroes a standard rite of passage, another, social, death.

The name she takes, Jewel, is elemental, and one of her powers is flight, of a sort, which puts her perpetually in potential transition between earth and air. Her first flight ends by plunging her into water, from which she has to be rescued by Thor. As a noir detective, she inhabits those most liminal of realms, twilight, darkness and shadow; in her comas, she inhabits, and is affected and instructed by, dreams.

One of the strengths of the book is the way that the artwork constantly changes, from contemporary grime and darkness to various shades of pastiche, many of them references to Marvel's Silver Age heyday or to manga, and to the cute innocence that Jessica has left behind her, along with her dreams of superheroing. Bendis' principal artist on the book, Michael Gaydos, is replaced at such times by other collaborators for pages or groups of pages. Most often Mark Bagley and Rodney Ramos, who draw *Ultimate Spider-Man* for Bendis, draw these flashback sequences in a deliberately retro way.

We know from hints that something terrible happened to Jessica a long time ago; we learn this in part from the sort of self-destructive behaviour that in popular media and the therapy industry is always the outward sign of inward trauma. Bendis exercises considerable restraint in not allowing us to know until the book's fourth arc precisely what that trauma was, and just why Jessica refuses to think of herself as heroic. He trusts the material enough to know that we will be genuinely shocked when we find out her story, because there is a sense in which we think we already know it.

Jessica is a woman, and the traumas of women, we think, are as predictable as those male crimes that create them, but in fact Jessica's back-story is both a standard tale of rape and abuse and something different and even worse. The failure of her relationship with Scott Lang is demonstrated by her refusal to tell him precisely what happened in her past: 'What a guy thing to say? A girl has a secret in her past – she must have been raped!'. Scott, like the reader, wants a story that fits neatly into understood categories; Jessica ends up committing to a relationship with Luke, who comes to know and accept everything about her, in a relationship workable because unidealized. He also waits to be told what Jessica's trauma is rather than assuming that he knows already.

As her past unfolds and her present spins out of control, we learn that a superheroine was never a very sensible thing to be; yet, and this is the journey of learning that Jessica takes in the course of the title's run, she comes to terms with the fact that in everyone's eyes save her own, she is, and always has been, a hero, whether or not she puts on a silly costume to fight crime. The simple fact that she survived what happened to her with her sanity more or less intact is heroism in itself, and the heroism of ordinary people as well as that of superheroes. Part of the heroism of ordinary lives is simply this: to survive experience.

Jessica is of course a completely new character who has no previous role in Marvel continuity; Jewel is posited, however, as someone who was at school with Peter Parker, as a girl who narrowly avoided being run over by the same sort of truck full of radioactive waste that turned Matt Murdock into Daredevil. Her parents were killed and her powers were given to her by the type of experimental military material that produced Captain America. The Avengers are in her past and she sleeps with Luke Cage, Carol Danvers is one of her best friends and she has J. Jonah Jameson and Matt Murdock as clients. When Jessica is in trouble, Murdock is her lawyer. We read her present in the light of a past that feels like a comic of the time that we happened never to read.

In an excellent paper delivered to the Wisconsin SF convention, Wiscon 2006 – 'The Secret Origins of Jessica Jones' – Karen Healey suggests that this story 'resonates as an echo of feminist efforts in history and biography, where the real women whose historical roles were often discarded or downplayed have recently been uncovered and brought to the light'. Jessica Jones is the Marvel Silver Age superheroine who was hidden from history. Healey sees this as an ironic comment, intentional or otherwise, on the way in which Marvel moved from pre-feminism to post-feminism without much of a feminist moment in between them.

I am sceptical of the idea that there is any consciously feminist comment intended here, given that Brian Michael Bendis has elsewhere shown little in the way of sympathy with anything that can be called feminism; he was the executor of the deeply misogynist strip-mining of Wanda Maximoff's continuity in *Avengers Disassembled* and *House of M*. His own work as an independent creator, in *Powers* or *Jinx*, say, shows no particular active commitment to either feminism or misogyny. I would place *Alias* far more in the context of his fascination with the preservation of individual autonomy and authenticity, and the relationship between actual and apparent truth. This does not rule out a specifically feminist reading, of course, as long as we are clear that it is not based in auctorial intention, save as a particular case of a general principle.

There is a further problem with reading *Alias* as a specifically feminist text, which is the way that Bendis seems to pose a dichotomy between Jessica as superhero – whether as the naive Jewel or the later mature version who finally resolves her problem – and Jessica as mother of an unborn child. In the last issue of *The Pulse*, it is to her child, now newborn, that Jessica addresses a long speech in which she talks of being a superhero as something that is now in her past. In earlier issues of that comic, Jessica is attacked by the Green Goblin and beats him viciously because she fears he has caused her to miscarry; later she discusses children with the iconic Marvel mother/heroine Sue Storm, and hangs on her every word as if she, Jessica, is unworthy. It needs also to be pointed out that the madness of Wanda Maximoff derives in part from her magical attempt to recreate children taken from her by a glitch in reality. It is not to make any negative statement about motherhood as a career decision by women to say that, in Bendis' hands, it is problematic.

I also think it probably more useful to regard this as an example of what I call 'the wisdom of continuity', the way that sometimes the presence of a gaping hole in what has been done and imagined hitherto will help individual creators make some of the right decisions. It hardly matters whether or not Bendis intended the sort of feminist comment on his chosen genre that Healey so effectively describes. He was driven by the logic of story and by the pre-existing complex continuity of the secondary universe he was working in. His original intention was to work with an existing female superhero – Spider-Woman – who has, especially as he writes her here and in his run of *New Avengers*, some quite significant issues of her own about being a superhero. Bendis has since written both an origin story for Spider-Woman in main Marvel continuity and a version of her in the Ultimate universe, in which she is Peter Parker's gender-swapped clone.

When he was not allowed at that point to make Jessica Drew, Spider-Woman, the central focus of his new project, Bendis created Jessica Jones rather than work with some more obscure but actually canonical female character. And the thing that makes Jessica Jones special, her back-story, derives perhaps less from any direct sense on Bendis' part that a feminist parable was needed than from the need to set himself story challenges that made this new character interesting.

For example, in the book's second major plot arc, Jessica is searching for a teen runaway who may have been the victim of anti-mutant hate crime; in fact, the reason why Rebecca has been isolated in a small bigoted town is not that she is a mutant, but because she is a lesbian. One of the reasons she has allowed her schoolfellows to think of her as a mutant is that at least having superpowers would render her vaguely cool, and because it happens that the local pastor has an obsession with mutants as the anti-scriptural abomination of the month. As a result of the Claremont period on the various X-Men comics, and specifically as a result of his *God Loves, Man Kills* (1982), anti-mutant prejudice has been so solidly coded in Marvel comics as a way of writing about homophobia in general, and religiously motivated homophobia in particular, that Bendis does not have to have been aiming for any great enlightened statement about gay teen angst to have come up with this plot.

Yet this arc, with its extended examples of the girl's scrapbook and artwork, is a telling portrayal of that angst of which Bendis and David Mack, who normally drew the *Alias* covers but produced several pages of Rebecca's artwork in collaboration with his partner Anh Trahn, should be rightly proud. The dialogue between Jessica and the smugly bigoted local preacher is particularly admirable, as is her clumsy fling with the well-intentioned local sheriff. Part of the arc's strength is that Jessica does not actually do very much; she is a long way from being a great detective. She talks to Rebecca's separated parents, gets drunk and has sex with the local sheriff, looks at Rebecca's work and talks to her schoolfellows, and is wrong-headedly suspicious of the local reporter who tries to help her. She fails to foresee or to prevent the murder of Rebecca's father; she only finds Rebecca – who is reading her poetry in a bar – because a neighbour boy knows where she is. She brings Rebecca back just in time to witness the arrest of her aunt and for the girl to be attacked by her mother. About the most impressive thing she does for Rebecca is an accident; driving her back, Jessica takes a phone call from Matt Murdock, who is having troubles of his own, and Rebecca, who hero-worships him, has a second of glee in the reflected glory of overhearing.

What we take away from this arc, though, is not any political message so much as an awareness that Jessica has, as one of her powers, one not usually thought of as a superpower but nonetheless important. She has the ability to empathize out from her own damage to other people's; she is an adequate detective in spite of the drink and the messy emotional life because she is motivated by other people's pain. Given a choice between her professional ethics as a private detective and moral behaviour, she always chooses the latter. Acting as a cyber-honey-trap for a gay married man, she gives him a serious talking to about the necessity of confessing to his wife as well as simply giving his wife the dirt. Typically, though, she pumps him for his psychiatric knowledge before coming clean.

Jessica, Captain America and the Nature of Heroism

In the book's first arc, Jessica gets caught up in what might be a standard narrative of blackmail and murder, but is given more point by her past and by the context of the superhero life. A woman whom Captain America has been seeing is murdered; Jessica finds herself with a film record of his secret identity that places him at the scene of the crime. Knowing that she is caught up in the machinations of people who will kill to serve the workings of their plot, and with no particular reason to feel warmth towards Captain America, Jessica does the right thing almost obsessively and at some risk to herself – she is tough but she is not invulnerable.

She is arrested on suspicion of being the killer and then assaulted by the actual murderer, a giant thug for hire whom she beats into giving her the name of his employer. The thug, Man Mountain Marko, is a Marvel Silver Age minor villain – Spider-Man beat him a couple of times – to whom Bendis gives unlovely sexual fantasies about his victims' corpses. The woman who originally hires Jessica spins a spurious tale of lost sisters that almost certainly directly references Chandler's *The Little Sister*; when Jessica tracks her down to a campaign headquarters, the reference is to Scorsese's *Taxi Driver*. The dialogue between her and her police interrogator again has Philip Marlowe's blend of intransigence and sarcasm, as well as a strong implication that she has been arrested purely so that a cop can play out a sexual scenario involving superheroines that is running in his head. The echoes of Chandler, associating Jessica with the virtues of the noir hero as described by Chandler, help demonstrate, even at this early stage, that Jessica is wrong about herself. Given the deeply misogynistic assumptions of much of Chandler's work, there is a conceptual wit in linking this flawed heroine to him, and yet Chandler's most famous description applies to her:

> Down these mean streets a man must go who is not himself mean, who is neither tarnished nor afraid. The detective must be a complete man and a common man and yet an unusual man. He must be . . . a man of honour. He talks as the man of his age talks, that is with rude wit, with a lively sense of the grotesque, a disgust for sham and a contempt for pettiness.[2]

Gendered pronouns aside, it is remarkable how accurate a description of Jessica Jones this is, honourable, sarcastic, foulmouthed and committed to a sense of herself as ordinary as she is.

---

[2] *The Simple Art of Murder* (1944).

In a few pages of investigation, Bendis references Jessica as superhero, detective, objectified sexual fantasy and vigilante; but as well as all these popular culture archetypes she is a vulnerable woman who picks Luke Cage up in bars, has a blistering row with him when she turns up unannounced in the middle of the night and is too scared to go into her own apartment. Jessica cannot forgive herself for the simple fact that she is a normal human being at the same time as being someone who can fight and fly; she sees contradictions where none exist. She has been made to question everything about herself and come up with some harsh answers.

The plot she has been embroiled in is less a matter of framing Captain America for murder than of revealing his identity and embarrassing a President who has been seen to favour him and other superheroes. This can usefully be seen as a comment on the culture of sexual scandal and the undercutting of heroes and authority figures that featured so heavily during the presidency of Bill Clinton, a period when his wife referred to a 'vast right-wing conspiracy' of the kind we see here. It would not work nearly so well with a character less iconically clear-cut as Captain America; Bendis is reminding us that even paragons have sexual lives, and, by extension, that Jessica can have a messy sexual life and still be a paragon. Even more importantly, Jessica is learning that even paragons are human and vulnerable.

The immediate potential beneficiary of the plot is a Democratic candidate; the men with whom real power lies are beyond party as they are beyond the law. Though not, as it happens, beyond the capacity of extra-legal authority to intervene: the security agency SHIELD has bugged Jessica without her knowledge and takes the conspirators down after a confrontation in which her life has been threatened and the threat taped. The usual sympathy of Marvel's editors and writers with a left-wing or liberal political position is thoroughly on display here, not least in the way that the conspirators are punished as they would not have been in life – we will see other examples of this political bias in the Marvel comics of the early 2000s, but it was hardly a new thing.

The fact that the plotters' scheme depends heavily on the assumption that Jessica will do the weak thing and the venal thing can be seen as a demonstration of the misogynist politics of such conspiracies, but is more usefully seen as a demonstration to the reader that Jessica is not what she might be, and has every excuse for being. She works for hire, but her soul remains her own; there are very good reasons indeed why she is unhappy with the idea that anyone might manipulate her.

One of the book's most poignant bits of dialogue comes when Captain America comes to see Jessica in his civilian garb as Steve Rogers.

CA: You didn't give up the tape

JJ: I guess, to everyone's shock – No, I didn't. But – to be honest – it didn't even occur to me to do that until he told me that was what they were counting on.

CA: Have we met before?

JJ: Yes

CA: Hey, yeah, you were at the Avengers mansion

JJ: A couple of times

CA: Ah, don't be insulted . . . Why don't you do it any more?

JJ Just don't

CA: No, I really want to know. I never met anyone who— I really want to know

JJ: Because. Well, because it became very clear that I could never be you. You, any of you. I just don't have what it takes. I don't have that thing. That thing that inspires people to be, I dunno, better than they are. That thing . . . So.

CA: Well, like I said before. I've met a million people in my life. And I honestly can't think of three who would have done this for me. What you did? You protected me when I needed it most. You did it. And that's – well, that's the stuff, so what I'm saying is that maybe you're being a little hard on yourself, huh? Okay?

JJ: You're not going to salute me or anything, are you?

Even as early in the book as this, Jessica gets an endorsement from one of Marvel's principal icons of folksy righteousness. Bendis avoids the trap of subtlety here: we know Jessica is too hard on herself, but it does not hurt that knowledge to have Captain America tell her so. Also, she is outside the standard model of reaction to superhero behaviour to the extent that she finds it embarrassing; she can take praise from Captain America, but an actual salute would be too much. One of the problems with the standard model of superheroing that *Alias* raises is just this – how can you be a superhero and self-conscious at the same time? The finest thing about Captain America here is that he is not too proud to acknowledge that he needed help and she gave it to him; this is the most important lesson he teaches Jessica. After a girls' night out with Carol Danvers, who is still a superheroine in spite of major traumas of her own – the scene is a *Sex in the City* exchange in which Carol portrays Luke as an obsessive, a 'cape-chaser' who only ever dates women with powers – it is back to the job for Jessica, investigating the gay psychiatrist mentioned earlier and a missing husband whose back-story is peculiarly relevant to her own.

Carol Danvers and Rogue

Carol Danvers discovered herself to be in an advanced state of pregnancy, which turned out to be the result of her being impregnated by a time-traveller who had abducted and seduced her, using mind control in order that she give birth to him. He then grew rapidly to maturity, in order to abduct and seduce her. Not only was she grotesquely abused by her lover/child (who then aged into senility as fast as he had matured), but her colleagues in the Avengers failed to notice that she was hardly in her right mind when she agreed to all of this, and let her go off without thinking things through. The superhero community has let both Carol and Jessica down, largely by being unthinking men with a tendency to think women capable of any irrational behaviour, and not to examine the possible causes.

Later, Carol Danvers fought the mutant woman Rogue at a point when the latter was still a villain – indeed, their fight precipitated Rogue's self-reinvention as a hero and an

Though it could easily be taken for a simple piece of plot machinery, Jessica's friendship with Carol Danvers is – seen from the vantage point of long-term Marvel continuity – something rather more; there are reasons why these two damaged women are each other's support mechanism beyond banter about men. For one thing, Carol Danvers has a history of alcohol abuse rather like Jessica's; she left the Avengers for a while in disgrace after drinking on the job. For another, she has a back-story as traumatic as Jessica's turns out to be, one that, like Jessica's, turns on her sense of self.

Jessica's involvement with Luke Cage is something that embroils her with continuity at a serious level, as well as being one of the many ways in which Bendis uses this comic to challenge unexamined orthodoxies. The relationship between Jessica and Luke starts off as casual sex, for one thing, and as casual sex that may have consequences, but not automatically negative ones. Interracial relationships are rare in comics to begin with, and, given their controversial status within the African-American community

X-Man (people who only know Rogue as the waif of the X-Men movies will be in some severe misapprehension as to her back-story). Contact with Rogue's bare flesh enables Rogue to steal other superbeings' powers for a while; Rogue's fight with Carol entailed, largely inadvertently, a far greater theft. Carol lost most of the qualia aspect of her memories – she was left knowing the facts of her life, but not how they felt.

Rogue, on the other hand, suffered for a while from a version of multiple personality disorder, and in the long term acquired a level of empathy that made simple villainy no longer an option for her. Carol has recovered much of her sense of self, but only gradually: the worst of it is that she is denied standard comic-book closure through violence by the fact that Rogue has reformed. When she confronted Rogue, the X-Men defended their new colleague and Rogue was genuinely sorry. There are reasons why Carol is a boisterous woman about town, though it is clear that, at least in Bendis' version of her, she is also quietly a haunted woman.

as well as among whites, have become a site of potential conflict since the 1970s, when Luke's white friend Iron Fist was involved with the African-American Misty Knight. It is probably the case that Jessica and Luke are the first such couple where the woman is white. Later, in *The Pulse*, after the birth of their child, Luke specifically refers to the issues surrounding their relationship as a 'biracial superhero couple' when proposing to Jessica.

Luke is not just any African-American character; he was one of the more durable products of Marvel's attempt in the 1970s to open out the traditionally white-bread superhero. He was, specifically, Marvel's take on the trash-talking, no compromises hero of blaxploitation films, a former criminal with a bad attitude and an invulnerable hide. His actual title lasted for 120 issues or so, and the character proved even more durable.

Jessica as Outsider

Jessica's next case involves Rick Jones, almost the living spirit of Marvel continuity; it was in saving him from an atomic test that Bruce Banner was turned into the Hulk and for a while Rick Jones was the angry monster's good angel. Later, when Captain America was defrosted, he was the trainee sidekick for a man out of his time; later still, he was the alter ego of the alien warrior Captain Marvel, changing places and dimensions with a clash of wristbands. In some mystical sense, Rick is the living embodiment of human evolutionary potential: he stopped a devastating interstellar war between the Skrull and the Kree with a few mystic passes. From time to time, he is kidnapped from his life as a mediocre singer-songwriter to be threatened, or taken hostage; he is one of the Marvelverse's representatives both of ordinary humanity and of the extraordinary potential that Stan Lee's liberalism sees in the ordinary. This section of *Alias* is interspersed with extracts from the 'real' Rick Jones' autobiography, illustrated by Bill Sienkewicz in a brightly coloured hyper-real style that offers a profound contrast to the noir, muddy style of Gaydos' work with its thick lines.

Jessica is hired by Rick's flaky wife to find him and, without any great difficulty, finds him playing his guitar; she is saddened to find him a paranoid mess, who sees alien enemies round every corner. For a while she believes, and tries to help, only to discover from the Avengers' butler that this is an impostor, that the authentic Rick Jones is still in LA. Yet her empathy with him and his wife is an empathy with real pain and disorientation, even if nothing they tell her is factually true; Jessica is always in good faith.

She has seen herself in this classic sidekick; she sees herself even more in someone who is not even a sidekick, but a crazy person who wants to be one, who wants to be more important than they are. 'People like to have a little bit of the fantastic in their lives,' the psychiatrist tells her, 'and they want it so bad that they'll put on hold any rational logic so they can hold onto it. They'll believe any crap you tell them, so badly do they want not to be ordinary.' Jessica, whom we already recognize to be extraordinary in a number of ways, applies this fallaciously to herself.

Talking to 'Rick Jones', she confides that she shares his sense of the huge excitement involved in actually being near or with superheroes. She cannot be a superhero herself, she claims, because if she were, she would not find this exciting. True, she has powers, but that does not make her special. Because this part of the conversation is placed out of chronological order, after she realizes 'Rick Jones' is a fraud, after her chat with the psychiatrist, we realize what she does not, which is that an epiphany that results from hanging out with a crazy person may not be as useful as all that.

The two extended conversations that end the second volume are ones in which Jessica finds herself at a distinct disadvantage, that she has entirely earned. Sharing a gig with Luke, acting as bodyguards to Matt Murdock – elsewhere in Bendis' work of the time Matt Murdock has been outed as Daredevil and is busy denying everything – she has to stand and take it when Luke spells out to her his point of view about how badly she has treated him. She raises the cape-chaser issue and he says, superficially sensibly: 'If I was a lawyer, I would probably end up fucking a lot of lawyers, but being in our profession, I am probably going to end up fucking a lot of people. In our profession.'

Jessica does not pick Luke up on this, but it is clear that he does not regard her as a civilian, describing, as he does, being a superhero as 'our' profession. And, of course, one of the reasons why she can take this from him is that Luke has never bought in to most of the stock but unneeded aspects of superheroing – the costume, the mask, the secret identity – and he has always been 'hero for hire', a mercenary. He is not Captain America, nor does he pretend to be; he is not the embodiment of an ideal, just a working stiff with powers. He is, in his own way, as Chandlerian a figure as she is and as totally a teller of unwelcome truths.

There is a clear contrast between Luke's bluntness when he tells Jessica that her behaviour is not adult and the elliptical way in which, on a first date, Carol's colleague in the Avengers, Scott Lang, asks Jessica not to drink. Scott Lang appears to be what Jessica needs in some ways: like her he has a past, in his case a term in prison, which he has got over to become a superhero. He also has a much-loved daughter Cassie, later to emerge as a superhero in her own right, as Stature of the Young Avengers. Scott Lang is always a possible permanent relationship for Jessica, though he lacks the down and dirty appeal of Luke; the interruption of their first date by a battle between a team-up of Spider-Man and the Human Torch, and Doctor Octopus, indicates that the exigencies of the superhero life may always be what comes between them.

Lang's suggestion that Jessica have a soft drink instead of vodka is rendered irrelevant by the fact that their waitress, who has presumably taken cover, is not coming back. And though his remarks about her drinking were phrased far less bluntly than Luke's more general criticism of her behaviour, she resents them more – 'it was totally rude' – even though she knows 'I kind of needed someone to do that for me'. For reasons of which we are not yet aware, Jessica has a problem with people who manipulate her and with people who assume authority over her.

Jessica and Female Solidarity

This becomes apparent in her dealings with J. Jonah Jameson, Marvel New York's crusading newspaper editor with the obsessive hatred of Spider-Man. He hires her to get the goods on Spider-Man's secret identity and sets her to work with Ben Urich, his investigative reporter. Like many others who work for Jameson, Urich has no especial brief for the editor's obsessions; he has known Daredevil's identity for a long time, and also turns out (in Bendis' later comic featuring Jessica, *The Pulse*) to have guessed Spider-Man's. He is only too delighted to cooperate when Jessica uses the newspaper's expenses money to do social work on the pretext of hanging around soup-kitchens and AIDS wards, spending Jameson's money on following spurious leads.

Just as she does not cavil at Cage's reference to 'our' profession, so Jessica bridles at Jameson's remarks about superheroes as much as she does at his insults to private eyes. Jessica's reaction to Jameson's combination of bullying and insults is not, though, necessarily an ideal response – however natural it is – to his insults of her both as former superhero and as private eye, because, as it happens, she turns out to have to deal with Jameson on rather different terms. After a brief incident – she is buying cigarettes and walks into a robbery, then has to keep the shopkeeper from hurting the robber, then has to pay for her cigarettes – which reminds her why she does not work as a superhero, Jessica finds a young, confused, angry girl wearing a Spider-Man costume in her apartment.

'Jessica?' the girl says, and 'They lied to me!' before staggering to the window, leaping through it and flying drunkenly off into the night, banging into adjacent buildings as she goes. Jessica takes refuge with Scott – who is only too keen to let her do so and thus score 'potential boyfriend brownie points' – and asks another ex-boyfriend, Clay Quartermain of SHIELD, for the girl's identity. When not giving her a hard time about dating an Ant-Man, Quartermain tells her that, of the three extant Spider-Women, this one is probably Mattie Franklin, an orphan who is J. Jonah Jameson's ward.

In subsequent retrospect, the Mattie Franklin affair turns out to be one that has even more ramifications for Jessica than we realize at the time. Her concern is misunderstood: Jameson mistakes her enquiries for a shakedown and Jessica Drew, the principal Spider-Woman, turns up at her apartment and hurts her simply for asking questions. Jessica Jones is forced to face uncomfortable facts about herself; the psychic Madame Web finds out about her past as well as prophesying danger in the imminent future. Mattie turns out to be in a type of trouble that Jessica knows more about than she realizes: Mattie has been hooked on drugs by a low-level gangster who, it is implied, is pimping her as well as leeching her blood to make the drug MGH, which gives its addicts temporary superpowers.

This is a case in which Jessica has to accept help, from her irritating would-be sidekick Malcolm and his extended social circle, from Jessica Drew, from the incompetent superhero Speedball. She also has to compromise on her relentless refusal of glamour: she needs to get into a dance club and does herself up to the nines to do so. Later, when she and Jessica Drew need to get into a hotel suite, they pretend to be a gangster's groupies and charm their way past a hotel clerk. Jessica has to compromise, and in moderation this is not a bad thing.

This is also a sequence in which we are reminded that a lifestyle like superheroing with its constant fights is one in which it is possible for even the strongest person – and Jessica is only in the Marvel Universe's low middle range of strength – to get seriously hurt. Taken by surprise by the gangster Denny's drug-induced strength, Jessica is beaten badly; returning home battered, she is attacked by Jessica Drew (whom she knocks down in retaliation) and briefly stunned by Speedball's psychedelic bubbles. The fight with the drug-empowered gangsters is one in which all three superheroes get hurt. Jessica Jones only survives because she is prepared to be seriously violent, smashing a television over Denny's head and then finishing him off with a phone handset.

Where most superhero conflicts in the comics are choreographed combats, the fight here has the messiness of real violence. Speedball does not even realize that the two women are on his side until Jessica

Drew suggests he pay attention to the fact that she and Jessica Jones have just 'kicked the shit out of everyone *but* you'. Speedball is there working with the police; Jessica Jones flies away from them with Mattie – the first time we have seen her fly. She has finally to use the powers she despises and she does so to help a young woman who has been drugged and victimised by a superficially charming man.

When we finally learn Jessica Jones' own back-story, we realize with a shock of recognition that in rescuing Mattie, she is rescuing her own younger self, carrying out a rescue that did not happen in her case. Mattie is important to Jessica's own cure, simply because they have so much in common. By making a story so close to her own come out better, Jessica starts to heal.

This arc has a brief epilogue: after a stint in rehab, Mattie turns up to thank Jessica, and we learn that Jameson has for once done the right thing and has praised Jessica's heroism in the *Daily Bugle*. This is an effective and charming little plot point – the thing about Jameson, his schtick in long-term continuity, is that he hates superheroes almost as much as the villains they fight. Later on, in the *Civil War* storyline, he faints from sheer rage on discovering that his long-term employee, photographer Peter Parker, is Spider-Man. Mattie's confused remarks about a mysterious 'they' who lied to her, her desperate search for Jessica Drew, these are never explained except as the result of her drug-addled paranoid fantasies; some bits of some plots never get resolved (though not, as it transpires, Jessica's own).

Scott Lang turns up and he and Jessica settle their differences. She is furious that he has not been in touch; he is furious that he is in love with this woman he does not understand; and yet somehow they talk it through. She tells him to stick his head up an ant's ass; he tells her that he is in love with her. And they agree to go out again. All of this is Bendis deliberately misleading us and setting up further hurt both in *Alias* and other bits of Marvel continuity. (Scott is one of the Avengers that Wanda Maximoff kills in her frenzy; his daughter Cassie is one of the Young Avengers who so admires Jessica as a role model.) Jessica is investing in people again, which means that she is becoming vulnerable; in letting herself have hostages to fortune she is starting once more to have something to lose.

The Secret Origin of Jessica Jones

The Secret Origin of Jessica Jones starts as one might expect, with the secret origin story for the superheroine she used to be, a pastiche of Marvel 1960s story-telling, full of referentiality. At school, Jessica is so anonymous that, when people are mocking Peter Parker for being 'Midtown High's only professional wallflower' they do not even notice her to taunt her on similar grounds. She is hung up on Parker, and ironically is just about to speak to him about this when he suffers the spider bite whose consequences we, but not everyone else, know. Distracted, she nearly walks under a truck of radioactive waste similar to the one that blinds Daredevil. Jessica is, at this point in her career, perpetually on the brink of something happening; she is living in the New York that produced so many of Marvel's superheroes at the time when that happened.

Her little brother catches her masturbating over photographs of the Human Torch – I suspect that Jessica is possibly the only superhero, let alone the only female one, who has been shown masturbating, however discreetly – and next day mocks her for it in the family car; the ensuing fight between them causes her father to take his eye off the road and crash, fatally, into an army lorry carrying 'hazardous experimental material'. Her parents and brother are killed, and Jessica spends six months in a coma before being ousted from it by a power-outage caused by Galactus and the Silver Surfer, presumably during their first confrontation with the Fantastic Four.

Adopted by a pleasant middle-aged couple – not her relatives, but otherwise remarkably similar to Parker's Uncle Ben and Aunt May – Jessica returns to school, to find herself no longer ignored, but the object of fascinated prurient interest and occasional mockery from the bully Flash. Peter expresses solidarity in the face of bullying, neither of them knowing for many years just how alike they are at this point, and she takes his concern for pity, and rejects it. Full of adolescent angst, she runs off into the long summer afternoon towards the next stage of her destiny.

All of this is part and parcel of the stock Marvel superhero origin story: the accident, the alienation, the sense that no one understands; and now comes the realization that one is no longer as others, that life has been radically reconfigured. Images flash through Jessica's mind as she runs – her dead brother, Peter on the brink of *his* destiny, Flash mocking her, her father about to die, her pin-up of the Human Torch. At this point Gaydos gives us a page of small-panel reprises of all of these images as they occurred elsewhere in *Alias*; this moment – fugally bringing in all sorts of moments and Jessica's state of abstraction – is known as fugue. She is thinking about sex, death and alienation, and suddenly all of this climaxes in her realization that she is many feet above the city, that she has run into the sky.

What happens next is what never happens even to other Marvel superheroes as far as we have seen: Jessica falls out of the sky and into the Hudson, and has to be rescued by Thor before she drowns. He asks how she came to be so far from land, but does not stay for an answer – too busy ticking her off for her cursing at what has just happened and too distracted by the adulation of people who are more interested in the saviour than the girl he just saved. Thor saves her life, but in important ways, he also lets her down now and later; his treatment of her demonstrates how flawed the sense of mission even of a god can be.

With J. Jonah Jameson denouncing Spider-Man on the television, for the first time in what is to be almost two decades of Marvel time, Jessica asks her adopted father what someone should do, if they developed powers, and why the public have such mixed attitudes to superheroes. 'Image', he answers her – people like the superheroes clean-cut like the Fantastic Four, while Spider-Man is too 'creepy'. As to the mission that goes with the image. 'Would I try to help people? We're supposed to. It's a society and all that. But . . . when it comes down to it, it's hard to know who's worth risking your life for.' Jessica gets far less sage advice than Peter does, but her subsequent actions indicate that she thinks she understands that same sense of mission.

In the event, the decision is taken out of her hands by events; she goes out to try out the extent of her powers, discovering her strength and becoming rather better at flying. She sees a robbery in process: the C-grade costumed villain, the Scorpion, is robbing the customers of a laundromat for the contents of their wallets and purses. Jessica descends from the sky and lands on him with a 'whump'. One of the by-standers asks her if she is 'like, a superhero?' and she confirms that she is. Jessica first accepts the title when someone gives it to her – someone who also thinks that costumes are a fad – and it really is as simple as that, in the beginning.

In the present day, Jessica is offered, through Murdock, a case almost surreal in its comic book aspects: she is asked to go to the Savage Land, a secret jungle enclave in Antarctica, and search for its white ruler's lost sabre-tooth. To take this case would be to place herself entirely back in the world of superheroes and their adventures, so of course Jessica refuses, claiming, untruthfully to some extent, that she hates to travel. But her superhero past keeps haunting her as a result of Jameson's positive news coverage; even her crank clients are men who think their wives are sleeping with the Hulk. Then she has a case referred to her from the Avengers' mansion, a request involving a figure from her own past. Gaydos' art is particularly telling as she listens to the answering machine: three frames of her looking down in almost identical drawings, then the machine, and then her face looking up with an expression of real anguish. Then she dashes from the room, in a series of frames that centre on the phone, and we hear the noise of her vomiting.

We still have no idea of what happened to her in the past, but for the first time we have a clue – the phone message mentions the Purple Man, Killgrave. It needs stressing at this point that before *Alias* we have never thought of Killgrave as a particularly interesting villain. He is a second- or third-string villain with an odd appearance and a mildly creepy power, who has been beaten by the likes of Daredevil. His power – compelling people to do what he wants – is interesting enough, but he has been shown as vulnerable to people with a will strong enough to overcome his.

Yet Jessica's reaction is extreme. She does what she would never normally do and goes to the Avengers' mansion to shout at Carol Danvers, who has given her name to these potential clients. Whereas in their previous rather superficial conversation in the first book, Carol was dressed as a civilian, here, when they are talking rawly about real things, she is, of course, in the superhero costume that is the essential truth about her. Jessica is furious and Carol refuses to regard her anger as legitimate; there are people whom Jessica can help and it is ultimately as simple as that. Interestingly, given how she is dressed at the time, Carol makes a distinction between 'the person you act like' and the person 'you really are', and ties their friendship very closely to her knowledge of that fact, also saying that Scott feels the same.

Carol may be right and she may be wrong – her talk of closure is perhaps a psychobabble too far – and it is clear that Jessica has always regarded their friendship as being about shared denial: 'What I need is for you to stop telling me what I need. I would never throw shit in your face about all the fucked up things you've . . .' What makes this especially telling as a demonstration that Jessica at this point regards friendship as being about shared denial is that Carol Danvers has, in continuity, a genuinely disturbed personal history. This is a good example of what I have called, in Chapter 1, texture; the reader does not have to know the back-story, just to feel confident that the writer does. This particular thread in Jessica's story is not entirely done with until issue 13 of *The Pulse*, when they discuss it while Jessica is in labour and Carol both acknowledges her past and makes a sardonic joke of it: ' But I really doubt that's going to happen to you now . . . Odds alone.'

Captain America appears and asks Jessica in for tea, but she is not ready to socialize in the Avengers' mansion. And she and Scott have another row, partly because he acknowledges that he actually knows all about Killgrave, it came up in the security clearance before they started dating. Jessica screams at him 'Respect my fucking boundaries' – which could almost serve as an epigraph for the entire series – and leaves him in the cab where he has joined her, growing from ant-size to normal to the annoyance of the cabbie, and without a wallet. Jessica flies up to a rooftop and is sick again, at which point she tellingly feels her stomach. This is typical of Bendis' economy and capacity to play fair with his audience – he is simultaneously referring back to the stress Jessica feels when thinking about Killgrave and to the pregnancy that we start to realize is a part of her story.

The scene in which Jessica confronts the families whose relatives Killgrave killed and has not admitted to is quietly gruelling; it helps set up the realization by those of us who have encountered the character in other comics that this is a far darker take on the man who can make anyone do anything than we have encountered before. It really does not matter that the specifics – he made the people in a diner stop breathing so he can eat in peace, and later that he makes people fight to the death for his amusement or to make a point – owe more than a little to the diner scene in an early issue of Neil Gaiman's *Sandman*; as Stravinsky once said, 'Good artists pay homage, great artists steal'.

The Jessica who acknowledges that she has prior experience of Killgrave and agrees to help the relatives' pressure group put things to rest is a quieter, less abrasive Jessica than we have seen up to this point. It is interesting that, when she returns the original call and agrees to meet them, she is looking at the photograph of herself as Jewel standing with a younger Carol; she is trying to pay attention to Carol's suggestion that she, like the relatives, needs closure. Bendis is a realist about the emotions. We next see Jessica waking up in some confusion after making a drunken idiot of herself in Luke Cage's apartment, flying in his window in the middle of the night, smashing his refrigerator and vomiting on her clothing. Embarrassment as much as the process of healing has made her ready to tell Luke the story of what happened to her – that, and his attractively abrasive, laconic attitude to Killgrave – 'Guy's a little fuck with an attitude.'

The time has come for Bendis to tell us what happened to Jessica, and Luke, partly because of his capacity for stillness, is the perfect listener. I have talked before of the skill with which Gaydos uses small, almost identical panels, to represent slow changes of mood, and this is particularly relevant here. What makes the back-story peculiarly unbearable is, of course, that it is represented in a light cartoony style, as a Marvel comic of its supposed time, in an earlier less gritty age, with the alliterative credits – 'Bashful Brian Bendis' and 'Magnificent Mike Gaydos' – that characterized Marvel's slightly tongue-in-cheek early years. Jewel is flying through New York, she hears a commotion, sees two men fighting and walks between them, into a personal hell.

Here and later, Killgrave is represented not only as a supervillain with the power to warp minds, as a misogynist whose first reaction is to tell a pretty girl to remove her top and as a selfish man who sends her out to beat up policemen in order that he can finish his meal, but as a critic of the whole superhero ethic. He asks Jewel for her name, 'Not your silly made-up name, your real name.' Killgrave understands the magic power of real names; he is not a magician, because his power is based on pheromones, but he acts as if he were.

The most chilling moment in Jessica's story comes in the interlude after this first tranche of back-story when Luke asks her how long Killgrave had her and she says 'Eight months'. Everyone – her friends and her colleagues and her family – simply failed to notice that she had disappeared and was in the worst place in the world. For eight months. It is also impressive that Bendis avoids the obvious – Killgrave did not rape Jessica. He constantly humiliated her in every other sexual way possible: she had to bathe him, she had to watch while he raped random pick-ups he had compelled to make love to him and (it is clear from the illustrations) to each other and 'on a rainy night, with nothing to do, he'd make me beg for it'. Jessica became Killgrave's whipping girl for every defeat he had ever had at the hands and fists of male superheroes. For eight months.

This is both terrifying in itself, and also sensitive. Rape would have been the cliché; it would also have been something that left Bendis open to the charge of being a man who did not understand the issues. By making the issue humiliation of a kind that is less gender-specific, Bendis writes with greater empathy and less chance of alienating his audience or writing crypto-pornography. To have one's will taken away, to lose the authenticity of one's own feelings, is one of the worst things of all.

All of this ended in a catharsis, when Killgrave, in a moment of petulance, sent Jessica out to attack the Avengers; interestingly, given his own history with the character, the victim of her apparently unprovoked assault is Wanda Maximoff. Bendis also reminds us of the actual consequences of violence, too often left prettied up in the Marvel and DC universes – Jessica's attack is met with deadly force by Thor. He misses, but then she is attacked by Wanda's android husband, the Vision, and he leaves her seriously broken and in a coma from which she takes months to awaken. The superhero world failed to save her, and then it nearly killed her.

Carol had failed her for eight months, but saved her in this moment. And people went on saving her, whether she wanted them to or not; in a dream drawn so that the characters have the big eyes and cute perky noses of Japanese manga comics, the psychic mutant Jean Grey befriends and wakes her, Carol and Clay Quartermain and Nick Fury offer her a dream job, as SHIELD liaison with the Avengers, and what seems like the entire superhero world apologizes to her. And Jessica refuses, because she is done with the superhero life.

This is a moment that Bendis reprises twice, in not especially obvious ways. In a thoroughly feeble – arguably deliberately and sarcastically so – 'What if?' comic, he shows us what would have happened if Jessica had said yes, and taken the job. She is a complete superhero, who spots early on that Wanda Maximoff is going off the rails, and is so perfect that she gets to marry Captain America. It is interesting that one aspect of this alternate world is that what is probably the worst storyline Bendis has ever been involved with does not happen. The other point about it is that in it Jessica moves from being a viewpoint character in whom the writer is heavily invested to being what is called, in the world of fanfiction, a Mary Sue, a mere surrogate for auctorial wish-fulfilment. Jessica needs to

The Pulse

The second reprise of Jessica's back-story was in the last issue of Bendis' *The Pulse,* offering another rebuke to the convenient pieties of the comic book. In a piece of retconning, which risked falsifying the achievement of *Alias* but is so well done that it does not, we learn that Jessica did give superheroing one last shot before becoming a moody drunken gumshoe. She dressed up in a dark, masked costume and called herself Knightress, for about a week. In one of *Alias'* several jokes with superhero time, it is suddenly the comics world of the late 1980s and early 1990s:

> Got myself a new look. I was in a much darker place. I tried to reflect that . . . And now I look back on it and I get that little throw-up in my mouth that I get when I think of my hair choices back then. And truthfully . . . *everyone* was doing darker costumes back then. Even Spider-Man went all black. It was the super hero equivalent of *leg-warmers.*

The fact that the look and name she adopts are closely parallel to those of DC's dark superheroine of the time, Batman's ally the Huntress, is a joke about the constant reworking of that character's origins.

Jessica as Knightress gets in on a fight with the C-list supervillain, the Owl, and is cut helping out Luke, whom she meets for the first time on this occasion, who is enough out of the loop that he has no idea of her back-story. We realize that this is part of his attraction for her. She also gives up this new secret identity in a flash when the children of a minor arrested villain need to be taken somewhere other than the police station and she needs to prove she is a responsible person. Jessica, even this damaged cynical Jessica, knows what is important and what has to be sacrificed for it; she empathizes with the children because she remembers how it was when she lost her parents. She still thinks at this point that she is 'a bad person'; when she falls asleep on Luke's arm – he has come to her apartment to help with child care and really is 'a different kind of superhero' as Marvel used to say – he looks down fondly at this woman he has just met and says 'Yeah, you suck.' This is, in this context, one of the tenderest of the many tender things Bendis has him say to her.

work through problems in a real way, in real time, not in the rapid turn-around and reset that is, alas, so often the superhero comic standard. Here is one of the real insights of this excellent storyline: that healing takes time and closure does not come conveniently at the end of a three-dollar issue.

Jessica's confrontation with Killgrave starts badly when he greets her as his 'favourite comic book character of all time', and goes downhill from there. It is never entirely clear how mad he is, whether his fourth-wall-breaking discussion of their relationship in terms of the comic book characters we know them to be is insanity, clarity or a strategy to freak out someone he can no longer get to with his psychic powers. In any case, whenever Jessica tries to discuss the victims he has refused to acknowledge, he describes her emotions in the third person, criticizes the development of her back-story and warns her against breaking continuity. The effect is memorably creepy, especially when he warns her not to turn to the end, because 'something really bad is going to happen to you'.

Bendis is both acknowledging possible criticism of *Alias* – 'One day you're a high-flying superhero who no one's ever heard of and the next you're the centre of the world' – both as a disruptor of Marvel continuity and as a Mary Sue story. He is also trying to go one better than the scenes between Clarice Sterling and Hannibal Lector in Thomas Harris' *Silence of the Lambs* and the Jonathan Demme film of the book. He is trying to control her again, but when she challenges him on the premise of his position – 'If this is just a comic book . . . why don't you just walk out of here?' – he points out that 'I'm not the writer'.

Jessica reports back to her client, who is hostile in the extreme, and then it becomes apparent that, for reasons unconnected with Jessica, Killgrave has escaped and is on the loose. Jessica is rightly terrified – has he not told her that something bad is coming for her? – and Bendis makes great play with the paranoid particulars of escaping someone who can control not only your will, but your perceptions. She rings Malcolm and tells him to leave her office, and watches while he does so alone; she is rung by Quartermain and offered SHIELD protection, but dare not take it for fear that

Killgrave is controlling him. She hides out with Lang, and wakes to find him apparently eaten by his own ants.

Killgrave is in the apartment; Lang has not in fact been eaten, merely paralysed and made to look at Killgrave with sexual desire. Killgrave continues his critique of the comic book they are all in 'Subtle yet expressive artwork, mainstream with just a touch of indy' before compelling Jessica to see Carol in bed with Luke and Lang, and then go with him into the street, where – to attract the attention of the superhero world – he orders passers-by to beat the person next to them until dead. He orders Jessica to kill Captain America, calling her a whore as he does so; Bendis deliberately prepares our sympathetic response to what follows by stressing the character's misogyny. [3]

At this point, in what comes close to being a *dea ex machina*, a version of Jean Grey, planted as a pre-hypnotic suggestion when she wakened Jessica years before, appears and tells her that her will is free, if she wants it to be. Jessica's will was corrupted by Killgrave before; what Jean Grey does is subtly different, in that she allows Jessica choice. And Jessica chooses to beat Killgrave almost to death. In the background, we see a shop, whose name is Mr Bendis Outlet; this is an acknowledgement that the author, like us, experiences this as catharsis.

Captain America looks on with approval, saying 'wow' at the brutal efficiency of Jessica's demolition of her former torturer. Once she is done, and standing with a look of fulfilment on her face, Jessica is embraced by Carol Danvers: 'Jessica, you did it, you did it, look at you'; she looks over her friend's shoulder at us with tears in her eyes. Whether or not she ever acts as a superhero again,

---

[3]   Earlier, in one of his comic book riffs, Killgrave accuses Jessica of acting like a whore for acting naturalistically in the full view of readers. He is not just a misogynist but a postmodern misogynist who knows enough to turn Mulvey's male-gaze theory on its head; Killgrave also echoes the Katherine Bigelow / James Cameron *Strange Days* by using its killer's trademark framing of 'shots' with his hands. For a full discussion of *Strange Days* and its use of gaze theory, see my *From Alien to the Matrix: Reading SF Film* (2005).

Jessica has achieved fulfilment in a moment of purging violence. As Killgrave is carted away to jail in an ambulance, she sits on nearby steps with a sphinx-like expression. The arc of Jessica Jones, superheroine, is for the moment done; she has dealt with her past and moved through it, in a moment that both accepts the convention of comic book violence and represents its full implications.

The book ends with a settling of Jessica's business as a human being, not a hero. She tells Scott Lang that she is pregnant, not by him, and he walks away from her; she goes to see Luke, who insists on telling her that he has fallen in love with her even before she has told him she is having a child and it is his. All of this could have been sentimental and mawkish, particularly in the afterglow of what precedes it. The fact that it is not is partly the result of Bendis' skill with slow broken natural speech in which people express their feelings by constantly interrupting themselves:

> Luke: The thing of it is, is I've grown quite . . . I worry about you. And I, when you told me all that shit about what happened to you . . . I found myself really caring. So, though I know you've got some shit going on with one of the Avengers or something. And I know me and you – we're all just how we are with each other. I just wanted to tell you that I'm here. And I'm, well, here. If you, I don't know. I just think about you a lot.
>
> Jessica: You like me?
>
> Luke: Yea
>
> Jessica: You mean 'like me' like me?
>
> Luke: We in high school now?

Jessica's arc in *The Secret Origins of Jessica Jones* began in high school and it is entirely appropriate that high school be referenced again during its hopeful emotional close. It also helps that Gaydos' dark, often gloomy art can light up and become entirely different when the browns and blacks suddenly centre on the pale grey of a toothy smile or an up-turned eye.

These two battered adults have suddenly found the wisdom to be together and the book ends with Luke giving that most perfect of comic book endings – 'All right then, new chapter' – perfect, because nothing ever ends in a superhero comic, even one that turns on its heroine's offering serious dissent from the entire superhero project and learning to take from it only those things that she needs. To adopt Graham Sleight's terminology, *Alias* is a perfect example of a terminable, end-stopped narrative within the interminable context of the Marvel universe. If it is a paradox that this particularly fine superhero comic should quietly subvert the form and its ideology, well, what else do you expect from a comic book? and specifically a Marvel comic book, because a significant part of Jessica's arc has to do with accepting that she is a flawed human being, whether she identifies as a superhero or not, which is to say that she moves towards the complexity of life in Marvel, and away from the shiny idealism of her earlier shinier model of being a superhero, which was partly a critique of Marvel's early days, and even more a critique of their major rival, DC.

3 *Watching the Watchmen*

Sharing a World with Superheroes

Superheroes Team Up

Particularly over the last two decades, one of the principal subjects of the superhero comic has been a reflexive examination of its own major premise. Superheroes, like masked vigilantes, are profoundly problematic individuals, at serious odds with some of the major assumptions of a democratic art form. Critics of the genre often assume, wrongly, that it pays no attention to the ethical issue at its core, whereas in fact it is obsessed with it almost to the point of cliché.

When Siegel and Shuster created Superman, the alien dressed in a circus strong-man outfit originally spent most of his time in unequal battles with ordinary decent criminals. The problem with this was, after a short time, that a story in which the hero's victory is inevitable is a story without suspense, which meant, in turn, that he and other superheroes had to be given opponents who were a serious threat to them. At once, the existence of such opponents meant either that there had to be powerful villains – Lex Luthor was added to the mythos at an early stage – or other superheroes with whom Superman could be tricked into fighting. It meant, in other words, that a world that was different in having one person with superpowers to cope with became a world in which ordinary people had to cope with many people with superpowers. It also eventually meant the creation of the superhero team.

The original purpose of the superhero team-up comic was to sell more copies, both of the new team-up comic and of the comics relating to each of the characters included, by persuading those fans who were interested in one character but not another to decide that they were more interested in both than they had thought. This much is obvious, but the very moment that decision was taken for commercial purposes, an artistic agenda inevitably had to kick in. When commerce and art mingle, it is not always the case that the latter will be damaged by subordination to the former, and one of the major reasons for this is that the needs of commerce will create

Superheroes v. McCarthy?

Interestingly, the early 1950s was the time of both the McCarthy/HUAC interrogations of left-wingers and, prompted by Frederic Wertham's Seduction of the Innocent, the Senate Subcommittee hearings – generally known as the Kefauver hearings from the presidential hopeful who chaired them – on the role of comic books in producing juvenile delinquents. When superhero comics deal – as, say, DC's older group the Justice Society of America (JSA) sometimes does – with what was going on in the early 1950s, the standard retconned assumption is that superheroes suffered during the McCarthy period. The JSA was retconned as the Earth 2 equivalent of the Justice League, some members of which got folded into the continuity of Earth 1 after Crisis on Infinite Earths. This is also the assumption of the relevant sections of George R.R. Martin's Wild Cards anthologies. In a piece of attractive reflexivity, the threat posed to the existence of the comics industry by Wertham and the Kefauver hearings gets amalgamated with the McCarthy era threat to the liberalism that is that industry's default politics; the long-term consequence of the hearings was the self-regulation of the industry, known as the Comics Code, from 1954 onwards. In the United Kingdom, the scare about comics was spearheaded by the Communist Party, somewhat abetted by George Orwell; the British affair is described in Haunt of Fears (1984) by Martin Barker.

formal parameters for art, and that interesting work will be done in the solving of the problems that this throws up.

What then, are those problems? As I have remarked above, if a comic is to put a bunch of the most powerful men and women in the world in a team, then there has to be a menace of commensurate size for them to fight. In the so-called Golden Age (1930s–early 1950s) this was simple, in a sense, because there were always the Axis powers to fight, though the teams involved were small groups whose relationship was never formalized. In the Silver Age (1950s–1970s), DC and, in due course, Marvel produced teams of superheroes which were larger and which tended to fight extraterrestrial menaces or superpowered villains rather than involve themselves in the Cold War.

Up until the 1980s, the menaces fought by superhero teams, both those assembled from characters with their own comics – the Justice League of America, the Avengers – and those who inhabited ensemble comics like the X-Men and the Fantastic Four, only inflated slowly. Much of the time the problem was supervillains whose agenda was to neutralize the heroes or steal their powers. My early memories of superheroes being used as chess pieces relate to one of these stories. Marvel often brought menaces from space, out of time or from mythology: the Avengers are brought together by a fight against Thor's evil brother Loki and later on fight the extra-temporal conqueror Kang and involve themselves in wars between interstellar empires like the Skrull and the Kree, who at this stage regard Earth as a primitive planet ripe for exploitation as a base, or a source of troops. Later on in the Marvel Universe, the empires that replace these two have learned to treat Earth with a certain respect.

The problem with all of this is that the point of diminishing returns eventually gets reached; as Alan Moore says, 'I had been thinking about why superhero team-up comics almost never work, and I think it is because you have to set your team against ever-escalating menaces.' One does not have to agree with Moore about the actual merits of all team-up comics to acknowledge that he has put his finger on the problem; none of this has stopped Moore creating further superhero teams.

This means, in turn, that there has to be another story for the comic that deals with groups of superheroes to tell, one that looks at the whole question of what superheroes are for, that performs the thought experiment of asking whether the world would be a better place if they existed, or, even more importantly, not. As the newspaper headline in a comic once asked 'Why must there be a Superman?' To a quite remarkable extent, this is the story that such team-up comics have been telling for the last three decades, especially since Alan Moore's own *Watchmen* comic, but to some extent even before this.

The Trouble with Superheroes

It is a story that relates to some degree to the very simple fact that superhero comics, even when they cross over with each other, have to deal in conflict, and are as likely to deal in conflict between superheroes, eventually resolved, as they are in alliances against greater menaces. This is so much a default – mostly a rather tedious default – that it has become one of the things most often mocked in the comics themselves. For example, when in *eXiles* the Alternate Universe-hopping team find themselves battling the Fantastic Four, the eXile TJ reflects, 'It's an unwritten rule. If two groups of superpeople unexpectedly cross paths, they punch first and ask questions later.'

This is partly a matter of pandering to the interest of some comparatively unintellectual fans in precisely how superheroes rank in power against each other, and thus a way of selling comics with a frame of the ensuing conflict on the cover. It is also, rather more interestingly, sometimes a way for a good writer to do something interesting with character and dialogue, by having individuals whom continuity has made three-dimensional banter against each other in a mode of combat that is as much verbal as physical. It is also a way of dramatizing the never-to-be-forgotten fact that these beings are not like the rest of us, that most of the time they bounce back when hit, unlike the buildings and other property that gets in the way of these combats.

One of the simplest points about the conflicts of superheroes and supervillains is that they normally do vastly more damage to the neighbourhood than they do to each other. When, in the course of the 1990s and 2000s, it became almost a cliché that villains would point out that superheroes are careless gods who render ordinary human achievement null and void, the point was not without merit. For example, this has become a major thread in Lex Luthor's claimed motivation, and part of the rationale for Maxwell Lord's destructive brainwashing of Superman in DC's *Countdown to Infinite Crisis*. It is also the rationale for the Superhero Registration Act in Marvel's *Civil War* storyline, triggered by a disaster – a disaster that quite specifically goes outside the normal assumptions of superhero comics – in which third-string superheroes try to capture a villain whose destructive power is beyond their capabilities, and get themselves, and a lot of civilians, killed.

Careless destruction, then, is one of the standard indictments against superheroes by the other inhabitants of the world they live in; another is that they are aliens, or gods, interfering in the working out of ordinary human destiny. Often this is phrased in terms of xenophobia and discredits the people who utter the view: Luthor is quite specifically represented in his period as President of the USA as appealing to the lowest common denominator in this matter (see for example the *Public Enemies* collection of Jeph Loeb's *Batman/Superman*), and many of the mobs who picket the Avengers' mansion at various points in the Kurt Busiek run are shown to be bigoted against, say, mutants or androids.

There is, however, a real point here. If superheroes chose, they could rule the world with a rod of iron, and there is a serious question as to whether this would ever be acceptable. Someone with powers is, after all, not accountable, and the general assumption of comics and the other materials that spin off from them is that absolute power corrupts absolutely, no matter how fine the intentions of those involved. In the television cartoon *Justice League Unlimited*, for example, the League find themselves up against an alternate world group, the Justice Lords, who themselves, having made a wrong decision a decade or so earlier, are brainwashing villains into niceness and treating democratic institutions as, at best, a rubber stamp. During the Kurt Busiek run on *The Defenders*, the Hulk, Submariner and Doctor Strange are mentally influenced into becoming petty tyrants; Marvel's alternate world group, the *Squadron Supreme*, originally run the world under the influence of alien mind control, but, after overthrowing those enemies, find it hard to relinquish the power they have taken.

We must not assume good intentions. In Mark Millar's Top Cow comic *Wanted*, supervillains took over the world decades ago and murdered all the superheroes; the most we can hope for is that we be secretly ruled by callous and exploitative villains rather than demented and sadistic ones. In the Jeph Loeb *Batman/Superman* storyline *Absolute Power*, time-travelling villains from the future have wiped out most of the Justice League and abducted Superman and Batman in infancy and childhood in order to bring them up as tyrants. In another storyline, Grant Morrison's *JLA Earth 2*, an alternate Earth is run by the Crime Syndicate – a brutal Ultraman, a version of Wonder Woman who is Lois Lane turned evil dominatrix, Owlman, a drug-addled Flash and so on – who rule selfishly and bicker constantly among themselves over sexual jealousy and so on. The corruption of the best is the worst, as the Latin tag says. Specifically, these are versions of standard superheroes who kill regularly and gratuitously, whereas normally they never kill at all.

When, as a result of Wertham's *Seduction of the Innocent* and the Kefauver hearings on comics as a source of delinquency, the comics industry produced, in 1954, the Comics Code, there was no particular requirement that superheroes not kill criminals. However, the various requirements to avoid sadistic violence and to avoid glorifying criminality are presumably part of the reason why, from that time on, Superman and Batman and many other DC superheroes were shown as avoiding killing in any circumstances. In the 1930s and 1940s, both heroes had occasionally killed criminals rather than handing them over to the law.

Marvel tended to operate by the same rules in its early days; one of the many interesting things about Wolverine on his introduction in the X-Men and elsewhere during the late 1970s was that he was quite prepared to kill, at a time when even the Punisher sometimes used non-lethal bullets in his vigilante crusade against crime. Generally speaking, the rule was that superheroes did not kill each other, and did not kill human beings; when it came to invading aliens or rampaging robots, the rules tended to be more permissive.

These rules have gradually eroded to a point where the various superheroes who stand by them in all circumstances are shown as doing so as a matter of personal ethical choice, but are admirable for doing so, most of the time. During the Grant Morrison run on *Justice League of America*, Batman threw Huntress out of the organization for a while purely on the basis that she had been about to kill Prometheus, a supervillain who had been prepared to murder a number of civilians as a side effect of killing off the League. Even when he is responding to a murderous attack on his kinswoman Kara, in Jeph Loeb's *Batman/Superman* run, Superman contents himself with imprisoning Darkseid in the Source Wall at the edge of the universe rather than kill him. In *Operation Galactic Storm* there is a serious dispute between the Black Knight and Captain America over the former's apparent execution of the Kree Intelligence Supreme for interstellar war-mongering and genocide.

Yet this ethic is often seen as problematic. Both the fake resurrected Jason of Jeph Loeb's *Hush!* and the genuine one of *Under the Hood* rebuke the Batman for not executing the Joker long ago and allowing him to continue to inflict misery and death on hundreds of people, including many of those closest to the Batman himself. After Wanda Maximoff's murderous rampage, several of the Marvel superheroes – though most notably the more morally ambiguous ones like Emma Frost – are prepared to contemplate executing her, simply for the safety of the world, and Captain America insists that this is not an option. Given that she imposes both the *House of M* and the *Decimation* on the world as a result of being left alive, Captain America's choice is shown as having serious consequences.

There are even times when the attempt by those superheroes who stand by this ethic to impose it on others is seen as dubious in itself, as having more to do with personal issues than with ethics. One of the few redeeming features of the generally wretched *Countdown to Infinite Crisis* storyline is just this: that when Wonder Woman makes the decision to execute Maxwell Lord rather than allow him to continue to control Superman mentally and use the Kryptonian to murder his enemies, she genuinely has no choice. She has used the truth-compelling aspect of her lasso to make Lord tell her how she can stop him, and he says 'Kill me'. Yet, as a result, her two closest colleagues reject her professionally and personally, rather than standing by her when a clip of the killing is released to the world's media. Both are keen to say that there must have been another way; neither of these two most intelligent of men comes up with any suggestion as to what that might have been.

However, they do have a point. Part of the assumption of many modern comics is that ordinary humans only tolerate the metahumans among them because they believe them essentially harmless and benevolent, and that that tolerance would disappear the very moment that belief did. Certainly Wonder Woman is shown as seriously discredited in the public mind by what happened – up to this point in the Greg Rucka run and before it, she has been treated as a secular saint in her role as ambassador from Paradise Island. In other comics, the idea that a superhero has killed or nearly killed is always a huge public issue. In *Hush!*, part of the nameless villain's plan is to trick the Batman into killing a Joker who for once is innocent; when, in Frank Miller's *The Dark Knight Returns*, the seriously injured Joker kills himself to frame the Batman, it is his death that finally makes the Batman a fugitive from justice, pursued by a Superman who sees his old friend as a threat to the mission they once shared.

In *Kingdom Come*, arguably the prettiest of superhero graphic novels – Alex Ross is for some reason particularly fine when drawing heroes in late middle age – Superman has retired after a young superhero Magog was acquitted after executing the Joker (for, among other crimes, murdering Lois Lane). The conflicts of superheroes and supervillains escalate to a point where they unleash an atomic explosion that devastates Kansas. Worse, the attempts by Superman and some of his allies to imprison all supervillains, and the efforts of Luthor to sabotage him, and of the Batman to work against both of them (for reasons too complex to spell out here, and which do not make entire sense without the beautiful illustrations of Bruce Wayne looking urbane and wise) create an Armageddon-like conflict that the human authorities attempt to resolve with nuclear weapons.

The point Ross, and Mark Waid, who provided a script for his visions – it is, for once, clearly this way round – are making is simply this: that the superhero project is one that always implicitly involves the use of deadly force, and will accordingly have, sooner or later, deadly consequences. No one elects superheroes or, come to that, supervillains; their actions are unaccountable except morally. Superman and those like him are at least aware of the issue of having duties as citizens that involve them in a project of restraint, as well as the use of their powers for good.

This is stated so powerfully here that it is in a way a shame that Ross and Waid went further, by making the apocalyptic strain in the narrative explicit. A preacher, Norman McCay,[1] who has already had visions, is recruited by the Spectre as a human witness to events as they unfold, and intones passages from St John's Gospel at regular intervals – not that the name Magog is without similar associations. In the aftermath of mass death, and the world's stepping away from the brink, Wonder Woman becomes pregnant with Superman's daughter, and Batman is asked by them to foster the child; the averted Apocalypse is to be followed by the birth of a

---

[1]   The character is modelled from photographs of Ross' father Norman Ross, but his name is also fairly obviously a tribute to Ross' influences: Norman Rockwell, the *Saturday Evening Post* laureate of Americana and Windsor McCay, creator of *Little Nemo*.

comic book messiah. One of the obvious ways in which superheroes can be made palatable is to present them in eschatological terms.

It is a given of the Marvel Universe that superheroes are resented by a significant part of the public; parts of the gutter press like J. Jonah Jameson's *Daily Bugle* are only too prepared to run anti-superhero stories, and Jameson's personal crusade against Spider-Man is one of that universe's most reliable constants. When Jameson is furious at Parker's self-unmasking during *Civil War*, there is a genuine issue here: Parker has, as Jameson points out, been engaged in a massive conflict of interest all these years, taking news photographs of himself making the news. This is even truer of Matt Murdock's relationship with the criminal law. Even those superheroes who are more or less normal have a difficult relationship with the normal rules of society.

Yet there is a pragmatic argument in favour of secret identities, which is that superheroes have friends and families who have to be protected from revenge. This is the point Captain America makes over the Registration Act – do you feel happy, he asks Spider-Man when they fight, that villains have your aunt's address? It is the main plot point of Brad Meltzer's *Identity Crisis*. In Moore's *The Killing Joke* (1988) the Joker does not shoot and cripple Barbara Gordon for being Batgirl, but rather because she is Commissioner Gordon's daughter and the Batman's friend. The running joke of the Batman comics is that the various versions of Robin are 'the boy hostage', but in a world in which there are no secret identities, every friend and relative of a superhero is a hostage to fortune. Of course, though, the same applies to every friend and relative of ordinary police and prosecutors, save for the particular resentment that masked vigilantes spark in their more or less deranged costumed opponents.

When Frank Miller had a television psychologist say, in *The Dark Knight Returns*, that the Batman is personally responsible for creating costumed villains as a reaction to his effect on the popular psyche, Miller was making a right-wing joke at the expense of social liberals. However, over the ensuing period, the argument became a reasonably common one. Miller's own *Batman – Year One* shows Batman fighting ordinary decent criminals, and Jeph Loeb's *The Long Halloween* and *Dark Victory* show a Gotham City in which, early in the Batman's career, costumed villains move into a power vacuum created when the ordinary human Mafia tears itself apart in civil war. Even in the *Gotham Knights* animated cartoons, we see supervillains making this claim, and, significantly, two of Batman's regular opponents, Harley Quinn and the Scarecrow, are renegade psychologists. To what extent, if there were no superheroes, would there be supervillains? It is a question that it is legitimate for the mundane characters in superhero comics to ask.

Astro City

Kurt Busiek has done a lot of work in Marvel, and more recently DC continuity, but some of his best work on this theme comes in his independent comic *Astro City*, whose inhabitants are proud of their superheroes, and to which tourists come just to gawk at them. Yet even here it is possible to spark resentment – just as much as in the world of Alan Davis' *The Nail* (the DC Universe apparently without Superman) or Marvel's *Civil War* – when the superheroes fail to catch a serial killer and the Mayor plays a sinister game of spin-doctoring, arguing that superheroes do not care for ordinary people enough to catch their killer, or that, perhaps, superheroes are secretly responsible for the deaths as part of some concern alien to ordinary people.

The Mayor – or to be more precise, the representative of an alien invasion fleet posing as the Mayor – makes particular play with his revelations about the nature of Astro City's equivalent of the Batman, the Confessor. In *Astro City: Confessions*, we gradually learn that this terrifying white-haired man who appears out of mist and at night to scare villains into submission is both priest and vampire, wearing a cross in order to mortify his undead flesh and fasting lest he commit the mortal sin of taking human life. He has, of course, a young sidekick called Altar Boy. What the aliens do not understand is that the Confessor really is a hero, who allows himself to be staked and destroyed in order to expose the aliens for

Even those comics in which most people, most of the time, regard superheroes as demigods show that there is a dark side to all of this public adulation. In Moore's *Marvelman*, the golden age that ensues when the Marvel family seize control is preceded by the nightmare few minutes in which the evil Kid Marvelman fills in the time while he waits for a final confrontation by killing as many Londoners as he can in the most brutal and sadistic ways he can imagine; the subsequent near-worship of his executioner Marvelman by the general public has something hysterical to it. One of the ways in which Moore makes this governance of the

---

what they are. One possible answer to the question of what superheroes are really good for is just this – they are prepared to sacrifice themselves every day for the greater good.

What is also interesting here is that Busiek achieves this quite powerful insight, and a tale of real emotional intensity, by playing intellectual games with the Batman mythos. In *Astro City* the Confessor is the closest thing that he gives us to the Batman, and the Confessor is both priest and vampire. This works as a joke, but it is more than a joke, it is a metafictional conceit of real resonance. Altar Boy is an attractive figure – a kid from the country who comes to town looking to be a sidekick, and who gets his wish. His name is a joke about the standard slash fiction assumption about the nature of the Batman/Robin relationship, particularly during the Dick Grayson period. *Confessions*, though, is a moving story of non-sexual love, initiation and vocation. Altar Boy trains himself to be the Confessor's successor.

In a 2006 single issue of *Astro City*, Busiek shows us how the hero Samaritan meets regularly with Infidel, a supervillain he has, for the moment, succeeded in imprisoning. The Samaritan hopes to persuade his enemy that virtue is the better game to play; his enemy lives in the hope that one day the Samaritan will tire of all this virtue and the common people whom he diligently serves. Both are aware that virtue and villainy are choices made for reasons that include both reason and emotion.

world by Olympians so tolerable is that it is preceded by some of the most graphically nightmarish images comics have ever seen; Kid Marvelman has a warped whimsical sense of humour in his murders, and the technique Marvelman has to use to dispose of him is itself more or less the stuff of nightmares.

In the prelude to his post-*Infinite Crisis* run on *Superman*, the miniseries *Up, Up and Away* (2006) Busiek shows a Superman who has been deprived of his powers for most of a year as a result of the *Infinite Crisis* and who has got used to being Clark Kent, and being a better reporter than when he had other things on his mind. He is also quietly domestic, but then his powers start to come back and he worries about the effect this will have on his relationship with Lois. Don't be silly, she ruefully tells him, I married a firefighter and sooner or later it was always going to be time for you to fight fires again. This would always have been a telling image, but is rather more so in the post-9/11 era. It is not just that with power comes responsibility, it is that the power and responsibility are matters of life and death – the lives of everyone on the planet, and sooner or later the death of the hero.

Being a superhero is not, in a sense, a choice; it is a vocation or a way of coping with oneself. Bruce Wayne needs to be the Batman to cope with the overwhelming grief about his parents' deaths and his impotence, as a boy, to save them. As the cost of his crusade – Barbara Gordon's crippling, the deaths of Jason and Stephanie – the survivor's guilt with which he is coping grows ever more intense, rather than being ameliorated. He is trapped in the sort of cycle of cure and consequences of cure and needing a cure for those consequences that we normally associate with addiction.

Moreover, the Batman needs to be Bruce Wayne, not only to be the tycoon whose money pays for all the shiny Battoys, but, I would argue, in order to retain a perspective on the world that is not entirely about the night and the superstitious and cowardly criminals who inhabit it. As well as servant and battlefield medic, Alfred the butler is there to monitor his master's sanity, and the balance between his two personae; in the first issue of Grant Morrison's run he remarks that the Bruce Wayne persona has been

Confessions of Spider-Man

Before the public self-outing of Spider-Man in *Civil War*, there came the points at which he was obliged to confess first to his wife Mary-Jane and then his aunt, both of which occasions are of interest. In the case of Mary-Jane, the revelation was designedly a damp squib: she had known for years, it was suddenly revealed, and had always held it against him that he did not simply tell her. She had not known because of any process of working it out – she had seen him leaving his home in costume and realized that the obvious was in fact the case. The issue then becomes, rather more interestingly, what the young couple do once it is accepted that she knows, and the answer is a long soap-opera about her coming to terms with what he does with his spare time.

Belatedly, during the J. Michael Strazcynski run on *The Amazing Spider-Man*, Aunt May finds out about Peter's activities as Spider-Man when he comes home too badly injured from a fight to put the shreds of his costume away in a safe place. Partly because of her friendship with Otto Octavius, the civilian identity of Doctor Octopus, and because of the death of Gwen Stacey, Aunt May had always been hostile to Spider-Man; after a day spent wandering the streets, she accepts the situation. Intelligently, Strazcynski has her and Peter confess to each other different versions of what happened to Uncle Ben – May had always blamed herself for his death for reasons almost as good as Peter's. He was killed when out at night after a row with May, by a criminal Peter had earlier let go. Both have feelings of guilt; neither is actually all that guilty.

We get as well, the almost obligatory scene where May tells Peter that she knew he had a secret and had assumed that it was that he was gay. The analogy between the secret life of the adolescent member of sexual minorities and the secret life of the superhero is one that partly explains the fascination for many queer teens of superhero comics, and probably helps explain the tendency of comics to a comparatively enlightened stance on sexual issues. And the joke remains a good one: Buffy the Vampire Slayer's mother Joyce asks her, when the truth of Buffy's late-night activities is revealed, 'Have you tried not being a vampire slayer?' (the joke is echoed verbatim in Bryan Singer's *X-Men 2*, because it is telling enough to be worth stealing).

acquiring rather too much of the Batman's growl and that the personalities need to be kept distinct.

The question of whether Bruce, the Batman or neither is the real person is one on which it is possible to waste a vast amount of ink, and the precise relationship is one on which no two writers seem able quite to agree, let alone readers. However, I would argue that we can all accept that the Batman engages with the world in the way he does partly as a choice to help the hopeless and partly because it is the only way he can live with himself. Moreover, he needs the light-hearted act of being Bruce Wayne to keep himself from being as psychotic as the villains he fights. Interestingly, there are major contributions to the Batman mythos that hardly talk of Bruce Wayne at all. Alan Moore's *The Killing Joke* is very specifically about a confrontation between the Batman and the Joker over the issue of whether a good man can be broken by 'one bad day', and we spend enough of it inside the Joker's head space that we actively need to see the Batman as he sees him, not as a person with another life. In the Frank Miller *Dark Knight* comics, the two identities have almost entirely fused.

If we compare the Bruce Wayne persona with some other secret identities from outside the superhero mythoi, another interesting point emerges. Both Zorro and the Scarlet Pimpernel – two of the models on whom Batman is in part based – pose as entirely worthless fops, whereas Bruce Wayne is an entirely effective businessman, even if he lets his business be run by managers on a day-to-day basis. On the other hand, as Bruce, he is always liable to be a target for crime in the same way as any other rich man in Gotham City; as playboy and tycoon, he is vulnerable in a way that he is not when the Batman. Much is made of this in some of the animated cartoons: in the episode *Chemistry* (in *Gotham Knights*) Bruce is seduced by a plant woman sicced onto him by Poison Ivy as part of an attempt on all Gotham's richest men and women. Ivy has no idea at all that she has caught the Batman. Being Bruce much of the time is not without its risks, yet the Batman needs to retain his other self.

Most supervillains are, after all, only supervillains, though there are many, many, exceptions. The Joker is never not the Joker – he does not spend half his time pretending to be a sane man; a majority of supervillains are in a sense representatives of humours or obsessions. In those cases where this is not true, the public persona is not a way of staying sane, or balancing the dark side, it is simply a way of interacting with the world in a non-criminal way. Luthor is always Luthor, though sometimes he pretends to be an ordinary businessman or politician rather than an evil super-scientist; Spider-Man's nemesis, the Green Goblin, is always present, even when whichever member of the Osborne family is currently using the mask is using their civilian identity and apparently in control and sane. The madness always lies behind the eyes, not inside the mask.

Far more than a career, being a supervillain is an identity; it is a choice that was made once and can only be taken back by an equally profound act of will. More supervillains become superheroes than become ordinary civilians when they tire of evil; this is for some reason more likely to happen in the Marvel Universe than in the DC Universe, where Catwoman is something of an exception, whereas in Marvel we have, for example, Emma Frost, Hawkeye, most of the Thunderbolts (though some of them rather equivocally) and even the Juggernaut (though not in the *X-Men* films). However admirable this is at a personal level, it does make it harder for the populace at large to keep clear in their heads who is good and who is bad this week; the world in which there are superheroes and supervillains is one in which it is harder for people to trust their saviours.

I would maintain, in fact, that the whole question that underlies the problem of superheroes in the world is the question of trust. Ordinary people do not trust them, any more than they trust their governments and for many of the same reasons. This is particularly the case when government gets involved in the creation and utilization of superheroes; Captain America was the successful result of a secret weapons programme, and when totalitarian regimes experiment on human beings, even volunteers, we tend

The Thunderbolts

The Thunderbolts are a particular case in point, as well as a classic example of how well Kurt Busiek works with continuity. During a Marvel event, in the course of which most superheroes disappeared to another world and were assumed dead, the Thunderbolts stepped up as superheroes, and were not what they seemed. They were, in fact, the current incarnation of that middle-range supervillain team, the Masters of Evil, posing as heroes as part of a vile scheme. In the event, however, some of them discovered that public adulation was worth more than loot, or did not want to disappoint a young recruit unaware of the truth, or simply made a pragmatic rational choice that this was a more sensible way to utilize one's skills. Currently, even their once and again current leader, Baron Zemo, has abandoned the Nazi ideology in which he was reared, and is behaving during *Civil War* in a way that is self-involved and arrogant, but hardly villainous, in spite of his multiple double-crosses of almost every faction.

Once Zemo has gone off to a dubious apotheosis, the Thunderbolts are taken over by the government as an assassination squad with the redemption part of the group mission largely abandoned; this reflects the cynicism of Warren Ellis, who took over the strip from Nicieza at this point, but is also indicative of the dark mood Marvel chose to adopt at this point. A Thunderbolts run by Norman Osborne and including Venom and Bullseye on its roster, as licensed government murderers, is so far from Busiek's vision as to be practically a new comic.

to talk of it as a war crime. Elsewhere in the Marvel Universe, a number of characters have their provenance in, or have spent time being experimented on by, government labs, including ones run by the USA and Canada; it was such a programme that vivisected the long-lived and self-healing James Logan and gave him his trademark metal skeleton and claws, and robbed him of his memory so that he became the psychotic Wolverine.

A particularly extreme example of this paranoia about heroes and their origins comes in Mark Verheiden's 1987 Dark Horse comic *The American*, a long-lived superhero based on a minor character from independent comics, but parallel to Captain America. Its premise is that this hero does not in fact exist. His identity is a front for a programme of suicide soldiers, altered by plastic surgery to look like the template, and treated as entirely expendable individually. Reporters who uncover the truth of the story are casually butchered, until one of the squad goes rogue and the former sidekick, Kid America, who has lost a son to the programme, helps him rescue a drunken reporter and bring the truth to light. Also involved in all of this are a still-living cyborg version of President Eisenhower, the now brain-washed former nemesis Bones and Eisenhower's daughter. *The American* makes some fairly predictable points about spin-doctoring and the dark side of American patriotism, but has an attractively bittersweet cynicism about its deeply flawed heroes.

Examples of this dark perception of superheroes and where they come from proliferate. The characters of Marc Gruenwald's *Squadron Supreme* are currently being given an equally cynical back-story in Straczynski's *Supreme Force* for Marvel's Maxx line – they are perhaps, though not yet explicitly, the Ultimate Universe's version of the Squadron. The Superman equivalent, Hyperion – Marvel's Squadron Supreme are deliberately far more cognate with DC's Justice League – is shown being brought up in an entirely faked version of the Kansas farm, where his parents are actors paid by the government and successive presidents have to have the vast expenditure explained to them. How else, after all, do you bring up a child who can incinerate his classmates with beams from his eyes, and how, save by giving him the perfect American adolescence on a Midwestern farm, do you try to ensure that this being sees himself as a loyal American rather than as a man among bugs? Straczynski is not sympathetic to what is done to the young Hyperion, and it ends in tears, of course, but he is sophisticated enough to see how government might not regard itself as having too many alternatives.

Supreme Force is a dark reading of the relationship between government and superheroes, but not an entirely unusual one.

When Hyperion becomes critical of the way he has been reared, the US government – specifically the Bush government – uses his alien background to discredit him, and to smear the Clinton administration at the same time, until he makes it clear that he will not back down and is powerful enough that they cannot make him. One of the subjects of their experiments with Hyperion's DNA uses his powers to become a serial killer; when other superheroes unite to trap him, the government recruits him as a one-man covert force to drop into the territory of enemies.

Governments, then, produce superheroes by inhumane experiments; they utilize them in illegal and covert programmes, and they treat them appallingly. This applies even when they are, at the same time, persecuting them for being, for example, mutants, or simply assassinating them for being potentially dangerous, as happens in Straczynski's other non-continuity superhero comic, *Rising Stars* for Top Cow (with the complication that the power of the superheroes in that particular comic is a constant and the more you kill, the more powerful the survivors become). Inevitably, this applies as much when there is only one superhero as when there are many: Kurt Busiek's non-continuity *Secret Identity* for DC has a protagonist who is the only person with powers, and has to spend as much time evading government kidnappers and vivisectors as he does on his good deeds.

A world with superheroes in it is a world in which menaces that would end life on earth are routinely turned aside. It is, however, also one in which there are malefactors as powerful and motivated as humanity's benefactors; there is clearly a principle of universal balance that applies. It is a world in which the process of saving lives and preventing crime and disaster is liable to be endlessly destructive of property, and the commitment of superheroes to saving life and never taking it is a personal ethical commitment rather than obedience to laws, laws that superheroes tend to think do not apply to them personally. It is also a world in which the populace is constantly tempted to quite unsavoury prejudices and mass hysterias, and in which governments will publicly stir up such scares, while also being tempted into extravagantly illegal and immoral actions by the convenience of having superheroes to use or to take the blame.

It is also a world in which superheroes themselves are subjected to quite extraordinary emotional pressures as well as the stress of dealing with the public and government, not the least of which stresses is their need constantly to take ethical decisions in which their extraordinary situation is a major factor. 'With great power comes great responsibility' said Spider-Man's Uncle Ben, and he might as well have been speaking to every single one of Peter Parker's colleagues. Add to this the maintenance of a secret identity, effectively a mode of self-chosen non-sanity, and the concern for relatives and friends should that identity be breached, as well as the particular problems that go with the individual superhero's condition and situation – being, for example, unable to touch your friends and lovers, as with Rogue of the X-Men, or the Batman's survivor-guilt – and it is clear that, intrinsically, but especially for the last 20 years, superhero comics have considered the rights and wrongs of their fundamental assumption with an obsessiveness that might almost be called neurotic.

Watchmen

Of course, a tremendous influence was Alan Moore's *Watchmen* (1986), in which we find classic treatments of almost all the themes I have outlined above. *Watchmen* was thought of at the time as the superhero comic that deconstructed the whole idea and made superhero comics redundant thereafter; this was not the case, but it did prompt some serious soul-searching on the part of everyone who wrote superheroes. It was an influence on much of the best work that followed it, which is really all one can ask of any work of art.

In the early 1980s, DC had bought up the intellectual copyright of the minor comics house Charlton, its continuity and its characters, and DC editors proposed to Alan Moore, whom they had recently hired on the strength of his work for the British comic *2001*, that he develop this material even more radically than he had the DC horror comic *Swamp Thing*. In the event, as Moore worked on the project, the idea of using the Charlton material became impractical, and in response he devised a plot that worked far better with entirely new characters. None of the Charlton characters found their way into his eventual creation, though one of them, the Blue Beetle, was to become a much-loved standby of DC continuity as a minor figure in the Justice League of America.

What started as a reinvention of forgotten characters evolved into one of the highpoints of the graphic novel. *Watchmen* creates memorable characters and a brilliantly visualized and thought-through setting; it makes effective but unsplashy use of the comics page in its deliberate and austere reworking of the traditional nine panels; it works complex variations on the superhero motif to a point where it can be seen, in retrospect, as having reinvigorated by its ingenuity and creativity a genre that it might have written closure to by its intimidating excellence. Like Moore's earlier *V for Vendetta*, it is also an intelligent political tract whose timeliness in the 1980s has not caused it to date.

Plotline

A not especially short summary is essential. In a slightly but significantly alternate 1980s, masked vigilantes had become an actual feature of American life in the late 1930s, many of them, as a group called the Minutemen, serving with distinction on the home front in the Second World War. An accident in a nuclear research facility in the 1950s created Dr Manhattan, a being of apparently infinite power and some remaining human motivations, whose presence tipped the balance of world power totally in the favour of the USA. One of the consequences of this was a successful campaign in Vietnam. Nixon is still President after the abolition of the constitutional amendment limiting the number of presidential terms, and – we are told in one of many almost subliminal references – through the suppression of the Watergate scandal through the state-sponsored murder of inquisitive journalists. Minor cultural differences include the prevalence of fast-food curry restaurants in the USA (the omnipresent 'Gunga Diner' chain), electric cars, spherical filters on cigarettes and the popularity of comic books about pirates. This last point is important, not to the plot, but to the way parts of the story are told.

In 1977, after a nationwide police strike, masked vigilantism was suppressed by law and most of the former superheroes, like Dan Dreiberg, the former NiteOwl, have gone into more or less anonymous retirement. The major exceptions to this are the Comedian, who remains what he has been for many years, a brutal government enforcer, and Rorschach, a more-than-slightly deranged outlaw. Laurie, who inherited the role of Silk Spectre from her mother, is Manhattan's live-in girlfriend and has given up other contacts with the superhero world save for a vague friendship with Dreiberg. Manhattan retains his role as the USA's major military asset, but is primarily interested in his scientific research. Adrian Veidt, who fought crime as Ozymandias, but ceased to do so several years before the law would have obliged him, is one of the world's richest men through his many investments, as well as its brightest and strongest.

These, along with the survivors of the earlier group of super-heroes, the MinuteMen, Laurie's mother and Hollis, Dreiberg's predecessor as Nite Owl, are the major characters of *Watchmen*. They are counterpointed, often literally, by a number of minor characters, most of them the proprietor and customers of a New York news-stand: a young comics fan, a butch woman cabdriver and her feminist girlfriend, a forensic psychiatrist and his wife, a group of young hoodlums, two homicide cops and the staff of a right-wing magazine.

The precipitating event of *Watchmen* – which originally appeared as 12 individual comic books – is the murder of the Comedian, thrown from his skyscraper apartment. Rorschach investigates, visiting former allies and opponents like the cancer-ridden ex-convict Jacobi, formerly the villain Moloch, treating his 'friends' with abrasive contempt and his 'enemies' with the casual extreme violence that is his hallmark. Increasingly he involves Dreiberg in his investigations.

These two figures, Rorschach and Nite Owl, are both riffs on the Batman – the psychotic avenger side and the gadget-obsessed detective side – just as Manhattan is a variant on Superman, and the Comedian a dark equivalent of Captain America. Rorschach has the contempt for criminals that is an important part of Batman's choice of costume – 'criminals are a cowardly and superstitious lot', the young Bruce Wayne says – where Rorschach refers to them more simply as vermin. Ozymandias is best seen as a variation on an older model of forerunner superhero in the pulps, Doc Savage for example, though he also has much in common with various supervillains, as we shall see. This tendency to echo and vary the pre-existent was already the case with the Charlton comics characters from whom, at several removes, they also derive.

Manhattan is disgraced by the imputation that most of those closely associated with him – his adversary Moloch, his former girlfriend Janie – have contracted cancer from his presence. He withdraws from human contact to sulk on Mars. This precipitates an international crisis, the Soviet Union moves troops into Afghanistan and war looms. A key image in 'Watchmen' is the Comedian's trademark smiley smeared with a drop of his blood; one of the many visual puns that characterize the book is between this and the nuclear clock standing at five to midnight. In one of the minor subplots, Nixon and his war cabinet consider the 'acceptable losses' of a nuclear war and retreat to their bunker as a deciding point looms.

Rorschach learns that the Comedian was investigating the disappearance of a number of creative artists and scientists; he is framed for the murder of Jacobi and remanded to a jail full of criminals longing for revenge on him. Laurie takes refuge with Dreiberg when Manhattan's departure puts her, his official girlfriend, out on the street, and they start to act in their old vigilante roles, commencing a sexual relationship as a by-product of this.

All of this is further countered by a television interview, in the course of which Manhattan is discredited; Laurie and Dreiberg's fight with the gang has the voiceover of the interviewer to describe it and the words of Manhattan's government handlers: 'battles, conflicts, whatever it is you super-people do – am I making you uncomfortable – the show's over – getting aroused – intimate moments'. The scene is at once terrifying, hilarious and deeply sexy.

Dreiberg proves impotent in an ordinary sexual encounter between him and Laurie, yet they are tender and touching when sex fails. He describes an experimental exoskeleton that broke his arm; Laurie comments, 'that sounds like the sort of costume that could really mess you up', and he replies, 'is there any other sort?'. They rescue people from a fire and then make love on the roof of his owl-ship, half in and half out of costume; they need to be superheroes, but they need to be their civilian selves at the same time. After making love, he tells her that they should rescue Rorschach; in case we had not noticed it, the sexual act and the acting out of superheroics are two activities that are closely intertwined.

In due course, they release Rorschach from a prison that has become a war zone because of his presence in it. By this point, their investigations have started to point to Veidt (interestingly, the means by which Dreiberg proves this involve cracking the files in Veidt's computer by guessing his passwords, a comparatively new plot point in the mid-1980s). Manhattan appears and takes Laurie with him to Mars; Rorschach and Dreiberg head to Veidt's home in Antarctica.

On Mars, Laurie tries to persuade Manhattan to involve himself in human affairs again. At first she fails because of his realization that she has left him for Dreiberg; she was his one remaining link to humanity. As they talk, she finally puts together the truth of her parentage – that the Comedian, whom she has always hated for his attempted rape of her mother, was also her father by an affair some years later – and is almost broken by this discovery. For Manhattan, however, it is evidence of the gloriously unpredictable aspects of human nature and the way it overcomes entropy, and evidence that he should help the human race to continue to exist.

Rorschach and Nite Owl confront Veidt; he reveals his master plan, which is to prevent nuclear war by providing convincing evidence of an alien invasion. He has, moreover, already put this plan into effect, killing or driving insane half of the population of New York in the process – specifically, killing all of the news-stand customers, with the exception of the right-wing magazine's staff. As a by-product of this plan, he has killed all his accomplices and given Manhattan's associates cancer to discredit him.

Nonetheless, Veidt's plan appears to have worked, and the world becomes a safer place. Veidt tries and fails to kill Manhattan, who is so estranged from human emotions that he does not even resent this; in the process Veidt kills the giant mutant cat which is the only being for which he shows any affection. Manhattan, Laurie and Dreiberg accept the situation; Rorschach does not and so Manhattan kills him in cold blood before abandoning humanity and its concerns forever. In a final twist, and the last frame, the office clerk at the right-wing *Frontiersman* magazine pulls the diary of Rorschach's investigations out of the nut file to make up a page . . . Manhattan's remarks about the glorious unpredictability of human nature may yet come back to haunt the world. As Manhattan says to Veidt before leaving the book, and the world, forever, 'nothing ever ends'.

Other concerns in this very complex plot include the back-story of Manhattan's transformation from an unimportant researcher to an inhuman quasi-deity, and the back-story of Rorschach's evolution from vigilante to near-madman. In jail, the forensic psychiatrist grills him about his past and Rorschach tells him how he avenged a little girl whose kidnappers fed her to hungry Alsatians – this section of the book is almost unbearably horrid and painful to read. Laurie discovers the secret of her parentage and is reconciled to her mother. Hollis is brutally murdered by the street gang as part of a growing public mood of paranoia about former vigilantes.

Allusions and Characters

The book's title is, of course, primarily a reference to Juvenal's *'Quis custodet ipsos custodes'*, usually translated as 'Who shall watch the watchmen?', and as such is seen in the book on several occasions scrawled on walls as graffiti or carried on placards. It is also a reference to Einstein's statement that he would rather have been a watchmaker; in a reversal of this, as a boy, Jon, the future Manhattan, makes watches as a hobby, and his father throws the pieces out after hearing of Hiroshima, telling his son to be a nuclear physicist. On Mars, Manhattan builds, and travels around in, a giant timepiece of glass fused from red sand, which Laurie eventually breaks; we are not told that a timepiece is the closest thing he now has to a heart, but this is the implication. He is, among other things, L. Frank Baum's Tin Man, a figure of pathos because, for all his infinite power and knowledge, he has lost empathy and moral compass.

He is a being of quantum energy caught up in the paradoxes of predestination and uncertainty. He tells Laurie that she will inform him of her affair with Dreiberg several minutes before she does so, but he only feels the anticipated emotional anguish of abandonment when she has told him. His status as a being beyond time, in one aspect of his nature, is closely linked to *Watchmen's* use of interleaved flashbacks and repeated images; he is one of several characters who can be seen as counterpointed narrators overall, in as much as the story reflects their narrative idiolects, and who tell parts of the story at a more literal level.

Einstein is most clearly referenced in Manhattan's career via the watch business, but so are various other nuclear physicists. Oppenheimer's quotation of Hindu scripture during the original bomb tests – 'I am become death, the destroyer of worlds' – is obviously relevant here, and the cold-blooded nature of Manhattan's interactions with humanity can be seen as related to Oppenheimer's rival, Teller, who helped create the concept of mutual assured destruction in our world. Manhattan's perception of the intricacies of the quantum universe and his sense of it as both fixed and unpredictable relates to Heisenberg's version of quantum physics. There is no very profound meditation here on quantum theory or the history of nuclear weapons; Moore was an averagely well-informed man of the 1980s, who picked and chose from available material what was useful to his narrative rather than making easily summarized points. Manhattan's name relates, of course, to the project, not the island.

All of the superheroes in *Watchmen* are deeply flawed human beings, even the comparatively sympathetic Dan Dreiberg, Laurie and Hollis, though in each case their flaws are balanced by corresponding strengths. Dreiberg has turned the dilettantism that might otherwise have paralysed him to the development of skills and technologies of actual use; Laurie's ability to go out and fight crime has stopped her being frozen by anger against her mother. These two are the closest thing Moore gives us to identification figures; it is significant that both of them are past first youth and that Dreiberg's retirement from vigilantism has left him mildly paunchy and deeply frustrated with his life.

Yet Dreiberg is shown to have the soul of a poet; Moore uses one of the appended chunks of prose at the ends of the individual issues to establish this clearly. Perhaps of all the characters, he alone has a sense of the sacred; it is worth quoting at length his remarks about his totemic owls:

> Perhaps instead of measuring the feathered tufts surmounting its ears, we should speculate on what those ears have heard. Perhaps when considering the manner in which it grips its branch with two toes behind and the reversible outer toe clutching from behind, we should allow ourselves to pause for a moment and acknowledge that these same claws must once have drawn blood from the shoulder of Pallas.

He and, to a lesser extent, Laurie make the decision reluctantly to accept what Veidt has done; they do not give up on responsibility, however, and plan to continue being masked vigilantes whatever the cost. They are not entirely admirable, but they are entirely likable; this is a book that avoids having a moral centre, but they are the closest thing to it in the sheer ordinariness that is a part of their heroism.

Three of the prose segments at the end of each issue are devoted to 'extracts' from Hollis' fictional memoir, 'Under the Mask'. Moore devotes considerable warmth to creating this figure of an earlier and kinder America with his folksy stories about cuckolded garage owners with a taste for opera, and his sense of the absurd about the pursuit to which he dedicated much of his adult life. Hollis is a useful foil to the younger superheroes simply because he is not even slightly neurotic; he is plausibly amused rather than disconcerted by the possibility that sexual psychopathology underlies the decision to become a masked vigilante.

Whereas Dreiberg and Laurie return to superheroing, the whole point about Hollis is that he gave it up when he grew too old for it, and was good enough at what he did that he lived that long. Yet he is also a victim of his younger colleagues and friends; the world is not kind to him. Just at the point when he has his post-retirement career as a garage mechanic planned, Manhattan releases electric cars that make his skills redundant. One of the reasons why young gang members beat him to death is that they were themselves beaten up earlier when they attacked Laurie and Dreiberg. Moore constantly reminds us that actions have consequences and that we cannot know what those consequences will be. Hollis is the most likable of all these characters, and is doomed by the others.

Rorschach is not likable at all, and is more or less clinically deranged. Damaged by his childhood, working as a vigilante has brought out in him an almost demonic brutality and capacity for violence. When imprisoned and taunted by fellow-convicts that he is, at last, locked in with them, he points out to them that, on the contrary, they are locked in with him. He has a way of looking at things that means that, when the prisoners come to get him in his cell, he tricks them to their deaths, carved or electrocuted by the acetylene cutter they planned to use to get to him and then kill him. Moore's scepticism about the superhero ethos is informed here by a balanced sense of the human possibilities that go with neurotic flaws – Rorshach is demonically clever.

A number of small details combine to represent him as unpleasant. His personal cult of President Truman, whom he believes to have perhaps been his unknown father or at least dubs him an exemplar of traditional virtue, sounds innocent enough. When we reflect that *Watchmen* is to an important extent a parable about nuclear deterrence, and the necessary ruthlessness of statecraft, and that Truman was the American President who ordered the nuclear bombing of Hiroshima and Nagasaki, Rorschach's cult of him looks rather less innocent.

Unlike the inner monologues of all the other characters, Rorschach's are represented as unpleasant by being scrawled on lines of exercise paper. His inner monologue is, indeed, the diaries he gives to the *Frontiersman*; at other times, he talks to himself, presumably aloud, and is allowed the standard small capitals script of the book's dialogue. It is clear from the sample scripts included in the deluxe edition that this distinction was something Moore

Steve Ditko

Rorschach is also Moore's tribute to the artist/writer who created the Charlton character, the Question, from whom Rorschach in part derives. Steve Ditko was one of the key figures in the early days of Marvel Comics, as important as Stan Lee in producing such figures as Spider-Man and Dr Strange, but less adroit in coping with the vagaries of the industry than Lee. Ditko was a figure of extreme political views, a follower of Ayn Rand's Objectivism and a right-wing libertarian.

As an anarchist of the left, Moore is at once attracted and repelled by Ditko, who quarrelled with Lee, partly over Marvel's liberal slant in the 1960s and 1970s, partly over Lee's desire to have the Green Goblin turn out to be tycoon Norman Osborne rather than, as Ditko wanted, a random nameless criminal. The scene where the police unmask the feared Rorschach to discover an unattractive little man of whom no one is afraid is possibly a reference to this row between Lee and Ditko, though Moore says he did not consciously intend one.

thought of from the beginning, rather than one of Gibbons' many excellent ideas.

Rorschach's back-story is interesting: he is the scrawny, unappealing son of a prostitute mother who often told him that she wished she had aborted him. He was the sort of child who is punished for retaliation against bullies, partly because his slight stature meant that he never 'fought fair'. There is a real sense in which he is a pun on the concept of the secret identity, because his identity as Kovacs is a person no one notices, including the reader. Rorschach dominates the first page of *Watchmen* with his apocalyptic rant as voiceover and, as a man with a 'The End is Nigh' placard, Kovacs traipses across the scene, trailing his feet through the Comedian's pooled blood on the sidewalk. It is still not until many pages later that we definitively make the identification of the two men. Talking to his psychiatrist, Rorschach says, and he is clearly right, that the incident with the kidnapped child fed to dogs changed him from Kovacs impersonating Rorschach to Rorschach.

As an antisocial man with a slant on human affairs that is at an angle to normal empathy, Rorschach is also a version of an archetypal fan of comics and science fiction. As a man living by himself, with odd enthusiasms (birdwatching, classic torch songs) and mildly out of condition, Dreiberg is another. Moore understands his audience well enough to know that they will respond positively to the mild teasing implicit in these portrayals.

Rorschach is to some extent Dreiberg's shadow self, and the fact that they are both aspects of third things – Batman clones, fan-boys – strengthens that fact. The few scenes in which Dreiberg talks about their relationship and how hard it is to be Rorschach's friend are genuinely affecting; the point at which Rorschach responds and acknowledges the respect he feels for Dreiberg, whom he normally mocks and carps at, is equally so. It is a good example of Moore's sense of balance that Rorschach ruins the moment by holding Dreiberg's hand a beat too long.

He takes his name from the piece of experimental fabric which he made into his mask, a piece of black and white cloth in which the black and white endlessly flow into patterns. He is not just a man with a face made of blots, he is also what we choose to read into those blots and the stories we tell about them. He is a hero, he is a Nazi and someone whose distaste for sexuality is itself a perversion; whichever we choose to see. Looking at blots for the prison psychiatrist, he claims to see a pretty butterfly when what he actually sees is a dead dog with its head sliced in half; in a sense, the world he has inhabited since the incident with the child and the dogs is the world he chooses to see.

He adopted mask and crime fighting as a response to the death (which actually happened in our world) of Kitty Genovese, raped and murdered while her apathetic neighbours watched. Moore does not let us simply or straightforwardly disapprove of Rorschach, because the world of thugs and demonic violence he inhabits is an all too real one. Significantly, Genovese's death is the only thing that happened in both our world and his, except for the Soviet invasion of Afghanistan; both crime and the threat of nuclear war are real issues, even if they are being discussed in a comic.

Rorshach's name is at one point misheard by the police over the telephone as Raw Shark. As such it relates to the literal sharks that the comics fan small boy at the news-stand reads about in his pirate comic, sharks that are harnessed by its protagonist to pull him and his raft of corpses towards his destination of damnation. The issue in which we learn his back-story is, because Moore never opts for subtlety when crudity is called for, named *The Abyss Gazes Also*, from the obvious quotation from Nietzsche: 'Battle not with monsters lest ye become a monster, and if you gaze into the abyss, the abyss gazes also into you.'

Yet, this man dies a martyr to the truth, in his own warpedly clever way. Earlier, trapped in his cell, he mocked the thugs who had come to kill him until one reached in to strangle him, and then tied the man's hands together with torn clothing so that his enemies could not reach the lock. When they cut their accomplice in half to get to Rorschach, he breaks his cell's toilet with a kick so that the man with the oxyacetylene torch is electrocuted by the water-splash on live wires. This is the man who goes to his death refusing compromise in the face of annihilation, knowing that he has already sent his diary of the investigation to the *Frontiersman*. As we see in the last panel of *Watchmen*, it may well be Rorschach who has the last laugh, and, through him the Comedian, whose death he has investigated to the end.

Which is as it should be, because Adrian Veidt is altogether too arrogant and smug in his attitude to the people he has made into his puppets for his absolute victory to be entirely satisfactory. He takes his name from Hadrian, the emperor in whose reign, and those around it, Gibbon believed human governance to have achieved its most successful flowering, and Conrad Veidt, the exiled anti-fascist who played so many memorable Nazi villains. His superhero name, Ozymandias, is the soubriquet of one of his idols, Rameses II, his other being Alexander. His arrogance and cult of these heroes make him more vulnerable than he realizes; Dreiberg breaks into the computer files which prove Veidt's guilt by typing in 'Rameses II' as a password.

'Ozymandias' is, of course, also the title of Shelley's sonnet, quoted in the title and epigraph to the eleventh issue, *Look on my Works, ye Mighty*. At one level, this title seems to endorse Veidt's critical stance to the actions of other superheroes; they have talked about saving the world, while he has taken action. On the other hand, it also links him to ultimate failure and futility: 'round the decay/ Of that colossal wreck, the lone and level sands stretch far away'. The sonnet also makes a direct link between the pharaoh and the artist who at once mocked him and commemorated him – 'the hand that mocked him and the heart that fed'; Moore is not simply condemning or praising Veidt and his actions. Veidt may be a criminal, but he is also a Maker, an artist in his way, at whatever vast human cost.

Veidt identifies with Alexander's cutting of the Gordian knot. The problem of the world as it is can only be solved by a single broad bold stroke, not by the piecemeal social engineering, to use Karl Popper's phrase, of taking out one supervillain at a time. Once he has made this decision, of course, individual lives start meaning as little to him as they do to Manhattan. The figures from the past with whom he identifies were both, of course, mass murderers once you choose to look at them in that way; Veidt kills several characters personally or indirectly, and millions of others through his plan, several of whom we also know. Rorschach, by contrast, whom we think of as far more obviously murderous, kills no more than five people in the whole of his career.

In his cult of personal excellence, bodybuilding and travels in faraway lands, Veidt is like an older tradition of pulp heroes, as I have said. His cult of the great of classical and Middle Eastern antiquity also links him to DC's version of Marvelman (Moore used a British recension of the character in his and Gaiman's book, *Miracleman*): the cry 'Shazam!', which replaces Billy Batson with Marvelman is, of course, an acronym for the wisdom of *S*olomon, the strength of *H*ercules and so on.

Veidt is also, as we eventually discover, the book's villain, all powerful in his wealth, his ingenuity and his ruthlessness. In a way rather different to that which applies to Rorschach, he has looked into the abyss and become a monster. As such he is Lex Luthor, of course – another Alexander, I need hardly point out – and perhaps most especially R'as Al Ghul, the Arabic-named master of conspiracy who is perhaps one of the Batman's most intriguing opponents because he comes closest to being his shadow double. Once Veidt has explained the final ramifications of his plot to Rorschach and Dreiberg, the latter begs him not to put it into execution and Veidt mocks him: 'Dan, I'm not a Republic serial villain. Do you seriously think I'd explain my masterstroke if there remained the slightest chance of you affecting its outcome? I did it thirty-five minutes ago.' Yet in some important respects, a serial villain is precisely what he is, a mass murderer of staggering ambition whatever his motivation. Bond's opponent Blofeld regularly appears stroking a Persian cat; Veidt's cat is sacrificed to his attempt to murder Manhattan.

In one of the novel's most effective moments of misdirection, Veidt is attacked by an assassin whose bullet strikes and kills Veidt's secretary. In the subsequent struggle, the killer bites down on a cyanide capsule, or rather, since the whole thing is a fraud, Veidt breaks one in his mouth. Dreiberg challenges him on this point:

'You couldn't have planned it. What if he'd shot you first?' and Veidt replies 'I'd have had to catch the bullet', looking sardonic when Dreiberg is incredulous. And later, when Laurie shoots him, he does catch her bullet in mid-air; 'catching the bullet' is of course notoriously one of the most difficult and deadly tricks in the stage conjurer's repertoire. Veidt is a magician, and a trickster, and is therefore also linked to comics' major trickster villain, the Joker.

One might have supposed that the closest figure in *Watchmen* to the Joker would be the Comedian, but he is not that sort of trickster. It is certainly true that the Comedian comes closest to wisdom in his many grim jokes. He is an unpleasant murderous thug, but when, after killing the Vietnamese woman who scars his face for leaving her pregnant, he points out to the disapproving Manhattan that Manhattan could have stopped him, the bitter jest he makes of it is true. When he tells the nascent Crimebusters group that their efforts are pointless, and sets fire to their chart of social problems, he is expressing the same sense of the pointlessness of what they do that comes to haunt both Veidt and Manhattan.

One of the reasons Veidt beats the Comedian personally and hurls him from a window is an earlier beating given him by the older man; another is that he shares with Veidt and Manhattan, whom Veidt also tries to kill, a certain capacity for wisdom. He is, to that extent, the double, the dark self that Veidt needs to kill, not least because the Comedian is honest about the vein of sadistic violence that Veidt is in denial about. The Comedian is a joker and a truth-teller through his bleak dark jokes.

Veidt is, however, almost entirely humourless, except for that sardonic silent look. He is like Manhattan in this; he does not share the other characters' taste for traditional superhero banter. Violence is a serious matter to him, not something to be celebrated: when Rohrschach and Dreiberg attack him, he in seconds reduces them to men bleeding and on their knees before him. All he says is 'Manners', rebuking them for attacking him at dinner; there is humour of a sort in that, but it is of a very dry kind. Earlier, when he kills the assassin he has himself commissioned, he is utterly silent, utterly effective, as he was when killing the Comedian.

When, knowing that his plot has succeeded and he has brought peace to the world, Veidt gloats, and where most villains would at least crack a gag at this point, he speaks in utter seriousness quoting Rameses' inscriptions: 'Canaan is devastated, Ashkelon is fallen, Gezer is ruined . . . All the Countries are united and pacified.' He is utterly serious minded, and for once the cliché 'deadly serious' actually applies.

Apart from his strength, athleticism and intelligence, he has the particular self-taught gift of coming to intelligent conclusions about the nature and future of society by viewing many television screens at once. He is – and this is another area where Moore is both attracted and repelled by his creation – a perfect creature of the age of McLuhan and intertextuality and Baudrillard and Debord. The opening of the eleventh issue of *Watchmen* is worth quoting at considerable length because it helps describe Moore's own working methods as much as it does Veidt's, who is speaking here:

> Multi screen viewing is seemingly anticipated by Burroughs' cut-up technique. He suggested re-arranging words and images to evade rational analysis, allowing subliminal hints of the future to leak through. An impending world of exotica, glimpsed only peripherally. Perceptually the simultaneous input engages me like the kinetic equivalent of an abstract or impressionist painting. Phosphor-dot swirls juxtapose meanings, coalesce from semiotic chaos before reverting to incoherence. Transient and elusive, these must be grasped quickly.

What Veidt does have in common with the majority of the book's superheroes is his isolation; he murders his core group of silent East Asian minions and kills his cat. Manhattan and Rorschach's isolation is something on which we have already commented. Hollis lives alone, as does the ageing Sally Jupiter, whose marriage collapsed and who had her child through an affair with a man who earlier tried to rape her, the Comedian. He in turn deserts and murders a Vietnamese woman whom he got pregnant, and lives alone. The only one of the original Watchmen who appears to have had a satisfactory emotional life was the lesbian Silhouette, who was purged from the group for her sexuality and later murdered. It is in this context that the potentially durable relationship between Dreiberg and Laurie is one of the few signs of hope in this bleak book.

The relationships of the minor characters are equally dysfunctional: the working relationship of the two right-wing journalists is one of abuse and contempt and almost until the end the newsvendor is a chameleon, telling each of his clients what he thinks they want to hear. The relationship between the cabdriver and her woman lover ends in violent abuse; the psychiatrist and his wife resent each other and have a social life in which their friends have a voyeuristic interest in his clients. One of the few relationships here that involves kindness is that between the newsvendor and the small boy who reads the comics on his stand; however, presumably the boy is sitting on street corners because he has nowhere else to go.

A male writer and a female artist who are part of Veidt's design team are engaged in having sex when he discovers the bomb that is about to kill them. One of the few moments of kindness in the book is that he does not tell her what he has found, allowing her to die unknowing and momentarily happy. In a sense, this is a description of the book's dark gloomy take on human relationships.

Watchmen as Thick Text

The story-telling of *Watchmen* is not simply a matter of its linear narrative. We are shown this world in vast detail and any aspect that we are persuaded to concentrate on is liable to turn into a plot point or a moment of emotional intensification. As Veidt says: 'An impending world of exotica, glimpsed only peripherally'. The omnipresence of fast-food curry restaurants in this alternate New York seems merely a gesture, until the moment when Laurie, contemplating the massed corpses Ozymandias' scheme has produced says 'Tandoori to go. That's all they went out for, these people . . . Tandoori to go.' And she breaks the reader's hearts with the inadequacy of her response to mass death, and its absolutely observed humanity.

Watchmen is heavily loaded with subplots: there are the lives of the people at the news-stand, all of which are to be cut short as the human cost of Ozymandias' plot to save the world, and the many flashbacks to the stories of them and other superheroes. A lot of incidents endlessly recur, seen from slightly different perspectives, so that we learn about the Comedian's attempted rape of Laurie's mother long before we realize that they subsequently had the affair of which Laurie is the progeny. Early in his career, Ozymandias tries to organize his colleagues and is mocked by the Comedian, who sets fire to his charts and organizational maps and mocks his aspiration to be 'the smartest guy on the cinder'. All of the characters have moments from their past that haunt them and of which we gradually learn the significance. 'Transient and elusive, these must be grasped quickly', as Veidt says.

This is also a text about texts. Each of the 12 issues, save the last, comes with an appended prose section – and the twelfth ends with a reader possibly about to discover the most important prose section of all, Rorschach's diary, of which we have had extracts in passing throughout. We get excerpts from Wallis' memoirs, Dreiberg's rhapsodic prose about birdwatching, the prison psychiatrist's assessment of Rorschach, a chunk of material from the *Frontiersman* defending masked vigilantes against their liberal political critics, and an article about pirate comics. All of these deepen the texture of the narrative.

A story is in order here about the complexity of Moore's method and the extent to which it is not entirely under his conscious control. When I interviewed him, about half-way through the production of *Watchmen*, he asked me where I thought the plot was going:

> 'Oh,' I said. 'You've set that up terribly neatly. Clearly the Comedian's killer is Ozymandias. And I suppose this is the Report from Iron Mountain plot about preventing nuclear war by creating a plausible alien menace.'
>
> 'What makes you think that?' he growled through his beard.

Tales of the Black Freighter

Inside the narrative, a young boy at the news-stand reads a comic book, 'Tales of the Black Freighter' (a title that refers to the stock translation of Brecht and Weill's song 'Pirate Jenny', whose *'schiff mit acht segeln'* becomes 'the ship, the black freighter'). In the story, which we get in fragments, but which makes perfect sense to us by the time we have read the whole book, a man is desperate to get to his home and warn people of a pirate ship; to get there, he becomes capable of doing anything – building a raft from corpses, harnessing a shark, killing a man for his horse – and comes to realize that the pirate ship is there for him, its new recruit, rather than anything else. He has become the thing he dreads in an attempt to save what he loves. The relevance of this to Veidt's trajectory is clear: as we come to understand the story, we get to understand his internal journey. The comic book is linked to Veidt intimately; its writer is one of the team he uses to create his extraterrestrial menace and then kills.

'Well,' I said, ' what put me onto it was the perfume ads.'

He looked bemused.

'All of the perfume ads, which are produced by one of Veidt's companies, have, as slogans, quotations from popular songs of the 1920s and 1930s. Except for one, which is a misquotation.'

'What?' he said.

'It says "Nostalgia, by Veidt. Gone is the fragrance that was so divine", and of course the lyric is actually "Gone is the romance that was so divine".'

'And?'

'The words of the song,' I said. '"What'll I do, when you are far away, and I am blue . . . With just a photograph to tell my troubles to . . . when you are kissing someone new". All of that happens to Manhattan – he is on Mars, he has blue skin, he talks to a photograph, and Laurie is kissing Dan. It is his situation exactly, and it's tied to Veidt through the ad, which means Veidt is responsible.'

'Well,' he said. 'That's very ingenious. But I didn't know I was quoting a song.'

'Tell me,' I asked. 'Did you ever see Robert Redford in *The Great Gatsby*?'

'Yes . . . ?'

'It was the theme tune.'

Moore's endlessly allusive mind constructs chains of reference so complex and reflexive that even he does not keep entire track of them. *Watchmen* is one of the things I always think of when I talk about thick texts, because it contains within itself large parts of the past and, as it happens, the future, of its chosen genre and is quite remarkably open to close readings, readings closer than Moore knew at the time. To describe it as the most profound of meditations on the world with superheroes in it is to limit a work that has many other meanings and many other axes to grind; it is nonetheless true. 'Who watches the watchmen?' the tag asks, and there is no ultimate answer; themselves, each other, the mundane world, the reader. No one, the anarchist Moore reminds us, is good enough to be another person's master; all superhero comics are implicitly considerations of power and how power brings with it both absolute freedom and a life in chains.

Dark Knights, Team-Mates and Mutants

Sustaining the Superhero Narrative

The Growth of Storylines to Runs

One of the things that, from the creation of the genre, defined the sort of story that a superhero comic could tell was the standard size of a comic, which was in turn dictated by such considerations as the availability of paper, what the distributors wanted and what advertising could be sold. Back in the Golden Age, when things were simple, the stories that were told could be simple too, and audiences were still amazed enough at the concepts they were meeting for the first or tenth time that they asked for little more. There were no stories that took more than one issue to tell, and for the most part issues contained more than one story; issues that contained only one story were the ones that were singled out as special 'book-length' issues.

Even then, though, relationships of hero and villain were explored over and over without a reset button and with occasional acknowledgements that they had history together. Increasingly, the particular encounters we saw came to be part of continuity; when villains recurred in the lives of a superhero, there was a sense of an ongoing antagonistic relationship. Partly as a result of this, the accumulation of continuity made it possible for things to become more complex. Marvel's habit of doubling up even some quite major characters in the front and back halves of issues when they had not yet earned their own comic meant that stories about them were more likely to become serials, albeit serials each of whose episodes could stand alone. Increasingly, the story of the next issue would start in the last few panels of the current one – every triumph of the hero was seen as temporary, with a new menace lurking round the corner. By the end of the 1960s, certainly by the mid-1970s, comics were getting themselves caught up in long and complicated storylines that were not just hero meets villain, hero and villain fight, hero takes villain to jail.

This meant, for example, that there could be long-standing story arcs, like the long delay before it was revealed precisely who was hiding between the mask of the Green Goblin. It meant that there could be strings of revelation like Doctor Strange's discovery that, behind his enemy Baron Mordo, there lurked the evil god Dormammu and that they had to be prevented not merely from seizing magic from Strange and Mordo's mentor the Ancient One, but from attacks on the fundamental principles of reality. It meant that the Avengers' quite casual connection with Captain Marvel could embroil the Earth in the war between the galactic empires of Kree and Skrull. It meant, in due course, that DC, most especially in its team-up comics, had to follow Marvel in telling longer stories. It meant that story-telling could be paced and that continuity could become more than one damn encounter after another.

It also came to mean that there could be, by the 1970s, the sort of event that I deal with below and the sort of run I deal with in the current chapter. It can be argued, to some extent retrospectively, that the first storyline consciously conceived of as such was Marvel's *The Avengers – The Kree/Skrull War* (1971). Once it became clear that comics were holding onto an audience that would consider first buying individual issues and then buying those issues collected into a more durable form, possibly with additional material in the shape of design sheets, introductions, or commentary, it became commercially viable to start creating short-run comics, or to find other ways to tell the sort of story that would work in permanent form.

Whereas back in the Golden Age comics buyers were primarily driven by their interest in the characters and what might be happening to them this month, increasingly they were as motivated by the writers and artists as much as the titles. This was in part a consequence of the cult of personality at Marvel – Lee and Kirby and Ditko and so on – but DC increasingly had its stars as well: anything Gardner Fox had a hand in was liable to be worthy of attention. This meant, in turn, that attention was liable to be paid when a new writer or artist came to a long-standing title, or when a long-established writer or artist was involved in creating one. Young writers could make a name for themselves and attention would be paid to what they were going to do next, especially when and if they changed jobs between the two major houses.

To some extent, before then, and certainly from the 1980s onwards, we are talking less about individual fine issues of comics or even one good issue after another, but about runs of comics where a long game was played, or special short runs when a writer and artist were allowed to do something remarkable. The fact that many such long runs, or particular short runs, are distinctly mediocre should not blind us to the fact that some of the best superhero comics of recent years were conceived of against the background of a strong probability that they would be sold as issues and then sold again in a trade paperback (a 'trade'). By the early 2000s, the only reason why individual issues still sold was a combination of audience sentimentality and a desire to know in a hurry what happens next; the future of comics, including superhero comics, is almost certainly in trade paperbacks, CD-Roms of complete runs and in a shift from illegal fan downloads to legal ones.

The market has never entirely abandoned the quick fix of the week's new issues and the monthly cycle of which titles come out in which week. A lot of fans are still hooked on that particular buzz, yet increasingly the trades are important and there are complications to that importance. Some comics do not sell especially well, month to month, and may tip the borderland of cancellation, yet sell particularly well as trades or digests: Brian Vaughan's *Runaways*, which Marvel aimed at younger readers, but which was a distinctly classier production than that might imply, sells better in collections than in its individual issues, and has sold well in deluxe hardbacks that combine three digest-size collections. There are also, it has to be added, writers who work better at the length of a trade collection than they do in slow-moving individual issues – Brian Michael Bendis is one of these.

In this chapter, then, I shall be looking at various specific runs of particular titles, and at some superhero graphic novels that were

Moore's Forty-Niners

Alan Moore's *The Forty-Niners,* a prequel to his police procedural superhero comic *Top Ten,* is interesting for a variety of reasons apart from its sheer quality – not the least of which is the interesting fact that it was written for publication as a finished trade book, but is divided up into chapters that are more or less precisely the length they would have been had they been published as individual issues. It is also a charming piece of story-telling that goes in directions we would not entirely expect, and yet know are coming because its hero is someone we already know, the ageing Precinct Captain of the earlier, but chronologically later, comic.

As above, Moore's reservations about working in the superhero mainstream have to do with the ownership of his creations, not with the utility of continuity in story-telling. Steve Traynor is a young, a very young, war veteran when he comes to town trailing behind him his glory days as JetLad; part of the fun is that we know he will end up a success, and that he will find love and lifelong partnership with fellow aviator Wulf (both of these characters referencing characters in the comics of the 1940s). And along the way Moore gives us some gloriously entertaining stuff about the vampire Mafia and some other aviators with views about how to run a city, views that in their authoritarian brutality remind us of *Watchmen*'s Rorschach, but also of another figure who looms over a rather different cityscape . . .

originally issued in monthly parts – this was, of course, also true of *Alias* and *Watchmen*, which I consider in Chapters 2 and 3, and of the various events and reboots that I consider in Chapter 5. Space dictates restricting this to three particular runs that I have selected on the basis that one is a classic graphic novel that helped redefine a character for two decades, one is a good example of what can be done by way of story-telling inside continuity without a second of radical reinvention, and the third is a brilliant re-imagining of characters and scenarios that had started to go very slightly stale.

Loeb's Batman

In the end, this was an arbitrary choice, and there are a number of similar runs that I considered and rejected with some regret. Jeph Loeb's various Batman titles, for example, offer a far sunnier version of the Dark Knight than Miller's or most others in the post-Miller era. *The Long Halloween* and *Dark Victory* show us the Batman as a detective working alongside the police and baffled by a series of murders of Gotham's old-time Italian-American mobsters; it offers a particularly inventive revision of Harvey Dent's continuity and does not make him less tragic a figure by suggesting that the charismatic DA had a dark side even before he became Two-Face. Loeb's *Hush!* has a storyline primarily designed to enable the artist Jim Lee to do utterly gorgeous takes on most of the Batman's cast of allies and enemies, and yet it was compelling enough to have determined continuity far more than may have been intended. It also has moments of tellingly neat psychological insight, as when the Riddler reveals that he has worked out the Batman's other identity, and the Batman points out to him that he will never tell, because that would spoil the enigma by sharing its answer.

Frank Miller's *The Dark Knight Returns*

In the early 1980s, Frank Miller made a name working at Marvel. He took the fading *Daredevil* and made it a title that excited people, introducing the blind vigilante lawyer's assassin ex-girlfriend Elektra, taking a podgy gang-boss from *Spider-Man* and making the Kingpin a satanic Godfather of New York's Hell's Kitchen and also, for example, taking a routine villain like Bullseye and making him the stuff of which nightmares are made. Miller also transformed the soap-opera aspect of the comic: Matt Murdock acquired Catholic guilt to go with his other problems, which included a mother who had left home to become a nun. There is a nervous energy to Miller's period on *Daredevil* that made it feel even more like New York than it had in other hands, and for the first time Matt Murdock was not only heroic, but sexy.

It is in the context of Miller's work on *Daredevil* that the news that he was taking on a Batman project was greeted with real and justified excitement. *The Dark Knight Returns* was not his first project for DC – *Ronin* combined his samurai obsession with his fascination with corporate dystopias and had some powerful imagery of dismemberment and emotional pain. What could not have been foreseen at the time of *The Dark Knight Returns* and *Batman: Year One*, the project that succeeded it, was that this was probably going to be the best of Miller, that misanthropy and a distinctly odd fetishist attitude to women would increasingly dominate his work thereafter. *Sin City*, his extended exercise in porno noir, is certainly not like anything else, and was admirably – if you can stomach it – filmed by Robert Rodriguez, but generally Miller's work of the 1990s and 2000s has been a disappointment: a sequel, *The Dark Knight Strikes Back*, tips all the way over into mannerism, incoherence and unpleasant right-wing point-scoring; *All Star Batman and Robin* is, if possible, worse, with the dementedly right-wing politics allied to the sexual fetishism and misogyny of *Sin City*.

The Dark Knight Returns has all of these things, but is the comic in which Miller kept his demons on a leash; it totters perpetually on the brink of insanity, but never falls. It has, it needs to be added, been much parodied, and deserves it for its various excesses, particularly those to do with the Batman's obtrusive voiceovers. Its unforgiving attitude to the effect of time on female bodies is unpleasant, but is at least balanced by Miller's creation of the first female Robin in the resourceful Carrie Kelly – who ends up rescuing the Batman at least as often as he saves her. It is, it has to be added, probably important that Carrie is a girl-child whose cute androgyny could not be further away from the pneumatic dominatrixes of *Sin City*, and that this remains true even in *The Dark Knight Strikes Back* when she has grown up to be the new Catwoman.

To summarize briefly: the Batman has not been sighted for 10 years. Bruce Wayne hung up his cape when the Joker killed Jason Todd, the second Robin, it is implied, and has been gratifying his addiction to adrenalin in other ways, such as – in the first page of the book – motor-racing, in which he takes serious risks in order to win. 'This would be a good death' he says, but not good enough; there is no woman in his life, nor any boy, because he is in love with death. Gotham City has gone from bad to worse and is largely under the boot of a vicious teen gang, the Mutants; Commissioner Gordon, who is about to retire, is a weary old man tired of holding back the barbarians. When two Mutants start to mug Bruce Wayne and think better of it – 'He's into it . . . Can't do murders when they're into it' – he decides to come out of retirement and starts a war on the Mutants.

Harvey Dent – Two-Face – has, supposedly, been cured, by having the acid-scarred side of his face restored, and is paroled; he promptly goes on the rampage, believing in his madness that both sides of his face are now scarred. The Batman defeats him; Gordon retires and is replaced by a young woman Commissioner pledged to suppress vigilantism. The Batman fights the Mutant leader inconclusively; he nearly loses and only survives with the help of Carrie, a teenage girl who wants to be the new Robin, more or less irrespective of what the Batman thinks about it. Subsequently, he engineers the freeing of the Mutant leader and this time beats him into insensibility. The Joker, again supposedly cured, escapes and goes on a murderous rampage; the Batman fights him and, badly injured, the Joker takes his own life in a way that leaves the Batman on the run for murder.

An international crisis that Superman fails to resolve leads to the detonation of an EMP weapon over Gotham; with the help of teen gangs who idolize him, the Batman restores order to the crippled city. On the orders of the President – a caricatured Reagan – Superman comes to Gotham to arrest his old friend. With help from Green Arrow, whom Superman maimed for his acts of environmental terrorism, the Batman beats Superman and dies of a heart attack in his moment of triumph. Alfred dynamites stately Wayne Manor. At the funeral, Superman hears a heart start to beat again, and says nothing; in the Batcave under the ruins, Bruce Wayne plots his next move with the help of Carrie and his other lieutenants.

All of this is told in a dialogue-heavy highly dynamic style, constantly interspersed with vox pops, fragments of television programmes, fatuous presidential speeches and short anecdotes about the effect the Batman's activities have on the public good: a deli owner is inspired to beat a mugger with a rolling pin; a paranoid goes on a rampage in a porn cinema; a mother hurrying home is blown up by the Mutants with a hand grenade in her purse. There are constant references back to the Batman's back-story – this is one of several classic Batman stories where we get the death of his parents as the psychic wound that constantly torments him.

Though it is notionally broken into four equal parts, and was published in four large issues, the act structure – *The Dark Knight Returns*, *The Dark Knight Triumphant*, *Hunt the Dark Knight* and *The Dark Knight Falls* – with the act breaks coming at the defeat of Harvey Dent, the defeat of the Mutant leader and Jim Gordon's retirement, and the death of the Joker – there are too many plot issues and plot arcs for this structure to feel wholly natural and organic. Miller was getting an unusual amount of space for each issue, and there is something quite arbitrary about the placement of some of the book's highlights. He was having to create a grammar of structured narrative different to the straightforward 20 or so pages per issue he and others were used to, and he was not entirely successful in making it work coherently.

The drive of the narrative is, however, sufficient that this is the sort of weakness that only occurs on analysis; when reading *The Dark Knight Returns*, one is swept away by its sheer mad intensity. Nonetheless, this structural tendency to the ramshackle is a problem with the later *Elektra Assassin*, where it is carried by the hallucinatory expressionism of Sienkewicz's art and some powerful fetishist images. This is a book in which attack gunships look more like high-button boots than any helicopter ever designed. It becomes a real problem in the vastly inferior *The Dark Knight Strikes Back*.

The constant monologue of the Batman, in which he monitors his physical condition in the middle of fights, is both intense and absurd: as he swings back into action, 'this should be agony. I should be a mass of aching muscle . . . the rain on my chest is baptism. I am born again'. This is the sort of thing much parodied in, for example, Dave Sim's free-floating *Cerebus the Aardvark*, where at one point the incompetent superhero Roach goes all Dark Knight on us (elsewhere Cerebus is the Moon Knight, the alien-costumed Spider-Man of *Secret Wars*, the Wolverroach and, when Sim decides to parody Gaiman, Swoon).

One of the reasons for this is that Miller's art is not especially kinetic – it is not insignificant that one of the key fights in *The Dark Knight Returns* takes place in a pool of mud that slows the Mutant leader down – and his writing has to carry a burden that another artist might have taken for him, the burden of showing action memorably. Yet it does not matter how static his drawing of fights is when his Batman says things like 'This isn't a mudhole . . . It's an operating table, and I'm the surgeon. Something tells me to stop with the leg. I don't listen to it.' This is overstated macho nonsense, but it is also magnificent in its way.

This static quality to Miller's drawing is one of the reasons why he uses so many talking heads; it is also why the moment when the Batman tortures a Mutant into giving him their plans is so specifically a question of removing a blindfold to reveal him suspended from a building in a sudden swoop of perspective. The climactic fights with the Joker and Superman are a sequence of monumental poses – Miller is not ashamed to have learned from Michelangelo and Blake, it seems. His character drawing tends to the sketchy; if there were not a long iconography of Harvey Dent, Jim Gordon and the Joker in our heads, it might be harder to keep track of who they are.

There is a deliberate contrast between the weird but comprehensible villains who return for one last time from the Batman's past and a younger generation who are far more monstrous. Harvey Dent's delusion is genuinely tragic: he believes that the Batman has engineered his mocking by a public who go along with the pretence that he has been cured rather than rendered more hideous. The Batman nearly kills them both in the process of preventing his blowing up Gotham's twin towers – and there is a historical irony for you – but does so in a mood of genuine compassion that contrasts with his attitude to all of his other opponents in this comic.

The Joker is shown first of all as near-catatonic; he is almost unrecognizable as he sits quietly while orderlies bicker round him in what is no longer Arkham Asylum but the Arkham Home for the Emotionally Troubled, and has traded in gloomy gothic for institutional white. He hears, on the news, reports that the Bat is back and his face suddenly stretches into his trademark rictus: 'Batman,' he whispers, 'Darling'. The world has passed him and Harvey Dent by; for 10 years they have sat quietly in their cells, having their psyches rebuilt by the foolish liberal psychiatrist Wolper, who believes that they can actually be changed, and that the forces of vigilantism are far sicker than the monsters they fight: 'Batman's psychotic sublimative/psychoerotic behaviour pattern is like a net. Weak-egoed neurotics like Harvey are drawn into corresponding intersticing patterns. You might say Batman commits the crimes using his so-called villains as narcissistic proxies.' Wolper's eventual murder in the course of the Joker's escape is almost contemptuously casual, yet the erotic charge of the Joker's relationship with the

Batman indicates that Wolper has seen, but misunderstood, aspects of their relationship.

The Batman and the villains he is used to fighting have enough back-story that they can understand each other at least; a newer generation of monsters are opaque to him. It is not even clear whether the Mutant leader is strictly human – he and a lot of his lieutenants are monstrously large and muscular, and he has a mouth full of fangs, something like a lamprey's, something like a shark's. Steroids and extreme punk hairstyles account for some of it, perhaps, but the teeth remain unexplained. One of the Mutant lieutenants is a staggeringly butch transperson called Bruno, and Bruno has almost Frankensteinian swastika bolts as piercings through the nipples of enormous breasts – outrageous bodily modification is clearly a part of Mutant style.

The Mutant leader talks less like a criminal than like a barbarian warlord. Harvey Dent demands a ransom – 'Five million – it would have been two but I have expenses' – but the Mutant is a different kettle of fish: 'We will kill the old man Gordon. His women will weep for him. We will chop him. We will grind him. We will bathe in his blood. I myself will kill the fool Batman. I will eat the meat from his bones and suck them dry. I will eat his heart and drag his body through the streets.' He is a figure of inexplicable, almost unstoppable aggression who bites the Mayor's throat out when the elderly bureaucrat tries to negotiate with him. The Batman almost admires him for the perfect animality of his strength and drive: 'He's fast, faster than I am, and stronger. And seemingly impervious to pain. But they do come smarter.'

One of the strengths of The Dark Knight Returns is the poignancy of its meditation on ageing: Jim Gordon is on the brink of retiring and is glad to be done with the struggle, Selina Kyle has become a podgy panderer whom the still-trim Joker mocks for the effect of time and forces to dress up in an unbecoming Wonder Woman costume, Oliver Queen (Green Arrow) is a balding cripple whose days as superhero are over. Superman talks of the past as glory days that are done – 'Diana went back to her people, Hal went back to the stars' – and of the Batman as someone who endangers everything that can still be accomplished by superheroes by insisting on overt behaviour.

Superman becomes one of Miller's mouthpieces for a distinctly jaundiced view of humanity; Miller manages this quite cleverly by making Superman voice it rather than Bruce Wayne. Human beings cannot bear the idea that 'there are giants in the earth', and the condition on which it is possible to help them and do good is that you take no credit for it. The specious arguments of a Benjamin Wolper, and the feeble leftism of Carrie's parents in which the Batman is callowly accused of being a 'fascist', are all then rationalizations of a fundamental resentment of inferiors towards superiors. Where Siegel and Shuster took the figure of the Superman from Nietzsche and reconfigured it for democracy, Miller has the iconic version of Superman voice as urbane weary wisdom a particularly crude version of unfiltered Nietzsche.

Of course, Miller is also playing, quite consciously, with fascist iconography: come the nuclear winter and the electronic blackout of the missile attack that Superman fails to prevent, and what does the Batman become in order to restore order? He becomes quite literally the Man on Horseback of Samuel Finer's model of authoritarian seizures of power, putting together a coalition of Mutants who have escaped from jail and the faction of former Mutants who have become the so-called Sons of the Batman, enforcing zero tolerance of petty offences with wire-cutters and napalm. Order is restored in the face of failures by the authorities and the normal social institutions: middle-class executives become looters and the one churchman we see is an ineffectual bigot who has to be saved by a boy he distrusts for having a loud boombox.

Even Gordon manages nothing more than a failed attempt to save from a fire a woman whom he thinks is his wife – his wife is in fact not in the burning building and they both survive. Earlier, he warns his successor Yindel not to think she can understand the Batman by thinking of him as a simple criminal. In a long speech he compares the Batman with Franklin Roosevelt and talks of the rumours that the President allowed Pearl Harbor to happen in order to force America into the Second World War. 'But a lot of people died,' he says, 'but we won the war. It bounced back and forth in my head until I realized I couldn't judge it. It was too big.' Yindel answers him, at the time, 'I don't see what this has to do with a vigilante'. Later, when the Batman is bringing order to the streets of Gotham, one of her men has a clear shot at him, and she holds him back, saying 'he's too big'. Normally, the Batman is shown as supplementing the forces of law and order; Miller shows him as something superior, who does necessary things that they cannot.

For Bob Kane, when he invented the Batman, the choice of costume was a simple matter of picking something that would scare the 'cowardly and superstitious' criminals, and this is the default way most writers see the Batman and his compulsions. For Miller, it is in large measure not a rational choice so much as possession by a dark monstrous Batspirit that may or may not have objective existence. One of the strengths of *The Dark Knight Returns* is that it regularly turns on a dime between dark comedy, coarse satire, action that is emotionally and viscerally impressive even where it is visually static and introspective gothic horror; it is too much of a caricature to be a reliable picture of a three-dimensional world, but it does have the richness and complexity.

Miller's version of the Batman is older, and conscious of it; he is even jealous of Carrie because she has years to learn to fight crime, years that he does not have any more. He is also far less of a detective and far more of a gunslinger – other versions of the Batman fight crime with forensic intelligence, whereas Miller's tortures suspects. In order to find out what the Mutants are planning, he suspends one of them from the highest point in Gotham by his feet, hanging sardonically next to him – this goes beyond the sadistic into the deranged. The disguises he constantly wears to gather intelligence or entrap people into crime are grotesque, where in most Batcomics they are as elegant as he is. His athleticism has become a chunky forcefulness: even the sleek Batmobile has been replaced by a tank. Where, in earlier runs, he had been what Grant Morrison calls a 'hairy-chested love-god', this Batman is almost entirely sexless – Alfred jokes sardonically about not needing to renew the wine cellar at Wayne Mansion, 'given your social schedule of late, the prospect of there being a next generation . . .'. The Batman has always been liminal in a number of ways, one of them that he was cut off from his parents by their early death; now he is cut off from the future as well, or so it seems.

Where most superhero comics take place in a rolling present, *The Dark Knight Returns* deliberately places itself in a period that is the Batman's future, but the actual present that it was written in – Reagan is President and the Soviet Union exists as the real threat that it was not even at the time the comic was written. Certain features of these 1980s are exaggerated and stylised: the Mutants and others wield unfeasibly big machine guns and some of the fashions – not only of the Mutants – are deliberately odd and estranging, Yindel wears a leather greatcoat of a size and shape so enormous it is hard to see how she stands up in it. It is a present day for which Miller and his Batman have little but contempt.

The attitude to the media is an area in which the satire is especially scathing – the Batman's every move is debated to and fro by talking heads who are none of them interested in the facts of the matter, even the ones who, like this overweight future Lana Lang, support him. These are media that are heavily censored beneath an appearance of being able to say whatever they like; part of the deal Superman has struck with things as they are is that he is never mentioned explicitly, and a link-woman is tut-tutted at for using the 'faster than a speeding bullet' catchphrase when he breezes unseen, but felt, into town. One of the reasons why *The Dark Knight Returns* has stayed fresh is that Miller's perception of new media as having become 'infotainment' was accurate at the time and has since become more so. Tragedy is the story of the fall of a great man, and these clowns twitter around the edges of it.

Nor are the audience for the media significantly better; the only person who applies the lessons the Batman teaches correctly is Carrie, his one true supporter, who becomes, like the dead Jason, a 'good soldier . . . who honoured me'. Even she only just about matches up to his standards; he regularly threatens her with dismissal for taking risks, for letting herself be seen by criminals they are trailing, even after she has exceeded her orders and saved his neck by doing so. Everyone else is cowardly – in this version of the Batman, it is not only criminals who are a cowardly and superstitious lot – venal and timeserving and obsessed with image at the expense of substance, from the President on down.

This is shown vigorously in the art, drawn by Miller, inked by Miller and Klaus Janson and coloured by Lynn Varley. Many of the pages have an unusual 16-panel grid, but this constantly opens out; the many vox pop and talking head characters are accordingly tiny and detailed, and thrown into unflattering contrast with a coarsely heroic Batman who on several pages takes up a single giant panel in a heroic pugilist pose. Much of the time Varley colours things – even the shell-suits the Mutants wear – in quite delicate pastels, which makes the sudden blocs of dark blue, dark grey or dark brown of the larger panels deliberately crude by comparison. This is a book in which Miller manages to be almost entirely the auteur of his own comic; anything that is here is here because he meant it to be. *The Dark Knight Returns* remains, with all its flaws and all the areas in which it makes us uneasy, one of the most impressive comic books ever written.

Kurt Busiek's *Avengers Forever*

Critics who are sceptical about the usefulness of an obsession with continuity to comics writers would do well to contemplate the career of Kurt Busiek. Busiek has serious claims as a creator of original material – *Arrowsmith*, *Secret Identity*, *Shock Rockets* – and of material that critiques and pastiches the obsessions of the main superhero houses – *Astro City* – but he has equal claims to regard for his work for both Marvel and DC. The miniseries *Avengers Forever* is a side-bar to the long period in the early 2000s when he was writing *The Avengers*, most of the run being drawn by the excellent George Perez, who also drew the *Justice League of America / Avengers* crossover that Busiek executed so tremendously. One of its characters – on the pretext that she is an Avenger at some unspecified future date – is Songbird, one of Busiek's running characters from his other major Marvel strip *Thunderbolts*, in which he took a lot of second-string Marvel supervillains and re-engineered them as quasi-reluctant heroes. Songbird, for example, had a previous career as Screaming Mimi until she decided to use her sonic powers for (more or less) good.

Using your powers for good is part of the mission statement of all superheroes, but the Avengers, created as Marvel's answer to the Justice League of America, are particularly keen to do so, saving the world from menaces and living in considerable style in a New York mansion provided by one of their number. The line-up of the Avengers has constantly changed and most superheroes who have been members are always liable to turn up to help out when they are short-handed. The hard core of the group has tended to be Iron Man and Thor, with Captain America joining as soon as he was defrosted. Janet Van Dyne has been a member much of the time, as has been, though rather less, her husband Hank Pym in his various manifestations as Ant-Man, Giant Man, Yellowjacket super-scientist and occasional violent spouse. The archer Hawkeye has often been a member, as have the formerly evil mutants Wanda and Pietro and the Scarlet Witch, up to the point where she kills several of her team-mates after going crazy. The android the Vision has likewise been a member much of the time: in the current New Avengers run scripted by Bendis, the line-up includes Spider-Man, Spider-Woman, Wolverine and Luke Cage.

Busiek's period on the comic lasted for several years; he made a particular point of bringing back favourite villains, several of them more than once. Pym's parricidal robot Ultron turned up a couple of times, for example, and the time-travelling Kang on two occasions – *The Kang Dynasty* and the side-bar *Avengers Forever*. Busiek's period was not one with major innovations, though he introduced some attractive new characters and stuck by his professed general rule of only inventing new superheroes if he could find a way of giving them roots in ethnic minorities. Part of the charm was that much of the run was drawn by the veteran George Perez, with his fine line and endless delight in vivid rendition of scenes with more recognizable characters in them than it is quite sane to be able to name.

Busiek has a strong sense of historical period – the short-lived and incomplete *Arrowsmith* is perhaps the best of all reconfigurings of the First World War into a magic universe with its young American hayseed aviator and sense of the tragedy of war – that feeds into the time-travel plot of *Avengers Forever*. In both *Arrowsmith* and the post-collapse *Shock Rockets*, Busiek demonstrates a real grasp of how military and quasi-military organizations function through

---

Marvels

Busiek's sense of period served him particularly well in his magnificent project *Marvels*, a showcase for Alex Ross' work in the Marvel Universe in a way that Mark Waid's *Kingdom Come* was for Ross' work on DC characters. The premise of *Marvels* is that an ordinary New York civilian – a news photographer who starts his career alongside J. Jonah Jameson – talks to us about all that he has seen in the course of a long life, a life which has overlapped with Marvel continuity from the patriotic adventures of Captain America and Submariner during the Second World War onwards. For once the standard floating present of superhero comics is abolished so that the revival of Captain America and the formation of the Fantastic Four and the Avengers happen in a particular period once and for all.

Marvels is a thorough-going hymn to the embattled and flawed decency of the average American coping in a world in which the concept of the average is changing as he watches. The central character is guilty of paranoid bigotry towards mutants when he reads about their discovery and stops being a jerk the moment he finds a mutant child in serious danger. *Marvels* is one of the best descriptions of how it would feel to live in a world with superheroes if they were real; the near photographic intensity of Ross' images works equally well in quiet domestic scenes or a picture of New York about to be engulfed by a Submariner-unleashed tidal wave. It is also, in its quiet and unshowy way, one of the most telling demonstrations of Busiek's solid inhabiting of the world of continuity.

that sense of mutual dependency and collective self-esteem that is usually called *esprit de corps*; all of his writing about the Avengers and the JLA (he has done short runs on the DC comic as well) is marked out by that sense of the group as a unit.

Busiek's obsession with continuity is not merely a comprehensive grasp of who fought whom when in which costume and for what stakes; for Busiek, continuity has always been about character and emotions as well as a fannish keeping of scores. One of the pleasures of his *JLA/Avengers* is that the interactions of the two teams are based on hostilities and camaraderies that feel anything but arbitrary. Thus, Busiek's Superman and Captain America get on amazingly badly at first because the self-righteousness that is a part of their outstanding virtue grates on each other, whereas his Batman gets on with Captain America almost on sight because of mutual recognition by serious people. When you think of this in the abstract, these are not the relationships that would occur to you, but when you read Busiek's take on it, you find yourself nodding in agreement and accepting that it must be so.

One of the outstanding characteristics of his work is Busiek's through-and-through emotional decency; this is a man who likes his characters and who wants them to behave well. This is why his run on *Thunderbolts* is better than those written by his successor – Busiek has an emotional investment in his former villains' redemption that makes him ingenious in finding different emotional paths for them to choose. Karla Sofen (Moonstone) finds herself drawn in the short term to a performance of virtue by pragmatism, sexual attraction to the Avenger Hawkeye and the moral influence of the alien artefact that gives her power; none of this takes in the long run, alas. Eric Van Joosten (Atlas) is influence by a desire not to disappoint Jolt, the one member of the team who is not a former villain and is unaware of who her team-mates actually are. It is this decency that makes Busiek such an ideal writer of Superman in both *Superman* and *Action Comics*, as well as the short-run *Up, Up and Away*; Busiek really means all this stuff.

In *Avengers Forever*, he set himself a quite remarkably complex problem, not least in finding the emotional truth of his characters, a task which his grasp of continuity in human terms makes possible. As well as a piece of incredibly complex plotting, *Avengers Forever* is a virtuoso display of character continuity, since its cast are a selection of Avengers from different time periods within the history of the comic, including, as I have mentioned, two Avengers from a possible future.[1] The Captain America in *Avengers Forever* is the depressed version who became almost entirely disillusioned during Watergate, which was far more complex in the Marvel version even than it was in reality. There are two versions of Hank Pym: one of them during the delusional phase when he believed himself to be the fun-loving Yellowjacket, literally on the eve of marriage to Janet; the other is Janet's contemporary and chastened by the failure of their marriage – through spousal violence on his part, and through her gradual emergence as a rather more hard-bitten woman with leadership potential – neither version of Hank can entirely cope with this older, tougher version of the woman they love.

The premise that makes this assembling of Avengers from all over the continuity possible is a storyline that also tries to rectify one of the more bizarre anomalies of the Marvelverse, the feud between the time-travelling immortals, the brutal warlord Kang the Conqueror and the intriguer Immortus, and the revelation, many years after they first appeared, that they were aspects of the same person. Kang spends centuries traipsing around the timeline creating an empire here and failing to create another there, and gets beaten every time he turns up in the late 20th century. Immortus, meanwhile, plays longer subtler games with history. Kang becomes Immortus when he is old and tired, and fiercely resents knowing that this will happen to him. All of this

---

[1] Of these, Songbird turned down the chance to become a reserve list Avenger in a *Thunderbolts* storyline subsequent to *Avengers Forever*, and is currently, during *Civil War*, acting in a quite morally equivocal way, so it is not guaranteed that Marvel intend to follow through on this. The other, Captain Marvel – Genis, son of the original Kree warrior – is currently intermittently connected with the Thunderbolts and has developed a rather different look to the one he has here.

and much else besides – Kang's clones and imitators, Immortus' secret masters – was accumulated over the decades, and Busiek sets himself the task of telling a story that will provide a Grand Unified Theory of Kang.

Because this is an Avengers epic – the first such epic was *The Kree–Skrull War* – it needs to have a space-travelling component as well as a time-travelling one. The book starts with a sinister flash-forward to an intergalactic empire whose genocidally brutal enforcers style themselves Avengers and wear uniforms designed after Iron Man, Thor, Ant-Man and Captain America; their leader has the face of Rick Jones. Back in the present, the then-current group of Avengers take a comatose Rick Jones, their on-and-off sidekick, for a consultation with the Kree Intelligence Supreme, at this point a prisoner of war on the Moon. This is the sort of comic book in which a trip to the Moon is a slightly inconvenient commute; one of Busiek's strengths, here and elsewhere, is his sheer enjoyment of the scale on which, in comics, it is possible to work. A book whose characters travel to the Old West, various alternate worlds and the end of time itself is not going to fuss unduly about the Moon.

Ever since Jones put a stop to the Kree–Skrull War back in the early 1970s by demonstrating mental powers he had not previously possessed, the Intelligence Supreme (a vast tentacled head in a container) has researched the young man's powers, seeking information on what genetic material might be extracted from him and other humans to kick-start Kree evolution. (The Intelligence Supreme has at this point destroyed the empire it ruled in order to force his people to struggle for greater fitness to survive – it is really not a nice being.) As the Intelligence Supreme watches, soon joined by the mysterious advocate of balance, the former supervillain Libra, Immortus' envoy Tempus arrives to kill Jones, swiftly followed by Kang, who prevents him, and Immortus, who raises an army from all over time to assault his younger self. Restored to consciousness in the middle of this, Jones is instructed by the Intelligence Supreme and Libra to summon Avengers from all over the timeline of the organization, and does so.

The Avengers and Rick are warned by Libra to get out of the standard environment of the time-stream, in which they are vulnerable to the paradoxes that are one of Immortus' main weapons, and head for Kang's citadel, Chronopolis, effectively the centre of time. It is being destroyed by Immortus' armies; as they watch, it falls and Immortus collapses its central citadel into an amulet of infinite power, the Forever Crystal. Pacheco's art, here and elsewhere, is particularly good in its portrayal of monumental citadels; for Busiek, part of being a villain is that you inhabit the endless rooms of an over-complex palace of mind. The Avengers escape in one of Kang's Sphinx-like time machines and decide to fight back; Immortus' desire to kill Rick puts them on any side that is not his. They intervene against his current projects: in the Old West, the 1950s and a possible future when the human race has been nearly exterminated by returning Wellsian Martians.

These three locations, and the engagement with them of the teams into which the Avengers divide, are a chance for Busiek to play with, respectively, Marvel's Western comics; the precursor, unrelated, Avengers created in a single issue of *What If?*; and the world of Killraven, leader of the human resistance to the Martians in a short-lived title about which enough people are nostalgic that it was revived for a short run under Alan Davis. Like the best virtuoso material, in comics as in music, there is emotional charge both to the display of skill and to the ends to which that play is put.

To complicate matters further, the apparent issue in the Old West is an invasion, using dinosaurs as shock troops, by a different earlier version of Kang — as Hawkeye remarks, 'I wonder if time travellers have to keep a list so they know who they're mad at in which year' — which other Avengers will shortly appear and deal with, which means that their actual target, as Songbird realizes, is a subtler attempt by Immortus to change events that we have already seen in earlier comics by different hands. Several of the gunslingers they attempt to ally with are Immortus' shape-changing pawns, the Space Phantoms, one of whom impersonates Songbird for a while.

Interleaved with this are two more straightforward episodes. The struggle against the Martians involves an alliance of Killraven's forces with old or immortal Avengers in whose time Captain America and Hank Pym are dead martyrs, but the actual campaign fought is a mopping up operation. It culminates in a moral lesson about choice – whether to pursue the last Martians or allow an alien race, and a robot child, to be born – of a kind that Marvel was very fond in early days and for which Busiek is clearly nostalgic. The 1950s episode lasts long enough for an initial confrontation with the 1950s team to turn to friendship, for Richard Nixon to be exposed as a shapeshifting Skrull and for Immortus to appear and declare this possible alternate world now surplus to his requirements, and wipe it out.

Janet van Dyne and Genis make a hairbreadth escape when this world is returned to unbeing; by making us care about the people we have briefly met, and whom Immortus has wiped out with a hand wave, Busiek has made us care about one of the central issues of the comic. Where the Avengers try to avoid mortal violence, even in self-defence, Immortus and Kang are utterly casual about entire worlds of possibility, and the Intelligence Supreme is hardly better. The central message of Stan Lee's Marvel has always been that sense that 'with great power comes great responsibility', and the whole point about villains like Immortus and Kang is that they are far too casual about wiping people out.

Immortus' base is a vast labyrinth, to wander through which is to risk despair or danger; the team find themselves separated and some of them have demons to confront, while others fight literal foes. Hawkeye gets stuck with the job of plot function, fighting and outwitting Immortus' servant Tempus and procuring an important plot token, the Synchronic Staff. The self-aware version of Hank Pym and Janet van Dyne work as a team; Pym's alter ego Yellowjacket comes to realize that everything that has been said about his real identity is true. Since he hates Pym – and the idea of being Pym – his dark night takes the form of a preparedness to betray his colleagues; captured by Immortus, he offers him a deal. Though he reconsiders this when more fully informed about its implications, the fact that Yellowjacket is prepared to do this takes Busiek into areas of moral complexity that his generally sunny approach does not normally touch on. Most often he is a writer who makes villains do the right thing, not heroes betray their comrades.

Captain America, who has thus far not been as central to the action as he normally is in the Avengers, finds himself confronted by his old ally Nick Fury, a version of Fury from a time between his period as a war hero and his stint as the all-knowing head of SHIELD, an intelligence agency that sometimes seems to rule the world, quietly. Fury, or what appears to be Fury, tells him that everything they do is pointless. To defeat Hitler is to replace him with new menaces – Captain America bridles at this. To beat Hitler is to prove to oneself that evil can be beaten, and if once, why not again, as many times as needed?

Captain America had talked himself into despair, but he now talks himself out of it. Songbird confronts her criminal past, and nearly despairs. Genis appears and tells her that in the time he is from they are together; her problem has been that she feels unworthy and she is told she has a future. It is worth pointing out, even if it is obvious, that the three big reversals of characters' moods that happen in this section all have to do with their coming to terms with time and change; beyond the belief of arrogant mortals that time is something that can be channelled and controlled, we are being shown, time is a moral force that changes us.

This is the lesson that Kang has never fully learned. In a prolonged interlude, Busiek shows us this villain in quite considerable depth, not only trying to make sense of everything that has happened to Kang in the Marvel Universe but to show what it felt like at the time. This is more information than we would usually get in comics about villains and their back-story and their emotions, but, without spelling it out explicitly, Busiek shows us the sense of entrapment that is crucial to Kang's character and behaviour. Bored by his own time, Kang created a personal cult of violence and ambition and has failed entirely to understand why nothing he does works for him. At an overt level, this section is a prolonged boast of conquest and intrigue and survival; at the level of subtext it is a hymn to a despair far more total than that to which Captain America and Songbird are tempted, because Kang knows how his story ends. Like Yellowjacket, he will do anything to change his destiny; because he has done so much, so futilely, already; we not only see him as trapped in endless repetitions, but see the path of villainy as essentially being just that. Yet, counter-intuitively, we find ourselves more sympathetic to Kang than to his older, more apparently pacific self, Immortus, simply because he is more vulnerable and more the occasional victim of violence as well as its perpetrator.

What follows – an extended piece of passage work in which the escaped Avengers realize how often Immortus has manipulated them – is the sort of virtuoso geekishness at which Busiek excels, but lacks the emotional force that, say, the recitation of Kang's career has. It is there primarily to allow Yellowjacket to make his deal with the devil, and he promptly appears and takes his friends captive on behalf of his new master. This master has, we now learn, masters of his own: beings from the end of time, the Time Keepers, propose to prune the timelines in order to ensure their own existence, justifying this with an at first plausible rationale of controlling the excesses that we have already seen the human race as capable of inflicting on other species. The space empire we saw in the book's opening frames, and have visited again with the Avengers whom Immortus briefly throws there, is a very bad thing, the sort of thing that, the Time Keepers argue, happens when humanity is allowed free rein among the galaxies. They have a right to protect their own existence and to police the multiverse, they argue, and humanity is too much of a risk.

Captain America and the others spot the fallacy in all of this: the Time Keepers apply double standards. They themselves are only one possible outcome – another is their evil equivalent the Time Twisters – yet they never assume that they ought to be prevented from existing or limited in the power available to them. The all-knowing beings who condemn humanity for its crimes are one of the stock tropes of SF as of theology; it is attractive that Busiek argues a contrary case and does it with some skill. Later on, once victory has been achieved, Captain America has the confidence to put the argument most effectively:

The Time Keepers feared what humanity could do – and in that at least they were right. We have to make sure that those dark futures – the tyranny and oppression visited on the galaxy by humanity – don't happen. But we have to do it as free men, not as prisoners.

This is, after all, one of the central arguments of Western philosophy, from Augustine and Pelagius onwards – are we saved by grace, works of piety or a combination of the two?

Of course, in order to get to the point where Captain America can sum up the question so succinctly, there has to be a big battle. This is a comic book, after all. The Time Keepers summon all the bad versions of the Avengers we have ever seen in continuity and Rick Jones, who has returned with Kang, Libra and the Intelligence Supreme as reinforcements, responds by summoning a vast horde of good Avengers, a greater number by some orders of magnitude, of course. The argument is in the end about the odds, and producing a larger army in defence of your side of the argument is, in such a debate, a winning riposte as well as a matter of having the big battalions.

Libra's role in all this has been very much that of Basil Exposition – he explains the rules of the game and agonizes about taking sides. Having been a comparatively ordinary supercriminal earlier in his career, he has become an occult representative of balance, and he realizes that even the forces of balance have in the end to choose a side. He is faced with the choice between the sterile restricted orderliness that the Time Keepers would force on the timelines, a wild chaos in which evil prevails, and the productive chaos of humanity's expansion as policed by the virtuous. The point of balance is not, for Busiek, to stick with neutrality and blandness and irresponsibility; it is to step outside those dichotomies that have been falsely proposed.

The Time Keepers have murdered their pawn Immortus for dilatoriness in killing the Avengers, and for being conned by Yellowjacket, who changed sides once he realized what the stakes were. They try to take back this petulant act by forcing the weight of time onto Kang, to turn him into his alter ego prematurely; by a supreme act of will, he resists and is split into himself and a far younger version of Immortus than we have ever seen, a version younger than Kang himself. Both of these withdraw once victory is achieved, to think about the way their destiny has been altered. We know from those Avengers who come from the future that this incident will be known as the Destiny War, and what Busiek shows us is that Destiny is not as fixed as continuity would seem to make it. The various Avengers return home, which, in the case of those whose home is the past means that they have no memory of all this; Yellowjacket returns to his marriage to Janet with no memory of the treachery to which he was tempted or of the reasons for it. Back on the Moon, the Intelligence Supreme has snaffled the Forever Crystal and lurks in the background, reminding us that it is a villain, just a very smart one to have profited from all this welter of confusion . . .

So, why is *Avengers Forever*, a short-run graphic novel in a broader continuity of near-infinite extent, something that should hold our attention? Obviously, for those of us who like such things, it is full of hair's-breadth escapes and sudden reversals, of constant telling allusions to much-loved storylines and guest appearances by favourite characters. But, further, I would suggest that part of the point is that it demonstrates how complex, both in terms of plot and in terms of moral weight, that continuity can be. Our sympathies shift between characters – even the villainous Kang acquires emotional resonance he has rarely had elsewhere in the Marvel Universe, prior, that is, to our meeting in *Young Avengers* with a teenage version keen to refuse his destiny in turn.

Part of its charm is that, under all the flash of its fights and adventures and confrontations, Busiek is making a point about the nature and purpose of heroism: the difference between villains and heroes is not just prowess or charm, but rather a concern to do the right thing even when it is difficult. The Avengers from 'our' time are quietly shocked by the future Avengers' preparedness to kill even the genocidal Martians and their cyborg quislings. The decision by the Black Panther that enough is enough, that a choice between life and more death has to be a choice for life, even at the expense of vengeance, is the result of appeals to him by kinder gentler Avengers who have not gone through his experiences, and he accepts that they are right.

It is in the context of this concern to do the right thing that the book's games with the concept of destiny become more than games. Rick at one point meets an older, one-armed bitter version of himself and learns that, if you cannot avoid fate, you can at least accept it with dignity; Yellowjacket – and it is worth stressing that Hank Pym has always been one of the more flawed of the team – nearly commits unforgivable sins in the name of flouting both destiny and his own real nature. Working with this vast cast, of whom his target audience knows so much, means that Busiek can work elegant variations and parallels on his central themes; we know that this mopey version of Captain America will buck up in due course, and the fun is seeing how it happens and how it plays out.

Another of the book's strengths is Pacheco's art – he is not one of the very best of the crop of comics artists working in the late 1990s and early 2000s, but he is assuredly at the top of the second rank. One factor in this is his effective use of large-scale composition on the splash pages that periodically break up his competent but unexciting use of a constantly shifting grid; he has learned from George Perez how dynamic you can be while also sticking in every single one of the characters and variants of characters that your writer has stuck you with. Pacheco has worked with Busiek several times, most notably on *Arrowsmith*; the slightly innocent, fresh-faced quality he brings to his characters works rather well with Busiek's moralized, charming, thoroughly decent take on them.

Grant Morrison's Period on *New X-Men*

The 40 issues Grant Morrison wrote of *New X-Men* in the early 2000s were quite specifically intended to kick-start into centrality a much-loved and popular group of titles that had lost their way a little in endless complexity and endless revisiting of the same characters' standard traumas. His manifesto/pitch document, handily included in the first hardback collection, makes the point that the audience to whom Marvel were attempting to appeal with their books in general, and perhaps with the X-titles in particular, was one that was used to the snappy dialogue and angsty plots of television shows like *Buffy the Vampire Slayer*. It is no accident that one of the writers who picked up on the X-Men when Grant Morrison had finished with them was Joss Whedon himself.

The main weakness of this run has nothing to do with Morrison's writing. Marvel pushed out the issues on a punishing schedule that exceeded one a month, which meant that, though most of the art on the Morrison run is perfectly fine, and some of it is lovely, not all of it reaches high, or even minimal, standards. Moreover, the run changed main artists several times over, so it does not achieve a consistent style and it is harder than usual to keep track of different artists' portrayal of the characters. Morrison's central cast are iconic enough that this is not a problem, but, for example, in Jean's vision at the end, it is only dream plot logic and his bad haircut that enable us to identify the man who advises her as the former rebel Quire grown to maturity.

Morrison was always the bad boy of the British writers, his long run on the Vertigo title *The Invisibles*, for example, used the freedom Vertigo gave him to create an occulto-anarchist primer in which an alliance of a tantric magician, a drag queen, a butch young dyke and others significantly outside the mainstream of superhero comics take on not only the apparatus of the British state but the metaphysical creatures of madness, conformity and nameless dread that lie behind it. His run on the more mainstream *Doom Patrol* was hardly more orthodox with its surreal villains trying to destroy consensual reality; the outcast status of the characters he inherited here meant that they could empathize with the sheerly weird enough to defeat it, and to have a bad conscience about doing so. *Animal Man* became a fourth-wall-breaking meditation on the nature of superheroes and whether one should even be in the business of writing them; it is the superhero comic whose hero has most serious conversations with its writer. Even his run on DC's flagship team-up, *JLA*, did some moderately radical things, like having the entire human race temporarily become superheroes to defeat an apocalyptic foe. His quite remarkable *Seven Soldiers of Victory* (2006) teams up a group of second-string superheroes who never actually meet, but separately fight different battles in the same war against particularly evil Sidhe invading from a version of Faerie.

Rather than provide a detailed commentary on 40 issues, we need to look at what Morrison did to the X-Men and their world in the course of his run. One of the crucial things was that he made the central issue of the comic the question of extinction: Hank McCoy and others discover that the human race is in its last generations, that a gene has emerged that will simply turn human history off for good. In a few generations, the mutants will be all that there is, unless humanity frustrates biological destiny by altering its own genome. Because Morrison has a dark streak, that sense of humanity as doomed means that efforts to exterminate mutants go into high gear. Morrison's occultist anarchism makes him less political a writer than other British writers of superhero comics, Mark Millar in particular, whose run on *Ultimate X-Men* is a useful point of comparison here, but his sense of paranoid dread is very British.

One of the first things Morrison does, in fact, is have Sentinel robots strafe the mutant haven Genosha and exterminate the 16 million who live there. One of the directions that other writers had taken the X-titles in was making there be more and more mutants all the time, and Morrison realized that, if mutants are a nation, your characters are simply under less threat all the time.[2] Rather than have this particular act be an overt declaration of war by humanity, Morrison created Cassandra Nova, a mutant predator more nihilist than any of the standard X-villains. Even Apocalypse

---

[2]   The later decision by Marvel to have the Scarlet Witch reduce the mutant population to 198 by magic is more or less an endorsement of Morrison's decision, which is one of a number of things he could not have done without permission.

has as his aim destroying society as we know it in order to force both humans and mutants to evolve under pressure; Cassandra kills for the sake of killing, to spite her twin brother Charles Xavier.

Again, by creating Cassandra, Morrison is not just making up yet another evil twin, though she certainly is that: a foetal Xavier, it turns out, strangled her in the womb and the being of pure energy that is Cassandra constructed herself a body over many years from his discarded cells. She is, in other words, quite literally the avatar of Xavier's bad faith. This famous pacifist killed his unheimlich twin before they were even born and at some level he has always known this; at some level this is the truth that underlies his endless struggle to be virtuous. This is the sort of complication of continuity that cannot be undone and no one wishes it undone – Cassandra is one of those villains who always finds a way of coming back and is effective even in less talented hands. Whedon uses her quite effectively in *Astonishing X-Men* and Claremont does something quite moving, in a kitsch way, with her and Xavier in *The End*.

Cassandra kills millions as an opening shot, and then moves to the specific, evicting Charles from his body in order to be more effective in destroying everything he cares about. She drives the Shi'ar empress, his wife, mad and sets the aliens to exterminate his pupils; just to be on the safe side, she also develops nano-Sentinels that will kill the X-Men from the inside out, and has one of his pupils bash Henry McCoy's brains in when he starts to suspect the truth. Cruelty is always more important to her than truth; McCoy's constant metamorphosis to an ever more bestial physiognomy makes him vulnerable to Cassandra's mockery. She has almost defeated him with her words even before she makes the unfortunate Beak hit him time and time again.

Cassandra is an effective villain because she is pure malice; she is only vulnerable because her nihilism makes her unable to understand sheer heroism. A Shi'ar warrior arrives, dying, in time to tell his comrades the truth; with his mind crippled by the neurological diseases with which she has crippled her own body before trapping him there, Charles Xavier struggles to get the truth out. And though she is a powerful telepath, she does not know people very well: she thinks that former villain Emma Frost is selling out her new friends when Emma offers her her body back as a refuge, whereas Emma is in fact trapping her in a mindless alien shell. 'Not my mind, my precious mind', Cassandra cries out like the Wicked Witch of the West, and is reduced to imbecility.

The X-Men are constantly betrayed by what is false within – one set of pupils engage in a riot that costs the life of several promising pupils, another set become the acolytes of a new teacher at the school who proves to be not what he seems. One of the central relationships of the Morrison run seems like a betrayal even if it turns out to be the last best hope for humanity and mutants alike: when the X-Men dig Emma Frost out from the rubble of Genosha, and Xavier asks her to work at the school, this is not a standard Marvel reconfiguring of a villain. Emma was always one of the leaders of the Hellfire Club and had used her powers for personal enrichment, spending much of it on cosmetic surgery and designer clothes; she is distinctly cynical about Xavier's mission as about almost everything else. The fact that Morrison gives her a secondary mutation that has saved her – about to die, she turned into living diamond – provides a handy metaphor for how little she is subject to other sorts of change; she is hard and glittery down to her soul. 'Once a villain, always a villain', McCoy says when he thinks Emma has betrayed them all to Cassandra, and he is clearly voicing a concern held by many of those who know her.

Or so it appears. When Emma first puts seductive moves on the depressed Scott Summers, whose marriage to Jean Grey is in that particular kind of trouble which comes from deep boredom, it seems as if she is merely 'playing with fire' – literally, since Jean Grey is the Phoenix – and trying to steal an old opponent's husband. She abuses her role as his psychotherapist to flirt outrageously, appearing in his mind in a version of Jean's old costume and referring to herself as 'Auntie Emma' as if she were sexually harmless.

Yet, as Jean finds out in amused incredulity, Emma has fallen in love and is vulnerable for possibly the first time since childhood.

Scott and Jean were teenage sweethearts and both have grown up into a far darker world than the one they inhabited when they were first together. One of the real strengths of the Morrison run is to interrogate a relationship that has become a cliché and make us understand that it is, perhaps, over. Another is that he takes one of the First Couples of comics and breaks them up, and does so without our feeling that anyone is particularly in the wrong; comics morality has normally more in common with soap-opera or tabloid morality, but Morrison insists on his characters acting like adults.

He does so with real wit – Scott's attempt to persuade himself that adulterous flirtation inside telepathically induced illusory scenarios does not count is by way of being a reference, I think, to Bill Clinton and 'I did not have sex with that woman'. This sometimes involves Morrison in corny but effective jokes: when Jean asks him whether he slept with Emma in Singapore, he answers that she kept him up all night. It is literally true, but not as effective a disclaimer as he perhaps intends. One of the most effective things Morrison does is show how Emma and Jean move from their original hostility to a warily collegiate relationship; in a series of pages without dialogue, they venture into Xavier's mindscape when he is trapped in Cassandra's body, and free him, acting as a highly competent team.

Morrison brought Emma into the centre of things partly because he wanted to write dialogue for her; she is one of the real strengths of his run simply because we are waiting to find out what she will say next. When her nose is broken by human vivisectors – part of a secret society who dissect mutants in order to transplant mutant organs into themselves and become something new – she says that she is 'very very cross indeed' and only Morrison's version of Emma could make this sound one of the most threatening lines you have ever heard. Further, he gives her a quintet of protégées, five adolescent girls who have done their best to become her clones in every respect, and who are referred to by everyone as the Stepford Cuckoos. When they turn on her, as they inevitably do, and call her a stupid old woman, Emma has a particularly effective dark night of the soul. 'I'm only twenty-seven, you ungrateful wretches', she says, but they are not listening, and she is clearly lying even to herself.

Scott Summers has always been a gloomy leader with a lot of doubts; over the years, this has become more and more of a cliché, even in the hands of the brilliant Chris Claremont in the period when he continued to produce X-Men material at a point when he had lost his edge. The default setting became to give Scott angst if writers did not know what else to do with him. Generally this meant Scott stopped being especially competent, but did not become interesting in the process; some of the most amusing and powerful scenes Morrison writes for him and Logan are ones in which the older mutant tells Scott to stop feeling sorry for himself, simply because Logan is speaking for most of the audience. It is something of a relief for someone actually to tell him that he has become so clenched that 'only dogs can hear you fart'.

The U-Men, the conspiracy of vivisectors, is one of Morrison's many wonderfully nasty ideas – like other villains before them, they see the school as a handy target, and plan to use it as their organ farm. Morrison has Scott and Emma confront their leadership as if they were civilized men, only to find themselves trapped; Jean is on her own in the school with the children, but of course Jean, and a bunch of mutant children, is quite enough to see off the merely average villains that all the U-Men, in the end, are. 'Define defenceless', Jean says as she goes to war, and the Phoenix's flames rise behind her. The problem is that a Jean who has to fight by herself is a Jean who uses all of her power; Jean Grey becomes clearly the Phoenix again, with all that implies in terms of the possibility that she will become a greater menace than the things she fights.

In the Claremont years, the only time Jean was cool was when she was doomed, and she never worked all that well after the Dark Phoenix storyline was taken back. In a piece of strip-mining, it was announced that the Phoenix had taken Jean's shape rather than possessing her, and that Jean had slept out the time of her supposed death, and Scott's marriage to her clone Madeleyne, in a cocoon beneath the sea. There is something inevitable to the fact that Morrison kills her off again because she was probably never going to be as cool again as she is in the best moments he gives her, though her gravestone says 'she will rise again' and, knowing Marvel, she probably will.

The theme of what is false within applies to several of the other storylines: Xavier and Jean are prevailed upon to help Fantomex, a mutant criminal on the run from one of the weapons programmes that have experimented on humans, mutants and Sentinels to produce ever more bizarre creations. Fantomex, for example, has a nervous system outside his body, in the shape of a flying saucer called Eva; he is also an accomplished liar: it takes some time for Jean and Xavier, two of the most intelligent and able telepaths on the planet, to realize that everything he has told them about his back-story is a lie, and that their visit to his aged mother was an illusion. There are times in the stories about experimental beings like Fantomex and the creatures who immediately precede and succeed him in the Weapon X series of experiments – one of whom acquires extra bodies every time he touches someone – when Morrison perhaps drifts too far into the sort of nightmare he used so effectively in *The Invisibles*. What he finds scariest, and makes most scary, are nightmares so ineffable as to be vague when you try and think about them.

This is why some of the most effective sections of his run are the ones that push the conventional to its limits, but not beyond. The Cassandra run, for example, and the school riot, and the attempted murder of Emma with a diamond bullet that shatters her into a thousand perfect pieces, are more like X-Men comics as we have known them than the Fantomex line, only better. Morrison clearly enjoys doing this sort of generic stuff – he brings in long-standing X-continuity characters, Bishop and Sage, to investigate the murder and has them largely fail. The gun was fired by the obnoxious slumgirl mother Angel; frightened of what might happen to her swarm of babies, she was made to do this by the influence of Esme, one of the Cuckoos. But they fail to discover who persuaded Esme to act in this, merely discovering that it was a tallish man. Since

McCoy and Jean literally reassemble Emma – 'Wake up,' she says to her rival, 'Scott needs you' – the whole issue is allowed to slide.

This is wrong, as it happens, because the attempt on Emma was merely one gambit of many. The gentle mystic Xorn, the man with a black hole inside his skull and a habit of preaching gentle wisdom to his class of pariah pupils, is in fact Magneto, returned yet again from the grave, and he seizes New York with his usual genocidal aims made more plausible by what happened in Genosha. He traps the various X-Men with a series of gambits – Logan and Jean are sent spinning into the sea, McCoy and Emma are marooned in the Pacific – that ensure their absence by appealing to their sense of mission. No matter how many times such calls for help or to arms turn out to be traps, it is the nature of heroes to answer them, and to try and survive. It is their own nature that is the thing most likely to defeat them.

By the same token, because he is a serious villain and not just a punch-bag for good guys, Magneto will always fail because of his own nature; a significant part of what defeats him, though, is that the world has moved on. Magneto is not what Xorn's pupils are interested in following, because for them Magneto is a dead hero on a t-shirt. The earlier rebels of Morrison's run – Quire and his gang – adopted the striped t-shirt and unfortunate haircut of an evil mutant in an old newspaper article; interestingly, because Morrison does not normally go in for *hommage*, it is an article and illustration we are shown in Issue 14 of the original run. It is also the article and illustration we see Phil Sheldon looking at in the Busiek/Ross book *Marvels*. Magneto is a figure from 1960s politics and Morrison puts him in a world of situationism and spectacle.

By casting aside his identity as Xorn, Magneto rejects much of the hold he had on his pupils: Beak and Angel were flattered by inclusion, but Beak has moral qualms when it actually comes to killing humans. Using the drug Kick to enhance his powers, Magneto becomes short-tempered and almost accidentally kills another of his followers, in a moment of rage at a stupid joke. When the renegade Stepford Cuckoo Esme reveals her infatuation with him – it has been blindingly obvious to everyone up to that point – he rejects the young girl brusquely; she attacks him and he kills her, plunging her earrings into her brain. By the time the X-Men actually arrive, he is already almost on the ropes, but manages to kill Jean before being gutted by Logan. Jean survived the sun by becoming the Phoenix but she is still human enough to die; she and Logan previously had the moment of total emotional honesty that was always pending between them, and without its being specifically sexual, Morrison makes it a *Liebestod* nonetheless.

Morrison delivers everything that X-Men comics are supposed to be about – paranoia about being a minority, operatic emotions and final tragedy. In an epilogue to his run, he delivers something more, a total nightmare. We are plunged centuries ahead into utter nightmare: humanity is gone save for one last boy and his battered Sentinel companion. A few X-Men are all that stands in the way of the entire destruction of life as we know it by a Henry McCoy turned into the monstrous vivisector and gene pirate that we know – from the world of Apocalypse and his alter ego there – that the cuddly avuncular scientist has the potential to become. Jean has hatched from the egg of the Phoenix innocent and all too prone to be his pawn. In a terrifying twist we learn that the drug Kick was nothing of the kind, it was an intelligent bacterium, Sublime, that has possessed pawns of its own with the aim of removing complex life altogether; when Scott and then Emma dropped out of their responsibilities, Henry took Kick in despair and was lost. Of the originals, only the immortal Logan endures, with the remaining Stepfords and Beak's grandson at his side; the desperate nature of the situation is such that even Cassandra Nova is at their side. They lose, and one by one they die in the most terrible of pain; Jean realizes too late who she is and what she has helped happen and breaks Sublime's control of McCoy so that he too can return to innocence and die.

Jean has a vision of a myriad future dead X-Men and knows what she must do; 'if you want to grow a new future to replace the one you just cut away', she is told by a man who might be Quire grown to maturity, or might not, 'you have to water it with your heart's blood'. She has already had a vision of the point at which the world took turn for the worst – Emma propositions Scott at Jean's graveside and he refuses her – and she influences events for the better. In the last full page of Morrison's *New X-Men* Scott embraces Emma and says yes to life for himself and the world.

5 Some Kind of Epic Grandeur

Events and Reboots in the Superhero Universe

Events and Reboots?

It took a surprising amount of time – until the beginning of the 1970s – for the occasional crossing-over of characters from one title's continuity to another's to be followed by the logical extension of storylines that moved from one title to another, so that, in order to find out what happens next to your favourite character, you might have to buy a comic you would not otherwise buy. It took even longer for such stories to evolve from simple two-parters into something more complex. Once Marvel had started issuing several X-Men related titles in the late 1970s and early 1980s, it became viable to run a storyline through all the related titles for several months, and in due course this became a quasi-regular occurrence.

What took even longer was the evolution of the 'event' storyline, which quite possibly has a short-lived run of its own, and also crosses over into a number of other titles. So-called 'event' storylines are one of the more obviously commercial ventures that superhero comics go in for – they are, after all, primarily there to persuade fans to buy more comics – and, by comparison with the best story arcs and detailed re-imaginings of individual titles, or groups of titles, tend to be less successful. In this chapter, I shall also deal with the reboots of their entire continuity that DC did in the 1980s and again in 2005–6, with mixed results. Inevitably, these have in common with other events the fact that they are stories that feel as if they were devised by an editor rather than a writer, and on which so many writers and artists collaborate, across a number of titles, that focus is liable to be lost completely. And, of course, there are exceptions to this rule, one of which, Marvel's *Civil War* has been, with all its faults and its slightly disappointing ending, the most intelligent piece of political comment, protest and analysis that the comics industry has ever produced.

The Death of Superman and some Batevents

One of the first, and in some ways least bad, examples of the non-reboot event is the so-called *Death and Return of Superman* (1993), which was widely publicized in the mainstream press (and is, perhaps, most important for being memorialized in the last movement of Michael Daugherty's *Metropolis* Symphony). Essentially, a mysterious silent being – who has no name, but is referred to by his opponents as Doomsday – batters his way out of imprisonment and proceeds to rampage across America, killing everything in his path; in one of several moments of near bathos, he allows a small yellow bird to settle on his hand, and then crushes it. A detachment of the Justice League turns up to oppose him, and are trounced and left more or less for dead. Superman arrives in time to save them, but makes no headway whatever against the monster. Moreover, he saves a family from death at the cost of a few minutes that might otherwise have enabled him to distract the creature from its principal goal: Metropolis.

The creature appears to grow stronger the more it is hit, and various bony protrusions sprout from its joints and facial features; one of the strengths of the sequence is that no attempt is made to rationalize Doomsday, to give it motivation or even to explain its attributes. It is death incarnate, pure and simple. And it is the Death of Superman, who batters it into quiescence but dies of the injuries it has inflicted, and is left a shattered, though still handsome, corpse cradled in the arms of Lois Lane, who has, of course, insisted on covering the story.

The second volume of this event, *World Without Superman*, is a strange mixture of the funereally pompous, the sentimental and the genuinely affecting. Superman gets a state funeral, presided over by the Clintons, and with most of the standard DC superheroes forming the cortege. Batman, of course, stays out of this procession and polices it from the shadows, because someone has to. Lois, Jonathan and Martha Kent and Lana Lang have to conspire to pretend that Clark Kent is missing, perhaps trapped or dead in the rubble of Doomsday's rampage, because, even after Superman's death, his secret identity has to be preserved, simply to protect those he loves from the vengeance of his enemies.

The sinister scientists of Project Cadmus have already tried to seize the body and now tunnel into Superman's tomb and steal it. They do this against the orders of their ultimate boss, Lex Luthor: Luthor has at this point in his career had his brain transplanted into a clone that lacks his baldness, has flowing red hair and beard, and affects to be his own son. Luthor had hoped that Superman would die or be defeated at his own hands, but is not in any hurry for a resurrection. He has his dupe, a shape-changing alien who has taken the identity of Supergirl, (who herself, rather more memorably and iconically, died in *Crisis on Infinite Earths*) steal the body and return it to its tomb.

In Smallville, Jonathan Kent has a heart attack from which he nearly dies, broken-hearted as he is by the death of his adopted son. In death dreams, he revisits the battlefields of his youth, attempts to harrow Hell and finally rescues Superman from demons who have posed as the inhabitants of Superman's native Krypton. Perhaps, he suggests, Superman's mortality was an illusion, produced by the Kents' limited perspectives when rearing him. Whatever the existential status of these dreams, he awakes renewed and, back in Metropolis, Superman's tomb is found to be empty.

The third volume, *The Return of Superman*, creates a number of pretenders to Superman's role, two of whom were to become long-term characters in the DC Universe. The African-American weapons designer John Henry, aware of the song of the same name, and attempting to expiate his design of a good cheap automatic weapon that his ex-girlfriend Angora has put out on the streets of America, builds himself a set of steel armour and a great hammer. Unlike the others, he makes no pretence of being Superman, but is merely an admirer who is trying to fill his shoes, as, in a small way, is the lumbering ex-thug Bibbo, who in a few scenes does his best to clean up his slum while wearing a Superman pullover.

The brash and brattish boy Conner insists on being called Superman, rather than Superboy, and has many of the right powers, while lacking judgement and skill. He is far too fond of hogging the limelight, but is essentially well-intentioned, when he can spare the time from flirting with the TV news reporter Tana, who becomes his Lois. It is clear that he is in some degree a clone of the original Superman, even though this appears to contradict the remarks of the Project Cadmus scientists that there were aspects of Superman's DNA that they were unable to unravel.[1]

We see another Superman born from a 'regeneration matrix' in the Fortress of Solitude. Mysteriously, this one has to wear dark glasses and has no sense of moderation in his pursuit of justice, killing or maiming villains unlucky enough to encounter him. He seems to know much of Superman's private past, but in a distant and detached way; Lois is not sure whether or not to regard him as genuine. He explains the changes in his personality as the result of his death, as does the next Superman pretender, a Terminator-like robot, a part of whose face is flesh and appears to be that of Superman. This proves to be Cyborg, a villain who has fused himself so totally with machinery and artificial intelligence that he functions, more or less, as a contagion, acquiring new bodies and machine parts as he escapes death time and time again. He

---

[1]   It gradually emerges in later comics that Conner is a chimera, whose DNA is a patchwork of Superman and Luthor. If readers are somewhat amazed to discover that Superman and his worst enemy have a child together, they are entitled to be.

destroyed Green Lantern's hometown and now he tries to trash Superman's reputation forever.

Of course, the authentic Superman rises from the dead, and of course the more admiring pretenders help him in his struggle with the more villainous ones. Various reboots of his powers ensued – for a while he acquired blue skin and affected a rather more Kryptonian mode of dress; the death had mythic power but affected nothing all that profoundly in the long term, save to demonstrate to Luthor that annihilation of the being he hates is not going to be as simple as all that.

Given the mythic power of the event that occurs at its core, *Death of Superman* is a long way from being all it might have been. One problem with it is that the decision to make Superman's nemesis a malign force of nature means that their conflict is essentially impersonal, whereas the most interesting Superman villains have been those like Luthor with a keen brain and a wicked tongue. Another problem is that the resurrection was handled uninterestingly and with a slightly mawkish religiosity – if you are going to use the resonant symbolism of an empty tomb, you really need to earn the cultural force of that symbol with your own contributions.

The four replacement Supermen are not especially interesting – John Henry has gradually become an interesting character over the years, but Conner never really acquired stature or dignity until the events leading to his death in *Infinite Crisis*. Nor is the grief of Superman's close associates made especially moving or powerful; the situation of their having to continue to protect his secret identity for fear of the consequences is a nice touch with potential for turning emotional screws, but is uninterestingly executed. The stateliness of the official proceedings is unrelieved by wit or humanity, it needed emotional complexity to work and that is very precisely what it does not get. *Death of Superman* was an interesting concept and a missed opportunity.

Much the same can be said of other major DC events, which include, for example, *Knightfall* (1993), the story of the crippling of the Batman by the monstrous steroid-freak Bane, who defeats him in hand-to-hand combat and breaks his back. The Batman is ill-advised in his choice of successor, appointing the vigilante Azrael, who takes the whole caped crusader thing rather literally, and when he recovers from his injuries the Batman has two enemies to overthrow instead of one. This sequence is one of several Batman events in which Miller's legacy of pretentiously posturing grittiness started to reach the point of self-parody; another is *No Man's Land* (1999), in which Gotham City is devastated by an earthquake and the US government is persuaded to leave it to rot. Ironically, this was mocked at the time – long before Hurricane Katrina – for the implausibility of any US government's doing any such thing. *No Man's Land* is an interesting missed opportunity for its Hobbesian perception that, once government collapses, the police and well-intentioned vigilantes become little more than another gang fighting for parity. There is also the previously mentioned more recent *War Games*, with its unfortunate tendency to kill off female characters and characters of colour – and make it their own fault.

The trouble with all of these Batman events is their tendency to the doom-laden and portentous. It is not calling for the return of Adam West-style campery to ask for a version of the Batman and his crew that is a little more nuanced, a little less Hobbesian. Even Miller's Dark Knight was known, after all, to crack a joke or two. DC have also grown over-fond of the Batman's having a cunning scheme as a way of setting up and resolving vast plotlines; given the terrible consequences of various of said schemes when copied and used by others – as has happened on a number of occasions – plausibility might dictate that he avoid them in future. Even since Stephanie triggered events that included her own death, in *War Games*, by misusing the Batman's game plan for a meltdown internecine struggle between Gotham's gangs, the Batman's various schemes to prevent his superpowered colleagues going bad – the creation of a nanobot-powered corps of sleeper soldiers, the OMAC project – have been used by the mysterious instigators of *Infinite Crisis*. One hopes, but does not trust, that he and DC will have learned a lesson from this.

Some Marvel Events

Marvel, meanwhile, had one of the first and most catchpenny of large events in *Secret Wars* (1984–5), not to be confused with the later, much better and almost entirely unconnected *Secret War* (2004). A powerful being abducted a bunch of heroes and villains to an alien planet and obliged them to fight it out, with their hearts' desires as the prize – this led to no very interesting character work and some very standard fight scenes. On the other hand, it sold a reasonable number of action figures, which was, apparently, according to the articles in the collected edition, one of the reasons why it ever existed in the first place. Though there was no reset button and no sense that it never happened, the only lasting consequence of importance that derives from *Secret Wars* is the black costume that Spider-Man acquired on the alien planet and wore for a while. Since it proved to be an alien symbiote, and has subsequently taken over – and driven mad – two of Marvel's grittier villains, Venom and Carnage, this is a detail relevant to the greater whole of continuity.

Most of Marvel's other events – *Inferno,* (1989) for example, in which New York City became for a while co-existent with Hell – also had few consequences. (*Onslaught* (1996), in the course of which most of the heroes disappeared from the world and had to be replaced, led to the creation of the Thunderbolts by Kurt Busiek.) Various X-Men-centred storylines have for a while replaced the whole of Marvel reality with an alternate world like that ruled by Apocalypse, but these are automatically reset when the time paradoxes that caused them are resolved. *The Age of Apocalypse* (1995) produced several unpleasant or virtuous characters who crop up from time – an evil vivisecting version of Beast, a comparatively sane and virtuous version of Saber-Tooth, the teleporting Blink who often leads the eXiles – but thus far these have been peripheral to principal storylines.

The *House of M/Decimation* (2005) storyline may prove an exception since it has had permanent consequences as well as significantly affecting the situation of a number of important characters. In the main comic run *House of M*, written by Brian Michael Bendis, there is a debate about the fate of Wanda Maximoff after her slaughter of several fellow Avengers. Various mutant leaders – notably Emma Frost – vote for her death and are over-ruled by Captain America with the plea that we do not do this to our own; the mere fact that Wanda's death is being considered leads her brother Quicksilver to suggest she alter reality drastically to save herself.

What Wanda comes up with is a world in which everyone is happy ever after, including her father, who won his war with the humans 30 years in the past and has ruled the USA and much of the rest of the world ever since, a world in which mutants have become the majority. In other storylines in other comics, we see a version of Peter Parker who is married to Gwen Stacey rather than Mary Jane and has passed his powers off as mutation-derived; an intelligent version of the Hulk is the de facto ruler of Australia; and so on. However, this is a fool's paradise; the child Layla, apparently a living embodiment of Wanda's sanity, jogs the memory of the superheroes she encounters and shows them the reality that has been lost. They confront Wanda again, and again she is rescued by her brother, who is confronted by their father, furious at what has been done in his name. No more mutants, she breathes, and the world changes again.

Now there are only 198 mutants in the world, a figure which does not include Magneto, Quicksilver or Charles Xavier; no one knows where Wanda is. Suddenly, all the bigots who used to hunt mutants are hunting former mutants and the Westchester campus of Xavier's school has become something between a refuge and an internment camp, with human-piloted Sentinels policing its borders. One miniseries, *Sentinel Squadron*, does a nice job of humanizing these troops, revealing that a couple of their leaders are themselves ex-mutants previously excluded from command roles as a result. Magneto gets power of a sort back in no small order; Quicksilver steals from the Inhumans the crystals that give them their powers and becomes a living focus of mutagenic energy, often afflicting the mutants he tries to help with extreme versions of the powers they have lost. Callisto, for example, gets back all her huntress super-senses, but to a degree of intensity she cannot live with.

One nice touch in all this across the whole of Marvel continuity is that those heroes whom Layla awoke remain aware of the truth of what has happened, whereas no one else knows. Ms Hill, the new post-Nick Fury director of SHIELD – Fury was sacked for exceeding his authority and fighting a private war with post-Doom Latveria in *Secret War* – finds out by having her psychics read Spider-Man's mind. Later, X-Factor find out and are furious with their former colleagues in the X-Men for not telling them. For once, in genre fiction, a secret is being kept that is genuinely huge and for which there is a genuine reason to keep quiet; this may be one of those plot strands that gets quietly forgotten about, but more probably it is going to have long-term consequences.

Someone in the Marvel offices clearly decided that the Marvel world had too many mutants in it and decided to rein back the endless creation of new powers and new characters, while doing so in a way that can be changed with a reset button by their eventual successors. What is attractive and impressive about this is that the consequences are largely seen in terms of their effect on character – Peter Parker, for example, is horrified to discover that, in Wanda's version of his ideal world, he is married to his dead sweetheart rather than his living wife, and his guilt over this and the non-existent children he remembers is another of his burdens. Quicksilver acts with incredible rashness in the first place and is not a man ever to learn from mistakes; on the contrary, he is shown escalating those mistakes constantly. The one obviously important new character to come out of all this, Layla, is a creepy child who hangs round the X-Factor mutant detective agency saying she knows everything, including where to inveigle a villain into standing so that he is killed by falling debris for planning to kill her. There is conceptual wit here and entertaining invention – she also says that one day she and X-Factor's current leader, the self-duplicating Jamie Madrox, will marry, and it is not clear whether she is prophesying, or merely teasing.

Civil War

The wit and invention are also present, to an even greater extent, in the *Civil War* storyline (2006–7, but ongoing in its consequences), which is the closest Marvel has ever come to writing political satire and protest. Back in the 1970s, the dislike of superheroes and the detestation of mutants by the general public were used as a handy place-marker for comments on racism and homophobia, but did no more than encourage imaginative empathy by doing so. *Civil War*, by contrast, is a detailed, nuanced and complex take on the assault on civil liberties under the presidency of George W. Bush and the War on Terror. It sets up divisions between much-loved and long-standing superhero characters, and it is impossible at present to see how this will be easily resolved afterwards. In so doing, *Civil War* allows a case to be made for both sides of the question of, say, imprisonment without trial, while clearly taking a view that is anything but neutral.

The set-up of *Civil War* is both very simple and highly complex; it has always been the case in the Marvel Universe that legislative and executive attempts to control superheroes are on the political agenda, only slightly outweighed and superseded by attempts to control those superheroes who happen also to be mutants. At various points in the few months before the *Civil War* storyline formally started, reference was made by some characters, for example Ms Hill – the new director of SHIELD – to a Superheroes Registration Act that would have, say, the New Avengers working directly under her authority rather than being what she regards as occasionally useful loose cannons (the characterization of Ms Hill, one of a number of far from indistinguishable unpleasant bureaucrats in the Marvel Universe, as someone quietly irritated by anyone to whom she cannot give orders is one of many minor details that Bendis and others handle effectively).

In a major but plausible retcon, it is revealed that some of the cleverer and more establishment superheroes have been engaged in a quasi-conspiracy that goes back to the aftermath of the Kree–Skrull War. Tony Stark (Iron Man), Reed Richards of the Fantastic

Four, Charles Xavier and Doctor Strange have been meeting regularly with Namor of Atlantis and Black Bolt, leader of the Inhumans; T'Challa of Wakanda is distinctly more sceptical about the value of such meetings: 'You just decided all by yourselves that you are the Earth's protectors'. Over the years, Namor warns constantly that he is waiting for humanity to destroy itself so that Atlantis can dominate again; Stark becomes keener and keener on the idea of an international superpowered police force and finally tells the others that they need to cooperate with legislation that will sooner or later become inevitable.

What makes it inevitable is, as he predicted, a specific incident: the young and underpowered New Warriors, who have become a superhero reality show, stumble across a covey of supervillains escaped from jail, one of whom, Nitro, uses his power of blowing up and reintegrating himself to destroy the New Warriors, the town of Stamford, Connecticut and 600 civilians, many of them children. Lobbying by the dead children's parents (the analogy with the parents' lobby that produced the anti-paedophile Megan's Law, mandating the right of parents to know of paedophiles in their area, is explicit) means that a Bill is rushed through, demanding that all of the superpowers reveal their secret identities and make themselves available to the authorities. Non-compliers are to be deprived of all civil rights and due process, and imprisoned forever in special jails. It is clear that this is only a first step towards conscripting all superheroes as a militia that will police America and the world forever.

What Marvel have successfully done with this is create, across some 70 or 80 comics, a storyline in which character work enables the writers to place much-loved heroes on different sides in what seems like a real conflict about real issues, rather than the factitious conflicts of *Secret Wars*. The analogy with current political phenomena like the PATRIOT Act and the camp at Guantanamo Bay is loose enough that no particular one-for-one correspondences can be made, and there are points at which earlier conflicts are specifically evoked. When Tony Stark persuades Peter Parker to out himself as Spider-Man, one consideration that weighs on Parker and his wife Mary Jane is whether he will be expected to 'name names' as in the days of McCarthy and the House UnAmerican Activities Committee. It is explicit that Reed Richards is in part motivated, in a telling piece of reverse psychology, by the fate of a favourite uncle destroyed in that period and a determination not to put himself in that position. The situation is polysemous enough that Reed is haunted by the Tom Lehrer song 'Werner von Braun', sung casually by a security guard – 'Once the bombs have gone up, who cares where they come down?'. Later, Reed reveals that he has developed a predictive mathematics of human behaviour that, he believes, demonstrates that his is the only sane course of action.

Other characters link the question of Superhero Registration to the Civil Rights issue and to slavery – Luke Cage justifies his non-compliance in terms of refusing to be 'shackled to the Man' – and to the draft resisters in the Vietnam War – Jessica Jones takes her and Luke's child and decamps to Canada for safety. Some characters justify compliance in terms of obedience to the laws created by a democratic government; others, like Guido of X-Factor, point out, not entirely accurately, that Hitler was elected. One of the things that make this an effective storyline is that we see the whole thing from enough points of view that we can respect, intellectually and emotionally, the positions of many of those whose side we ultimately condemn.

This is one of the things made possible by spreading the event across so many of Marvel's titles – *New Avengers*, *Ms Marvel*, *Amazing Spider-Man*, *X-Men*, *X-Factor*, *Thunderbolts* and so on – as well as running the two *Civil War* titles, *Civil War* and *Front Line*. The last is peculiarly interesting in that it is that relatively rare thing, a superhero comic in which superheroes comparatively take a back seat. One of its running plot segments concerns two journalists: Ben Urich of the *Daily Bugle* is a character with much Marvel back-story, and the ex-alcoholic radical journalist Sally Floyd was the central character of the *Decimation* comic *Generation M*. Ben does his best to uncover the truth while working for Jameson, whose editorial line is all in favour of Registration, and Sally, rather more inclined than he to see conspiracies everywhere, finds out the hard way that the Registration Act suppresses freedom of the press and Habeas Corpus. One of the things that Busiek's *Marvels* demonstrated was that sometimes the interesting story is the one told from the sidelines.

The fact that the Registration Act criminalizes people who only have good intentions is what sticks in the gullet of Captain America, perhaps the closest thing the Marvel Universe has to a moral centre. He objects to the Act not because of analogies with other situations, not because of what it may become in the future — the time-travelling Cable tries to warn the President (who is not

---

The Case of Speedball

Another segment of *Front Line* is the one dealing with the surviving New Warrior, Speedball, who previously has always been the irritating twerp he was, for example, in *Alias*. Here though, he becomes a figure of quiet authority; he regrets what happened in Stamford, but he will not say that he was wrong. His friends died trying to arrest a murderous villain, because they were heroes; he will not defame their memory. Deprived of his powers by the blast, he is thrown into a federal prison to be brutalized by guards and prisoners (and by implication raped); he is disowned by his family and, on recovering his powers, thrown into the prison camp Stark and Richards have built in the Negative Zone. Yet he will not capitulate, and becomes quietly admirable. A system that tries to break this good young man cannot, we and his lawyer Jen Walters (She-Hulk) realize, be right. Reed Richards tries to get him his day in court, and this results in Speedball's attempted assassination.

In a further moral complexity, Speedball, left by this attack with returned powers and constant agony when he uses them, decides to dedicate himself to atonement for his accidental crime. He takes the name Penance, dresses in a black plastic costume that goes far further into the realm of fetish clothing than any previous superhero costume, and fights through the pain. He does this in the new government-sponsored incarnation of Thunderbolts, alongside some of the worst villains Marvel has ever produced.

drawn as G.W. Bush) of dire consequences and is rebuffed with talk of the November mid-term elections – but because he thinks it wrong. When he sets up a resistance movement, Captain America is not joined by his old friends like Iron Man, but by his former partner Sam Wilson and Luke Cage and another hero of colour, Black Goliath. He is joined by the Young Avengers, whom he tried to keep out of the superhero game; Spider-Woman, the double agent whom every side has betrayed, also sides with them. We know, because he is Captain America, that he is right.

There are many, many side issues to all of this: Zemo regards it as a side issue to a forthcoming battle with the Grandmaster that he does not expect to survive. Wolverine tracks Nitro, and then the trail of those who employed him; this seems to be Damage Control, the firm that rebuilds after superhero battles, but it is not clear who lies behind them. Peter Parker agonizes about his loyalty to Stark and whether he has taken the right side, eventually deciding that he has not and going on the run after apologizing on television to the American people. Sue Richards walks out on her husband after the cloned copy of the long-missing Thor that he and Stark have built and programmed kills Black Goliath. What is impressive is that in all of them the intellectual conceit, the satirical agenda and even the constant pages of heroes hitting each other are secondary to the human story, and to the long-built emotional weight provided by continuity. To pick an example I have mentioned elsewhere, Zemo demonstrates his change of heart to Captain America, who fought his father before him, by returning, via a time bubble, the mementoes of Captain America's life in the 1940s, which years earlier Zemo had destroyed in front of him.

The culmination of all of this is somewhat less impressive than the set-up. At the height of a final battle between pro-Registration forces and the resistance, Captain America realizes that he has lost the battle for the hearts and minds of the American people and orders his forces to stand down, handing himself over to the police. Even though they are aware of the extent to which Iron Man has both orchestrated and profited by the social forces he and Reed regard as inevitable, Ben and Sally abandon their exposé; during an interview, Sally tears into Captain America as an elitist who has lost touch with reality. Some of the resisters – Sue Storm, for example – apparently make their peace with the authorities; others, like Spider-Man, continue the struggle. Does Millar intend an analogy between Captain America's backing down and the way Al Gore did not pursue the question of the Florida vote in the 2000 election? It is interesting to consider this.

This storyline has been commercially very successful – Marvel deferred publication of the later issues of *Civil War* in order to maintain the quality of its art rather than hand pages over for completion to lesser artists. It is also, clearly, the lead-in to other storylines: the invasion of Earth by the vengeful Hulk and the inhabitants of the planet to which the Illuminati exiled him; the creation of a 50-state initiative in which every part of the USA has its own superheroes; the corruption of the Thunderbolts into a government-sponsored assassination squad. Clearly, there is a sense in which it is still too early to judge the long-term effects of the story on the Marvel Universe.

Nonetheless, at a time when most of American popular culture was avoiding political issues like the plague and when even quite casual protests against the Iraq war – like the remarks made by one of the country band the Dixie Chicks – were greeted with howls of vilification, it is interesting that superhero comics produced a work of significant protest art, significant because it supplied a lot more than protest. It is also emotionally powerful – the last issue of *Civil War: Front Line* shows us a Tony Stark who is apparently entirely victorious and yet deeply troubled. He is the new director of SHIELD, and the journalists who might have exposed his machinations have congratulated him on them; his old friend-turned-enemy Captain America is in custody. Yet he throws his Iron Man head-piece across the room and drops to his knees in anguish; in successive frames, the viewpoint pans up and away from him in his penthouse suite, until he is an insignificant mark in a cityscape.

In a Bendis side-bar comic, *Civil War – Confessions*, Stark delivers a monologue on his motives and we realize at the end, as he says, 'It wasn't worth it', that he is standing over the corpse of the assassinated Captain America. Earlier, though placed later in the comic, Captain America has asked him whether it was worth it, and Stark has refused any answer save 'You're a sore loser'. There is genuine tragedy in the breaking of this always uneasy friendship.

DC and its Crises

In fairness to DC, the event/reboot that also appeared in 2006 only seemed less radical in its implications by comparison with *Civil War*'s extremes. Where its predecessor *Crisis on Infinite Earths* (1985) was only, if magnificently, an attempt to rein in what was seen as the excessive complication of the DC Universe, *Infinite Crisis* tried at the same time to rejig the universe so as to simplify the complexities that had resulted from its predecessors' less felicitous adjustments, and to do so in ways that created space for changes, such as more superheroes of colour and other innovations, like an explicitly lesbian Batwoman.

Infinite Crisis also had at its heart acts of great destructiveness perpetrated with good intentions by those who wanted to return matters to a kinder, gentler, more old-fashioned state of affairs; we learn that the ends do not justify the means even when perpetrated by the best and brightest. In the context of Bush's America and the struggle of red- and blue-state America, it is hard to avoid the conclusion that here too a moral, even a satirical, comment was, if not intended, at least available to interpretation, especially when the villains of the piece turn out to include recensions of Superman and Superboy, and not, let us be clear, evil twins like Ultraman either.

Crisis on Infinite Earths

To explain the logic of this, it is necessary to go back to the grand original of reboots, *Crisis on Infinite Earths* in 1985. It was felt by a number of the DC creative team that their universe had become too complex for new readers to follow, and it was also decided that certain quite popular characters should be killed off for good; Julie

Schwartz put it with his usual forthright succinctness – 'Every ten years', he said, 'we need to give the universe an enema'.

The resulting 12-issue comic was one of the most impressive pieces of work George Perez has ever drawn and was effectively, if not memorably, scripted by Marv Wolfman, demonstrating as often before that his forte is for powerful scenes rather than either great story arcs or great individual lines. One of the obvious criticisms of the series is that Wolfman's storyline has at least one climax too many: the evil Anti-Monitor not only comes back from apparent destruction rather often, but revises his plan of universal destruction each time he does so. Another problem is that the entire concept is paradoxically and at the same time metafictional and crude.

The premise is that the universe was originally intended to be one, but that attempts to observe its creation by an Oan scientist, Krona, resulted in its splitting many times over, into many timelines in a universe of ordinary matter, and also a universe of anti-matter where evil, in the shape of the Anti-Monitor, becomes dominant. The good Monitor of the universe of ordinary matter tries to set up lines of defence to save at least some of the worlds, while knowing that an ideal solution will be to return things to the unity they once possessed in the process of saving them. They are called Monitors and Krona, but they might as well be called good and bad editors. To complicate matters further, part of the Monitor's game plan involves his own death at the hand of one of his assistants, whom he knows to be possessed, some of the time, by his opponent; the ruthlessness with which he allows her to be lumbered with this load of karmic guilt is only excusable by his own decision to die; religious analogies clearly apply at some level.

Many, many timelines are devoured by the Anti-Monitor's device before Barry Allen, the Flash, sacrifices himself to destroy it, appearing dying in a variety of times and spaces to his friends in the process. Supergirl fights the Anti-Monitor to a standstill, dying in the process. One of the two Wonder Women dies in the last moments of the fight with an Anti-Monitor resurrected for the last time, her essence travels back through time and becomes the spark that imbues the other Wonder Woman in infancy (the starting point for Perez's memorable stint on *Wonder Woman* in the immediate aftermath of *Crisis on Infinite Earths*). These three were to be only the most important of the vast number of DC characters polished off, or drastically revised in the course of this series.

Flash was replaced, almost instantly, by the former Kid Flash who stepped up to take on his mentor's role. Supergirl, on the other hand, was absent from the DC Universe almost until the very eve of *Infinite Crisis* some 20 years later – a cynical person might regard the decision to sacrifice her as having a certain amount to do with the disastrous *Supergirl* film of 1984 and the potential franchise's consequent loss of worth. The covers Perez drew for successive issues, of the Superman of Earth 1 cradling the dead girl in his arms, and of Flash facing his titanic opponent with resolution, are particularly strong images; some of the covers for *Crisis on Infinite Earths* have the remorseless busy-ness that is the downside of Perez's facility with large crowds of characters, each drawn as individuals, but not these two.

One of *Crisis on Infinite Earth*'s surprising strengths is the way that Wolfman and Perez manage to play off two recensions of Superman – the somewhat ageing one of Earth 2 featuring heavily in the story – against each other, with a version of Superboy simultaneously in the mix. Even when cooperating, as here, they have subtly different approaches to things: the older version is even here (unknowingly foreshadowing his role in *Infinite Crisis*) subtly more naive and idealistic than his younger self. His position after the destruction of his world – large parts of it have been edited into Earth 1 – including many of his colleagues in the Justice Society, is peculiarly painful and poignant, especially when his cognate persuades him that it is his duty to help and survive in this new world.

The plot relies a little too heavily on touching every single base in DC's continuity, from prehistoric savage characters to a mage in pre-deluge Atlantis and various points in the far future and the – at this point simple, compared to what it became – supernatural world. More worryingly, it relies a little too much on a variety of *dei ex machina*; the resurrection of the Earth 2 Lois to share her husband's exile is a sentimentality too far. The complex role of Alexander Luthor, the son of a virtuous alternate world Lex, is too much a matter of plot mechanism for easy summary – for this entirely to work, he needed to be a memorable character and Wolfman never makes him one. The attempt by various villains to exploit the situation is a plot strand too many and never goes anywhere terribly significant; one cannot help but feel that a less ambitious, tighter plot might have been preferable.

What *Crisis on Infinite Earths* does provide us with is a sense of the tragic far too often missing from the DC Universe: existence is saved, but at a staggering cost. Entire universes die and are seen to die with moments of real pathos and heroism taking place along the way; the evil Crime Syndicate Ultraman goes into non-existence with courage and grace, fighting to the last, as he has done all his life. I have mentioned the deaths of major characters, but many of the minor characters who die get effective touches like this along the way. One of the strengths of Perez's work in this is that as well as the large and sometimes over-busy panels, much of the story-telling is done in tiny intricate frames on a grid that constantly changes – many of these grace notes come in small gemlike thumbnail panels of a face and some dialogue. It has also to be added that *Crisis on Infinite Earths* was trying to do a number of things at the same time – a commercially driven reboot of a property as well as a piece of epic story-telling – and managed to do most of them effectively, in spite of the fact that it was doing many of them for the first time.

Zero Hour

DC's next attempt at a reboot, *Zero Hour*, eight years after *Crisis on Infinite Earths*, lacked the sheer power of much of this and had comparatively few lasting effects. A villain with the unmemorable name Extant is messing around with the single timeline of Earth and removing most of the DC Universe's future-time locales. He turns out to be working for the renegade Hal Jordan as one of the latter's schemes, in what we are told to think of as his madness, to alter the past so that Coast City was never destroyed and with it much of his personal life. In a subsequent major retcon, this is reconfigured as his having been possessed by Parallax, the 'yellow impurity' that the Guardians imprisoned in their power battery; by this point, Jordan has sacrificed himself to save the world and spent a time as the spirit currently possessed by the Spectre, which is in turn corrupted by Parallax. One of Jordan's successors, Kyle Rayner, brings back the Guardians, whom Jordan had destroyed, and re-establishes the Green Lantern corps – he also brings Jordan back from the dead, sane, purged and redeemed. None of this is foreshadowed, or indeed had even been thought of, during *Zero Hour*, one of a number of areas in which the 1990s reboot has not importantly affected what follows.

It is also significant that, in the 2006 reboot *Infinite Crisis*, characters feel they have to explain the events of *Crisis on Infinite Earths* to other characters who, in the nature of things, are unaware that it happened. No one ever feels that they have to talk about the events of *Zero Hour*, which are never mentioned, nor even significantly alluded to in the extended discussion between DC editors and creators that is included in the collected trade hardback of *Infinite Crisis*. Nor, accordingly, will it be discussed any further here.

Infinite Crisis

Infinite Crisis rebooted the DC Universe in a number of ways, not all of which are yet entirely clear. It followed on from a number of storylines, some but not all of them explicitly part of the *Countdown to Infinite Crisis* event that preceded it, and was followed in turn by the relaunch of most of DC's titles with a rubric that indicated that the starting point for all of them was a year after the events of *Infinite Crisis*. At the same time, DC produced *52*, a weekly comic that covers the events in the continuity within the missing year, with varying results in terms of interest and quality.

Various superheroes have died, or die in the course of *52*, and are replaced by new characters who take on their costume and role and are in many cases significantly less white bread than their predecessors; the new Blue Beetle is a young Hispanic man, for example. Notoriously, the new Batwoman is a lesbian and ex-lover of long-standing character, the former Gotham City cop Renée Montoya, who as *52* proceeds becomes a masked vigilante in her own right, replacing the Question when the original Question dies of cancer.[2]

Infinite Crisis has one of its roots in the events of *Identity Crisis*, the death of Sue Dibney and various other characters and the revelation that earlier on some of the Justice League mind-wiped the rapist supervillain Doctor Light, leaving him somewhat incapacitated; they also removed 10 minutes of the Batman's memory when he disagreed with this action. In *The OMAC Project*, one of Batman's subsequent schemes for controlling his peers in the Justice League should they go too far is subverted by the telepath Maxwell Lord into the creation of a million cyborged superbeings with a brief to destroy all superhumans. Lord also murders the current Blue Beetle and brainwashes Superman into his personal killing machine; Wonder Woman kills Lord as the only way to be sure of defeating him, and her execution of him is widely broadcast. She quarrels with Superman and the Batman over her decision.

In other storylines in the so-called *Countdown to Infinite Crisis*, most of the important alien races find themselves fighting a war for territory when the geography of the galaxy is radically reconfigured; various Green Lanterns attempt to hold the peace, and at the start of *Infinite Crisis* many characters, surplus to the requirements of plot, head off to help them. In *Villains Unlimited* Luthor puts together a coalition of supervillains out to lobotomize the heroes before the heroes do the same to them; a smaller group of villains, led by the mysterious Mockingbird, oppose this coalition out of general bad attitude. To complicate matters further, it becomes clear that Mockingbird is the real Luthor and 'Luthor' an impostor. The Spectre, currently without a human host, goes crazy and tries to destroy magic.

---

[2]   Times have certainly changed: when DC decided not to use a page of art depicting love-making between Montoya and a pick-up in *52*, they thoughtfully allowed the pencil sketches to appear on their website.

These dark doings are used, in the early issues of *Infinite Crisis*, by the elderly Superman of Earth 2 – one of the characters left over from *Crisis on Infinite Earths* with a full memory of what happened – as an argument to himself that he is justified in deciding that the Earth produced by the crisis is a botched job. His ageing wife Lois is dying and he believes that only a recreated Earth 2 can save her. He is encouraged in this belief by his two companions, Alexander Luthor and Superboy, but is, as we gradually realize, their dupe, not least because much of what has gone wrong, has gone wrong at their instigation. It is Alexander who has impersonated his virtuous father's evil cognate, for example, and Superboy who has moved the galaxy around.

Alexander has rebuilt one of the Monitor's machines, using parts of the Anti-Monitor's corpse; he kidnaps various superheroes to power it, among them Power Girl, whose identity has always been unclear but who is now definitively revealed to have been the Power Girl of Earth 2, but who refuses to cooperate in the destruction of the world which has adopted her. Lois dies on the new Earth 2, and her husband is persuaded by his younger cognate that Earth 2 is not the perfect world he wants – 'A perfect world would not need a Superman'. Repentant, the older Superman becomes the ally of Earth's superheroes against Alexander, who is trying to create a perfect world by mixing and matching elements from all the disparate Earths of the multiverse, and a demented and homicidal Superboy who merely wants his own homeworld back, and is prepared to destroy everyone and everything to get it. Quite specifically, and as a signal of this, he kills Conner, who may be less motivated, and may be a chimeric clone of Superman and Luthor, but still understands the difference between right and wrong and is prepared to die for it.

Superboy is tricked and defeated and deprived of his powers by his two older selves; the older Superman dies of his wounds and the Superman of main continuity loses his powers for a while; the mad Superboy is imprisoned to become a plot device another day. Alexander Luthor escapes, but is murdered by Luthor and the Joker, the latter having been insulted by Alexander's failure to recruit him. The result of his manipulations is a new Earth, devastated by all that has happened, and with important bits of its nature changed in ways that we will only gradually discover; for example, the time-traveller Booster Gold discovers, before his death in 52, that his knowledge of events that are historical in his time of origin no longer applies.

Obviously a part of one's judgement of *Infinite Crisis* depends on one's view of the consequences of the changes that have been made, and to some extent of the particular storylines and writing and art on the various titles most affected. Certainly Kurt Busiek has recharged Superman with significance, and Grant Morrison's intelligent lightening of the Batman's sombre tone is very effective; on the other hand, much of 52 is frankly dull, particularly in its earlier stages.

I have commented in Chapter 1 on my serious reservations about *Identity Crisis* and *The OMAC Project* – they retrospectively damage much-loved characters and storylines without earning the right to do so. I should, though, in fairness comment that Gail Simone's *Villains Unlimited* is glorious amoral fun in its bloodthirsty way, and has a nice moment of confrontation between Catman and Green Arrow where the villain tells the hero that the heroes need to remember that they are supposed to be the good guys, and act like it.

What, though, of the seven parts of *Infinite Crisis* judged as an autonomous work of art? Somewhat to my surprise, as happened with *Crisis on Infinite Earths*, I was rather more impressed when reading it as a whole than I had been when reading individual issues, specifically the incredibly complicated plot, which I have so very briefly summarized above, made a lot more sense as a whole. One tendency of the comics industry is that the rise of trade paperbacks as a significant part of the industry means that many writers think in longer paragraphs than they would for the individual issue; individual issues can thus now be less impressive than the whole run. At the same time, with the exception of one or two scenes, like the death of the older Lois, it never quite delivers the requisite emotional punch – the point of this story is, after all, to break our hearts a little as well as to revive a franchise.

I was impressed by the book's slow demonstration of the extent to which exile and resentment have corrupted its two major villains, both of whom were heroes at the time of *Crisis on Infinite Earths*. Superboy in particular has become a monster, his slaughter of various heroes and of his cognate Conner Kent is seriously unpleasant in an artistically justifiable way; the worst things come by corruption of the best, and Superboy never accepts that he is no longer even slightly the good guy in all of this. If one of the important themes of the superhero comic is the responsibility to use great power with great moderation, then his arc within *Infinite Crisis* is an important discussion. The decline of the more or less heroic Alexander Luthor of the earlier event into the satanic intriguer here has also something of the tragic about it – he decides that his nature is essentially flawed and determines to be a villain.

Just as much of the strength of *Crisis on Infinite Earths* came from George Perez's artwork, so *Infinite Crisis* stands or falls on the quality of Phil Jimenez's work. Incidentally, this is another reason why the collection is so superior to the issues, in that particular panels have been redrawn and radically improved and altered with considerable care. Jimenez is so notoriously a passionate imitator of Perez that, on their first meeting, Perez greeted him with a cry of 'Son!'; their art is similar enough that the few pages of flashback and of revived alternate Earths that Perez drew for *Infinite Crisis* gel with Jimenez's work in a way that the interpolated work of other pencillers does not.

Like Perez, Jimenez can at times be too busy; a vast scene of superheroes attending a ceremony in a cathedral is well-drawn but mostly notable for the sheer number of quite obscure characters he gets in. You spend too much time ticking the faces off to feel very much about the occasion that has brought them together. On the other hand, Perez has also taught him how to use small panels for moments of intensity like Conner Kent's final agony, and how to open them out on the next page into iconic whole-page panels like the one of Earth 1 Superman, Batman and Wonder

Woman reunited in grief as Wonder Girl sobs over Conner's corpse. Nor do these moments have to be static – a double-spread in which both Supermen tackle a revived Doomsday is dotted with thumbnail panels showing particular moments within this broader single conflict. Like Perez before him, Jimenez turns a script less accomplished than ambitious into something with real epic scope just by the intensity of his best art; with all my reservations about it, and the larger revamp of which it is part, I have to acknowledge that *Infinite Crisis*, like *Crisis on Infinite Earths* before it, has a loopy magnificence.

If, in the end, I prefer the more humane scale and the intelligent politics and deep sense of emotional betrayal that characterize Marvel's *Civil War* event – the sense that quite ordinary and admirable people like Carol Danvers and Peter Parker can become for a while the accomplices of atrocity without turning into red-eyed monsters – that is in part a compromise between my love of comics and my fascination with the issue of how close they can come to the real while preserving their essential nature. And the fact that the two continuity universes can both support work on this scale, and to some degree also this level of accomplishment helps explain why I still feel the love for the partly delivered promise of superhero comics that I felt when I was 10.

6 Gifted and Dangerous
Joss Whedon's Superhero Obsession

Whedon and the Fanboy Creators

It ought to be a truth universally acknowledged that artists working in popular media draw their influences from other popular media as much as from the canons of great art. One of the reasons why we do not always stress this fact is that there is often an element of apologia in our work on popular culture, an implied bid to have it admitted to those canons or not to have it unthinkingly dismissed by high culture's gatekeepers as unworthy of attention. If, writing about television shows, we ignore the influence on those shows of, say, superhero comics, we not only end up understating the sheer richness and allusiveness of our texts, but may also end up misunderstanding and misrepresenting the artistic personality of the writers who are our subject.

To be specific: some career decisions by artists may seem perverse at first glance, but then, more fully considered, reveal themselves as connected closely to the driving forces of their work. Joss Whedon's decision to divert his attention from more personal projects not only to develop a project – in the event an abortive project – based on the DC character Wonder Woman, but also to become the writer on the comic book *The Astonishing X-Men* (2005–7) is one such decision. I have called this chapter 'Gifted and Dangerous' because what I am arguing is simply this. The two six-issue runs of *The Astonishing X-Men* published as volumes under those names should be as central to our sense of the artistic personality of Joss Whedon as any of his television and movie scripts, as well as something we can enjoy as much. I also intend to show that his comics obsession is the source of much of what is strong in his work, as well as of some of his weaknesses.

Whedon earlier worked on the script of the first X-Men movie, but it is known that only a couple of, admittedly very typical, lines from his script made it into the final version – it is normally assumed that one of these is the point at which Wolverine convinces Scott that he is the genuine article and not a shape-changer by saying 'You're a dick'. Work on this movie could be seen as merely another piece of Whedon's work as a script doctor, but this would be an error, given his often-stated devotion to this particular part of the comics universe. Far from being perverse, these decisions are logical extensions of interests that have dominated Whedon's work from the beginning and which help us understand both the strengths and the occasional weaknesses of his more celebrated work.

Whedon is one of a group of youngish creative writers – most of them working primarily in television or film – whom Jennifer Stoy has termed the 'fanboy creators', suggesting it as a term not only for Whedon, but for Rob Thomas, Ron Moore, Ryan Murphy and Kevin Smith. J.M. Straczynski, the show-runner/auteur of *Babylon 5*, is working on a number of Marvel titles. Allen Heinberg, who wrote several 2004–5 issues of *Young Avengers* for Marvel and, in 2005–6, *Wonder Woman* for DC, was a writer on *The OC* and had Seth in that show attempt to sell a comic book to Wildstorm Comics. Common characteristics of this group would include an obsessive habit of popular culture intertextuality in their dialogue and plotting, a constant moving back and forth between forms, and the use in their core work of tropes derived from the favourite reading and viewing of their youth; the British writer Russell T. Davies might usefully be seen as a UK equivalent, though his obsession is with *Dr Who*, which he now show-runs, rather than with comics.

I would further argue that this early reading and viewing has trained these writers in the skills necessary to use those – often quite complex – tropes effectively; negotiation and parsing of the tropes of popular culture produces a competence cascade, the flowering of many talented individuals where once only one or two flourished. The unabashed influence of earlier texts on their work is one of a number of ways in which the productions of the fanboy creators are thick texts, which is to say they are texts whose contingent, collective and polysemous nature renders them especially satisfying. The fanboy creators are also a variant form of their favourite reading and viewing matter's assumed ideal reader/ viewer.

It is also, unfortunately, the case that their creations are often flawed in precisely the ways that comics are often flawed, by unexamined use of default clichés and by over-fondness for storylines that return to a status quo ante – in *Star Trek* fandom this is often referred to as the reset button. Nearly all of them have an almost morbid fondness for torturing their protagonists with unhappy love affairs that drag on for an implausibly long time – the on-and-off relationship between Logan and Veronica in Rob Thomas' *Veronica Mars* is a good example of this. Whedon, in particular, has a remarkable tendency – for a professed sympathizer with feminism – to associate sexual fulfilment with death, and this again is something he may have learned from comics.

One element in the contingency of their works is the choice of form and of genre. Where a writer like Neil Gaiman made his name in comics before also producing songs, novels and screenplays, Whedon and Smith made their names in television and film before adding the writing of comics to their CVs. In all these cases, but especially the latter two, this implies an absolute refusal to regard any one literary form as superior to any other. I would suggest that this is another defining characteristic of the fanboy creator – that comics are a defining influence on their work and a form in which they feel entirely at home.

At this point, I would stress that the use of the term fanboy accurately depicts the situation. The reasons why no women fall into the category almost certainly reflects glass ceilings in the relevant industries rather than any gender-determined matters of taste and inclination. Given the growing presence of women in, say, the comics fanbase, I would expect this situation to change.

In the absence of any real knowledge of what his take on Wonder Woman would have been or of the details of his script for the first X-Men film – which seems to have been available online at some point, but is no longer – I will concentrate on Whedon's use of superhero tropes in his better-known work, the extent of specific influences from well-known comics in this work and on the extent to which his work on the Buffyverse-linked comic *Fray* and on *The Astonishing X-Men* reflect his interest, one might legitimately say his obsession, with the figure of the superhero. Not only is he currently working directly in the comics and film superhero genres, he has always centred his attention on characters who are either best, or at least relevantly, considered in the light of superhero tropes.

We know, specifically, that the adolescent Joss Whedon was a fan of comics in general, and that he was a fan of the Chris Claremont period X-Men in particular. He has said as much in his introduction to the collection of *Fray*, and the influence of Claremont's work would be obvious even if he had not. We need to look at his work, and at Claremont's and see what Whedon might have learned from Claremont's example. More generally, we need to look at the driving dynamics of superhero comics and see how they emerge in Whedon's work for television and film, as well as in his comics.

Superhero Comics as Influence on the Whedonverse

Buffy is a superhero; it is one of the most obvious things about her. Of course it is also relevant to consider Buffy as the heroine of a high-school film: she has the rivalries, the short-lived but intense emotional entanglements and the difficult relationship with the school principal of the central characters of teen film from the John Hughes sextet and Lehman's *Heathers* onwards. But then, so did Spider-Man, though the relevant comparison in his case was with the world of *Archie* comics. Joss Whedon has linked Buffy specifically to the blondes in slasher films and made a particular point of the extent to which she is his answer to the Last Girl, who in the classic slasher film survives where her frailer sisters die. Much has rightly been made of her as a variation on motifs from the world's major religions; she dies for humanity, she harrows Hell and so on.

However, this last point links her to that other linked category of people who die for humanity and harrow Hell. It should not be forgotten that among the rival saviour cults of the first two centuries of the Common Era was the cult of Hercules, the character of Greek literature and mythology reconfigured as a saviour demigod, Hercules Soter. There is a large area of carryover in Western culture between the Redeemer and the superhero. And, of course, Buffy is a redeemer and so are several of her friends and associates – her opponent turned lover and then friend, the ensouled vampire Spike, for example, dies to save the world and adopts a posture of crucifixion as his inner fires burn him.

Buffy has gained powers that are massive extensions of standard human abilities – strength and athleticism – as a result of becoming a Slayer. She has died twice and been reborn, her liminal status is undoubted. She spends much of her time in twilight and darkness, and has lost her original kin either through death (Joyce) or desertion (Hank). She has a family of the heart in Dawn and the Scoobies, and a shadow double in Faith, whose own oscillation between good and evil is a standard superhero trajectory. Buffy has prophetic dreams; her dreams also link her to other Slayers, notably Faith, dream is another place of twilight.

She has a secret identity only in the sense – though it is a very important sense – that no one expects a slightly ditzy blonde schoolgirl to save the world on a regular basis; she is one of what Alice Sheldon, the SF writer better known as James Tiptree, called 'the women men don't see'. She has a sense of duty that leads her into endless trouble with the authorities at her various schools and universities and which she has to put ahead of her feelings for various lovers, most notably Angel whom in 'Becoming Part 2'

(2.22) she has to kill to save the world. When, later on, she decides that she will attempt to save her sister, even if the world ends as a result of her failure, it is as a consequence of all the other things she has sacrificed to the mission rather than mere selfishness.

Buffy is a paradoxical being: in order to fight the creatures of the night she becomes someone who haunts the night herself; to save humanity she has to struggle to retain her own humanity and risks becoming merely the embodiment of the struggle. Those of her schoolfriends who acquire powers also do so in paradoxical ways: the logical computer hacker Willow becomes an all-powerful witch, and one of the most dangerous aspects of her magic is the habit of cutting laterally through to a solution to problems – a skill she acquired from hacking – her return of Amy to humanity is essentially a hacking of the original spell's operating system. Cordelia, the queen of consumerism, becomes someone who renounces wealth, looks, love and even humanity for the sake of the mission; a teenager almost sociopathic in her lack of consideration for the feelings of others becomes an empathic clairvoyant who feels the pain of beings in trouble.

Especially in the early series, Buffy has a profoundly antagonistic relationship with the Sunnydale authorities; she is arrested for Kendra's murder and expelled from school at the behest of Mayor Richard Wilkins, himself precisely the intially shadowy super villain in whom comics regularly trade. Challenged by Xander in 'Selfless' (7.5) over her decision to execute Anya when the latter turns back to evil, Buffy says 'I am the Law', echoing both Batman and the English comics character Judge Dredd.

The Slayer is, almost by definition, a vigilante protecting the run of humanity from supernatural menaces of which they are for the most part blissfully unaware (in this way, Slayers are not so much like standard superheroes who combat menaces of which the public is aware as they are like Tolkien's rangers and wizards). On a day-to-day basis she protects individuals and occasionally she confronts Apocalypse. Buffy, partly because she survives so long, learns to carry out her mission with discretion – she spares Spike and Harmony on several occasions because of her intuition that this is the right thing to do. This is often compared to Bilbo and Frodo's decisions to spare Gollum; it is also cognate with, for example, Matt Murdock's advocacy of the rehabilitation of the Gladiator, whom he had defeated as Daredevil.

Buffy acquires a support group in the Scoobies, several of whom become or are significantly powerful beings in their own right. Not only would they have died without her long before they developed those powers and abilities, but they would, as we see in 'The Wish' (3.9), have become particularly formidable vampires. In various of the alternate worlds beloved of Marvel Comics, we have seen figures of righteousness such as Iron Man turn to the bad; I have already mentioned how, in Alan Davis' *The Nail* for DC Comics, even as harmless a figure as Jimmy Olsen is shown to have serious potential for evil without the positive influence of Superman and Clark Kent.

One of the standard, though often debated, assumptions of the modern superhero comic is that, for many of us, moral standing is a product of contingent circumstances, that what it takes to change people to the dark side is what the Joker, in Alan Moore's *The Killing Joke*, calls 'one bad day'. Though the Batman of *The Killing Joke* disputes this, and the Joker's experiment in driving Commissioner Gordon mad fails, it is clear that a standard comics assumption is that some become evil by choice and others have evil thrust upon them — if not at the time, then in one of the reconstructions of continuity that make comics too complex. Hal Jordan, the Green Lantern who became the murderous Parallax, had more recently been shown to have been possessed by Polaris, an ancient evil being, and to have had no control over his actions. And the influence on Batman himself of a single trauma in his past indicates that the Joker, like a number of his adversaries, has that real insight into his personality that comes from being in part one of his shadows.

This sense of evil as a contingent circumstance is important to Joss Whedon's view of vampirism, though is only a partial description of it — you can see him as being in dialogue with the comics version of this sense. On the various occasions when Angel gets his soul back, he is near-broken by the guilt of Angelus' actions;

it is as if he were not personally responsible. Spike, on the other hand, has less guilt because he accepts responsibility for his killings, when in the *Angel* television series he is nearly dragged into Hell from Wolfram & Hart ('Hell Bound', 5.4) he does not regard it as especially unfair. Yet in 'Damage' (5.11) he and Angel discuss the extent to which evil was something that was done to them as much as something they are.

By the same token, it is possible for supervillains to reform. The difficulties involved making this career change – not least in deciding what 'good' is, in the context of the lack of moral compass that made them villains in the first place – has kept various comics titles, notably Busiek's *Thunderbolts,* going for some years. Of Buffy's associates, Angel, Spike, Anya and, rather more ambiguously, Illyria, Darla and so on have this trajectory; Andrew both has it and parodies it. The vicissitudes of human–mutant relationships have caused the X-Men's nemesis Magneto to move backwards and forwards between good and evil on a regular commute. Again,

---

Vampires as Superheroes

Vampires, more or less by definition, have superpowers. When vampires choose to work for good, especially when the object of the enterprise is their own redemption or a loyalty to friends that transcends their personal status as good or evil, then those vampires become superheroes almost automatically. Marvel's version of Dracula is a supervillain, as is the vampire Baron Blood, but other characters such as Blade and Hannibal King are vampires who work for righteousness, as is the Confessor in Kurt Busiek's *Astro City* comic, a Catholic priest turned creature of the night who wears a large silver cross in order to mortify his undead flesh. Morbius is a scientist infected with pseudo-vampirism and desperate for a cure – he only fights superheroes if they get in his way. Jeff Mariotte has said that, when he went to work on the *Angel* comic, Joss Whedon specifically asked him to explore the idea of Angel as superhero.

reformed villains in Joss Whedon's work, as in comics, are always prone to backslide and be forgiven.

Faith, who refers to herself and Buffy at a point when they are finally reconciled after years of estrangement as 'hot chicks with superpowers', has a fairly standard arc for a superhero, being tempted over to the dark side and then working out her redemption by going to jail for some years. If you are a superhero, and jail cells are not built to hold you, staying in jail is an act of redemptive will, a penance imposed by your conscience rather than the state. Staying there is also a good that has to be weighed against the possible consequences of crises in which you are needed – the moment Wesley tells her (in 'Salvage', *Angel*, 4.13) that she is needed to deal with Angelus, she breaks out of jail on the instant.

Spider-Man was told by his doomed Uncle Ben that 'with great power comes great responsibility'. Most superheroes work for free and even the very small minority who do not do pro bono work much of the time, Buffy is, as an adult, always broke, as is Spider-Man. When, in 'After Life' (*Buffy*, 6.3) Anya claims that Spider-Man takes money for saving the world, Xander corrects her, not merely because he is a geek, but because he regards it as an important moral truth that Buffy, as a superhero, has to live by.

Dawn: You can't charge innocent people for saving their lives.
Anya: Spider-Man does.
Dawn: Does not.
Anya: Does too.
Dawn: Does n— (*catches herself*) Xander?
Xander: Action is his reward.
Anya: Why are you never on my side?

Of the major characters of *Buffy the Vampire Slayer*, Xander and Andrew are clearly identified as comics fans, and both Dawn and, more improbably, Cordelia in her later appearances in *Angel* show signs of continuing acquaintance with comics. The alternative is that the renegade power, Jasmine, who possesses Cordelia, is the comics fan – Cordelia's reference to the Heaven where she has been trapped as 'Misty Magic Land' (a reference to Alan Moore's

---

Willow and Kitty Pryde

One particular area of *Buffy* in which the influence of Chris Claremont is obvious is in the characterization of Willow and the indulgence Whedon and his team sometimes show to her. Some fans have assumed that this is merely a matter of Whedon's personal affection for Allison Hannegan, but it goes deeper than this. Whedon has said: 'There were few interesting girls in comics young enough for a twelve year old to crush on . . . Until Kitty Pryde. She was such a figure of both identification and affection, I even forgave her her inability to think of a decent name for herself.' Elsewhere he has said of Kitty, 'I love her logic . . . and her power, which is both cool and visual'. Kitty Pryde was one of the Claremont period's additions to the X-Men, a bright teenager and computer geek with the power to walk through walls, but whose contribution to the X-Men had far more to do with her intelligence than her comparatively lightweight powers. For the first few seasons of *Buffy*, it is Willow's intelligence as much as her growing skill in magic that is her crucial contribution to the group.

People sometimes ask why Willow is Jewish, given how rarely this is mentioned or impinges; one of the best reasons I can think of is that Kitty Pryde is. The convenience of the computer skills they both share is obvious. One of the strengths of Claremont's period at the X-Men was that his characters regularly thought their way out of trouble as well as fighting

---

then-current *Promethea* series) is entirely appropriate thematically, if surprising in character terms

Another of Claremont's strengths was ensemble writing; the whole point of the X-Men when first devised was that they be a young team, still coming to maturity and identity, as opposed to other Marvel teams like the Avengers, most of whom had their own mature adult identities and, indeed, their own comic books. They were not just about whatever the mission of the storyline was, they were about their complex interactions, their crushes on each other, their desire to have relationships with missing or rejecting parents and their need to study, as well as to save the world. The

their way out, or relying on creaking plot machinery, and Kitty was as much the brains of the outfit as their mentor figure Charles Xavier. And, of course, when Joss Whedon came to write *The Astonishing X-Men*, just about the first thing he did in the comic was bring back Kitty from the semi-retirement other writers had put her in, and start her snarking away at the powerful telepath Emma Frost (who in Joss' hands mostly sounds like Lilah Morgan, but in her confrontations with Kitty sounds more like Cordelia Chase).

It is also perhaps worth remarking that it is widely believed in the fandom that Claremont's original plan was to have Kitty grow up and come out as a lesbian. It was further believed – I do not know with how much authority – that Claremont was overruled on this by his editors at Marvel who felt, in the early 1980s, that it was untimely for the book to go in this particular direction. Certainly her relationships with Storm, her dance teacher Stevie and her aspiring evil mentor Emma Frost have a degree of emotional intensity at least equivalent to her notional romance with Colossus. And, in defence of Marvel, it has to be noted that Kitty was notionally underage at this point in her career. In any case, the vexed question of Claremont's intentions towards the character was sufficiently discussed in fandom that that too might be an influence on Joss Whedon, part of that fandom, in having Willow in due course come out too.

Claremont period X-Men are at least as relevant a model for Whedon's Scoobies, and for Angel's detective agency, and for the crew of Serenity as the original Scooby-Doo team. It is of the X-Men, rather than his own characters, that Whedon has said 'Take a few characters and really fuck them up . . . The mission statement is always "Why do I love every single character? What makes them worth writing about?"'.

I should also mention briefly that whereas for Ridley Scott, Ellen Ripley was an ordinary person capable of great heroism, and for James Cameron she was an aspect of the triple goddess, and for David Fincher she was a woman promoted beyond her talents, for

Joss Whedon, when he wrote *Alien Resurrection*, she was a superhero. She is a liminal being with a bad attitude to authority, and the scene in which she demonstrates her power during a basketball game is a classic superhero response to being bullied.

Joss Whedon's mild infatuation with Willow is one example of perhaps the most negative aspect of his infatuation with comics: Buffy and Angel, but perhaps even more so Willow, are cut too much moral slack. All three of them are to some extent examples of what Jennifer Stoy calls 'superhero exceptionalism'; their actions have consequences, but allowing us to disapprove of them for those actions is not one of those consequences. Buffy's brutality towards Spike in, say,' Dead Things' (*Buffy*, 6.13) has no real consequences for her; Angel's mind-wipe of his colleagues in 'Home' (*Angel*, 4.22) does not lead to major disasters and, had there been a sixth season, he would have been seen coping with the consequences of his Samson smash of Wolfram & Hart rather than condemned for the deaths it caused; Willow's abuse of magic is spun as an addictive

---

Serenity

I mention the crew of Serenity here briefly, partly because of the way Whedon's film *Serenity* and late episodes of his TV space opera *Firefly* such as 'Objects in Space' reconfigure the show to some extent, from being about its Clint Eastwood-like captain Mal to being about River, the mad girl to whom he gives refuge. When I first heard about *Firefly*, I described it as a cross between the pirate scenes in *Alien Resurrection* and *The Outlaw Josey Wales*, and that was a reasonable description as far as it went. When the show starts being about River, it moves from being a Western to being a superhero origin story, because a superhero, with her telepathy and programmed fighting skills, is what River is clearly in the process of becoming. Much of what I have said about Buffy as superhero applies to River – powers, bad relationship with the authorities, liminality (she is both mad and terrifyingly sane, and is first seen rising from a box which might as well be a coffin).

weakness rather than a former victim of bullying's unhealthy interest in power. Faith's attitude to jail as a personally imposed penance rather than submission to democratically constituted authorities is a more attractive version of the same tendency.

One of the strengths of good comics writing is the inexorable working out of continuity and its consequences; one of the worst flaws of comics writing and television writing is an excessive use of the reset button. Whedon never uses the reset button at the crude level of plotting, but his shows are sometimes prone to it at a moral and emotional level, particularly, it has to be acknowledged, when his overseeing of them became less close. The fact that it never became something on which he cracked down when other people were running his shows on a day-to-day basis indicates at least that he was comparatively unconcerned about it.

Joss Whedon's fascination with alternate universe versions of his own continuity – 'The Wish' (3.9) and 'Normal Again' (6.17) in *Buffy*, 'Birthday' (3.11) in *Angel* – can be seen as influenced by *Star Trek*, of course, but it is a trope most especially associated with comics in general, Marvel comics (which had for many years a title *What If?*, devoted to such stories) in particular and the various X-Men titles even more particularly still. Claremont's *Excalibur* spin-off had a storyline called 'The Crosstime Caper' and the more recent title *eXiles* deals with alternate versions of X-Men characters teaming up to repair the timeline of alternate worlds that have gone seriously wrong.

One of the current X-Men line-up, (though not appearing in Whedon's team), Rachel Summers, is quite specifically the daughter of Scott Summers and Jean Grey from a dystopian future which she time-travelled to prevent that future existing. Moreover, the changes effected by her interventions have allowed a set of circumstances in which Jean Grey can never have been Rachel's mother, having been dead at the time as a result of becoming the Dark Phoenix. The circumstances of Dawn's existence as Buffy's sister – she is essentially a supernatural artefact, the Key, reconfigured as Buffy's sister by the order of monks who protect it – are rather different, but equally causationally dodgy.

Sticking with the X-Men and getting ahead of ourselves for a moment, another intermittent member of the group, Lilyana Rasputin, was kidnapped to a demon dimension as a small child and briefly snatched back when rescued. In the time it took for a groping hand to find her again through the mists of the portal, she experienced the time to grow to maturity and become a powerful and morally equivocal mystic warrior in her late teens. Again, the personal history of Connor, Angel's son, is different, but has, shall we say, a family resemblance.

Various others of Buffy's circle have direct cognates in the world of comics superheroes and other characters. Rupert Giles' back-story as revealed in *Buffy* in 'Halloween' (2.6) and 'The Dark Age' (2.8) is closely paralleled by the back-story of the mystical adventurer John Constantine, originally created by Alan Moore in *Swamp Thing* and subsequently the central character of his own comic *Hellblazer*. John Constantine is a seedy adventurer with a provincial accent, striving to atone for the deaths of his original colleagues during an exorcism in Newcastle, the circumstances of which remained vague for some time. The parallels between what happened in Newcastle, and what Giles and Ethan had to do with the demon Eyghon in 'The Dark Age', are loose, but directly similar in this: both Constantine and Giles are haunted men with something to atone for.

The most obvious parallel, apart from the career of Buffy herself, is the career of Willow, who moves from being a mousy hacker to becoming a witch with the power to shatter worlds. This gradual evolution is paralleled by the way that Jean Grey came into the fullness of her link with the abstract cosmological principle, the Phoenix, over a period of many months and issues, before becoming its entirely amoral and murderous aspect, the Dark Phoenix, and choosing to die rather than continue to destroy her friends. Of course, there are differences. Jean Grey's sudden access of power came from sacrificing herself for her friends and being reborn, whereas Willow's came from rising from a coma to re-ensoul Angel. The first hints of Jean's darkness came during a period when she was under the sway of hallucinations of amoral power induced by the Hellfire Club – in turn, of course, a reference to the classic British TV show, *The Avengers* – whereas Willow's came when she tried to take revenge on Glory for sucking out Tara's mind ('Tough Love', *Buffy*, 5.19). Those of us who had grown up reading the X-Men could nonetheless recognize the tropes from an early stage, and worry about them.

During Willow's rampage, Andrew specifically references Dark Phoenix in his remarks about her. The somewhat disappointing handling of this matter in the show relates in part to the fact that Willow pulls back from the brink without having to pay the level of consequences that Jean Grey did. At the time the Dark Phoenix saga first appeared, it was assumed by all concerned that she would stay dead, until someone thought through the implications of her being the Phoenix. Interestingly, though, Chris Claremont, the writer, had apparently not especially intended Jean to die in expiation of her casual acts of world-shattering and had the decision imposed on him – at a stage when his original version of the script had already been drawn – by an editor concerned that the comic preach a consequences-based morality. Even in Claremont's version of the plot arc, Jean Grey was stripped of her superpowers. In the long run, of course, she came back; another thing Joss Whedon learned from Claremont in particular and comics in general is that death really does not have to be permanent when you are dealing with superheroes.

The chastened earth-linked power of the later Willow has much in common with Jean Grey's abilities. Like Willow perceiving the growth of individual flowers, Jean Grey draws on the essence of the natural order; just as Willow in her dark phase starts to suck the life out of the earth itself, Jean Grey as Dark Phoenix sucks dry the energy of an entire solar system. Often, when writing about such matters, Claremont modulates the standard rodomontade of comics into a more thoughtful mode; he is an obvious influence on Whedon on the rare occasions when the latter has to go mystical on us.

There are other elements in *Buffy* and *Angel* that can be seen as deriving from comics. The amalgamation of the Scoobies into a

---

Teen Titans – Another Parallel

In the 1980s, the X-Men's major DC rivals were that other group of superpowered teens, the Teen Titans, who were going through a particularly fine run scripted by Marv Wolfman and drawn by George Perez. The storyline collected as *The Judas Contract* reveals that a long-term member of the team, Terra, is actually the mercenary Tara who has infiltrated them at the behest of the assassin Deadshot; her malignity is revealed in scenes where she smokes, uses bad language and wears eye-liner. I find it hard to believe that a comics fan like Joss Whedon did not have this in mind when creating the characters of Faith and Tara, or the entire Angelus arc of Season Two of *Buffy*.

---

single superslayer to defeat Adam (in 'Primeval', *Buffy*, 4.21) can be seen as parallel to various precedents, but perhaps especially to the fiftieth issue of *Excalibur*, a title started by Chris Claremont though at this point written as well as drawn by the English artist Alan Davis.[1]

Obviously, we can legitimately assume that more recent comics are relevant to Whedon's work as well, since he regularly praises current comics writers: not only Alan Moore, but also Warren Ellis and Garth Ennis, for example, in his introduction to the collected *Fray*. The empowering of all potential Slayers in 'Chosen' (*Buffy*, 7.22) is paralleled by, for example, the sudden forced evolution of the entire population of Earth into superheroes in order to fight an alien menace in the World War Three storyline of Grant Morrison's tenure of *Justice League of America*. In 'Chosen', the cutting between a number of powerless and then suddenly empowered potentials all over the world is precisely the strategy that comics would adopt at such a moment. The way that, throughout the early part of Season

---

[1]   *Excalibur* was, at the time, as again currently, a team split off from the X-Men and based in England; most importantly Kitty Pryde was one of its leading members.

Seven of *Buffy*, we see potentials we have never met before suddenly slaughtered in each episode, is likewise a very comics-influenced piece of shorthand, and again, quite specifically, something that Claremont does on a regular basis. There are interesting parallels to be drawn between the serial story-telling technique of comics and television shows, and almost certainly a significant set of back-and-forth mutual influences. These are, after all, the two current artistic forms in which serials are the dominant mode of narrative. But this is potentially too vast a subject to do more than touch upon here.

I do not propose to discuss at length the extent to which the narrative rhythm of the Whedon television shows are negatively influenced by those of long-running comics titles in their failure fully to deliver a satisfactory pay-off. Comics are, after all, titles that are intended to go on for a long time, and even after the genuinely tragic end of a run like the Dark Phoenix saga, or the doomed love affair of Daredevil and Elektra, there always has to be a next issue, in which something else happens. Once the decision had been made that Buffy's story not end with her death, there was always going to be something provisional about any season end, not merely because the story goes on in our heads, but because it goes on in that of its creator.

The perfect ending of a television show – that of *Six Feet Under*, for example, where one after another the show's family of undertakers are seen dying, often a long way into the future – is one that gives us complete closure; it is incredibly rare for a comic to end that totally. Neil Gaiman more or less manages it in *Sandman*, but only by very careful planning from an early stage in the comic's run and by the use of Shakespeare's plays as part of his plot, ending the entire sequence, as he does, with the dying Shakespeare's composition of *The Tempest*, whose epilogue becomes his own. Joss Whedon's decision to allow the creation of a post-'Not Fade Away' Angel comic book, and his involvement in the comic *Buffy Season Eight*, indicates the extent to which any end to the television show and the broader story is provisional. I cannot say this without a shadow of a doubt, but I have a strong suspicion that those of us who grew up reading comics and obsessing with particular storylines are less prone to dissatisfaction with the way the stories of Buffy and Angel worked out than those who did not.[2]

Whedon as Comics Creator

Though various of the shows' writers and actors – notably Jane Espenson, Doug Petrie and Amber Benson – have written or co-written runs of the Buffy and Angel comic books, Joss Whedon's only direct contributions to the comics version of the Whedonverse come in the *Tales of the Slayers* and *Tales of the Vampire* anthology comics. In the latter, Whedon provides a linking narrative in which a vampire tells a bunch of Victorian trainee Watchers a group of stories, most of which are set in the 20th century; he also provides a somewhat by-the-numbers tale of a young Goth Tolkien fan who feels empowered by becoming a vampire. Jane Espenson and Drew Goddard's contributions to this collection are significantly better than Whedon's.

The same cannot be said of *Tales of the Slayers*, good as Espenson's Austenesque tale of a young girl and her sinister suitor is. Petrie's story about the New York Slayer is interesting for giving her a name, Nikki Wood, which is subsequently confirmed as canon. Whedon contributes a tale of the first Slayer, which discards much of what was said of her in 'Restless' (*Buffy*, 4.22) – the implication, for example, that she is prelinguistic – in favour of the more historicized version of her that appears in 'Get it Done' (*Buffy*, 7.15). The other Whedon contribution to *Tales of the Slayers* is a missing scene from *Fray* in which the Slayer of the future finds a bunch of old Watchers' diaries and the Scythe nestling among them. This at least explains how, between one issue of *Fray* and the next, Melaka Fray acquires the Scythe, because in the comic, even as collected, there is no explanation whatsoever. One of the besetting

---

2   I owe this insight to conversations with Lesley Arnold.

sins of Joss Whedon that he did not learn from his comics-reading youth is his occasionally cavalier attitude to continuity.[3]

Fray

Fray, then, is the story of a moderately amoral underclass woman in a city of the future who has never questioned why she is strong and has never had any dreams of fighting vampires. Vampires exist openly in her world, and killed her twin brother, but they are not thought of as supernatural, just as a variety of mutant or alien that it is smart to stay away from. The death of young Harth has alienated the thief Melaka from her cop sister Erin, whose job Melaka regards as that of protecting the upper classes rather than society as a whole. Erin is half concerned to bring down a sister who is a threat to her own hard-won position, half-concerned that one day Melaka will get herself into a situation out of which she cannot fight her way.

Then everything changes. A mysterious man – from the pathological cult that is all that remains of the Watchers' Council – burns himself to death in front of Fray. A demon, Urkonn, informs her of her mission to fight vampires. This she is disinclined to do, until one of her sidekicks, a young girl with one arm, is brutally murdered. It transpires that the master vampire is her twin Harth, who got the Slayer dreams and is trying to open a Hellmouth; she defeats him, with help from Erin, but he survives to fight another day. By this time, Fray has realized that Urkonn has a demonic agenda of his own, and that he killed her friend to motivate her; she executes him: 'He was a good teacher . . . even a friend . . . For a friend, I make it quick.'

Fray is an astonishingly assured piece of work. Whedon and his artist Karl Moline strike exactly the right balance between fast story-telling in multiple panels and splash pages full of an appropriate

---

[3] The letters columns of Marvel's titles in its classic period in particular were always devoted to nit-picks and positively Jesuitical suggested rationalizing fixes for them – famously always rewarded with a 'No-Prize' from the editorial staff.

sense of wonder; we first see Fray leaping off a roof in the middle of a heist with air cars buzzing past her. If there are areas of clunkiness – Urkonn has to pause the action at some points to explain to Fray the nature of her world – well, exposition has always been one of those things that a paradoxically fast-moving and kinetic form like comics has had a problem with. Whedon learned from Alan Moore how to repeat a panel in a different context to demonstrate the ongoing nature of traumatic past incidents – the events leading to Harth's death – and from Claremont how to manage ensemble: one of Fray's strengths is that for someone who thinks of herself as a loner, she has a lot of people who will come out and fight the vampires when she says it is necessary, including her sister and a whole bunch of other police patrolpeople.

The relationship between *Fray* and the rest of the Slayerverse is complex. The first issue's opening sequence takes us to the barren wastes of a demon world where Urkonn consults with his masters among mausolea and flayed corpses; if anyone has ever wondered what a post-Apocalyptic demon world looks like in Joss Whedon's mind, they could do worse than check this more or less canonical version.

The back-story of Fray's world is that at some point in the early 21st century, a Slayer and her allies rid humanity's Earth of their supernatural predators and closed off dimensional portals for good, with – it is implied but not specifically stated – themselves on the other side. Since then, potentials have been born and have come into their power, but without recognizing what it is; the Watchers have become a cargo cult of fanatics. The presence among humanity of various sorts of mutant – Fray's fence Gunther is a water-breather who looks rather like the Creature from the Black Lagoon – means that super-strength is just another oddity among many, and that when vampires reappeared, they were just regarded as another minority of the odd-looking and dangerous. Fray's world is, in other words, an interesting reconciliation of all of Whedon's shows; this future of slums where the sun hardly shines, and of upper classes moving above them in aircars is not inconsistent with *Firefly* and we can, I think, take it that the back-story of the last active Slayer is at least a closing storyline that Whedon at one point considered. The early issues of *Fray* appeared in 2001, even though later issues were delayed until 2003, appearing either side of the *Buffy* TV episode 'Chosen'.

Fray herself is more like Faith than she is Buffy, while having a sense of guilt about her brother and a sense of responsibility for the other denizens of her slum that is not apparent in the dark Slayer. She steals from the rich, and to a very large extent gives to the poor; what she does have in common with Faith is foolhardy confidence in her own abilities and a pronounced degree of self-love as well as self-loathing. She loves the thrill of action – something that Moline captures brilliantly – and also the excitement of finding moment-to-moment solutions to problems. I would suggest that a major influence on the way she improvises descent from lethal heights by swinging from cornice to passing car owes a lot to classic Spider-Man and Daredevil. Of all the comics spin-offs from *Buffy* and *Angel*, *Fray* is perhaps the best, certainly until the new *Buffy Season Eight*, because it is least constrained by TV continuity, freest to draw on the great comics of the past.

The Astonishing X-Men

Whedon's work on *The Astonishing X-Men* (not all of which has been published at time of writing) is as caught up as any other Marvel comic in 40 years of continuity, and revels in the fact. In the first pages of Whedon and John Cassaday's 24-issue run, Kitty Pryde returns to Xavier's school where she was trained and, as she walks through its halls and drifts through its walls, she and we reminisce about the past, reliving past images of Kitty's arrival at the school and occasional teen rebellions against Xavier. The past is most especially relevant, since one of the reasons she has been asked back is because Emma Frost, formerly the White Queen of the Hellfire Club, has asked for her. Emma needs, she claims, someone without recent loyalties to her as a team member to watch her. Kitty does not need to watch her, Pryde says, remembering past encounters, 'I can smell you'.

The recruitment of Frost to the team after years of villainy and at best neutrality is one of the relics of Grant Morrison's particularly fine run on the comic. Many fans were suspicious of Whedon's handling of Emma Frost, given his past form with strong morally complex figures like Lilah in *Angel*. They saw what he did in issues 12–18 of his run as essentially taking back Morrison's innovation and retrospectively making Frost's turning away from the dark side a mere stratagem, and not even hers. In the event, Whedon managed to have his cake and eat it: Cassandra had implanted a suggestion into Emma, as Emma trapped her, which had become a full-blown manifestation of survivor-guilt and fear of returning to evil. Emma is betrayed by what is false within and plays on the worst fears of her team-mates, fears that each of them manages to survive and overcome. She returns to herself in time to put the nearly awakened Cassandra back in her box and that, for the moment, is that. Emma and her colleagues are then abducted by their alien enemy Ord and have to defer any post-mortem on her actions until later.

In the long run, Emma may even have done them a favour. It is clear, for example, that the seduction of Scott Summers, the team leader – which Morrison showed as starting on a mental level long before the death of his wife Jean – has become something more; Frost may destroy Summers, because it is in her nature to do so, but it is clear that she has feelings of a sort for him, even as she apparently blasts his mind. The Scott who survives this is a significantly more effective leader than he has been for some time.

There were always clues in what Whedon showed us that things were not entirely as they seemed. When, at the end of Issue 12, we have what appears to be a reveal of the Big Bad, with Emma joining up with a re-established Hellfire Club that includes Sebastian Shaw and Cassandra, there are clues for those of us who were paying attention that this is a delusion in Emma's mind. One of the club is a grey-faced Goth girl, who was, as it happens, the dead child whom the X-Men found in Emma's arms when they dug her out of the ruins of Genosha early in Morrison's run – she is a clear signal not only of delusion but of survivor-guilt. Whedon plays fair, but only if one is paying attention.

The antagonism between Emma and Kitty is one of the strongly written personal relationships that Whedon has brought to the mix. As I say earlier, relationships are always what this comic book has been about when it has been any good, in the hands of Claremont and others, as much as its wonderfully lurid storylines about risks to the fate of the world, the universe and the human race. Because consummation of the Summers/Frost relationship was the reveal on which Morrison ended, Whedon had, along with the writers of the other titles in X-continuity, the job of showing the reaction of other team members to it. Wolverine, for example, arrives in Scott and Emma's bedroom with a viciously sarcastic 'Which stage of grieving is this?' and he and Summers promptly fight, leaving Emma Frost to complain of being stuck in perpetual rivalry with the dead woman her lover still cares about enough to fight over.

It is not that Whedon brings to the comic a psychological realism that was not there before; on the contrary, he is not signally better at this than Morrison, or than Claremont, even the tired and repetitious Claremont of now, as opposed to his glory days in the 1980s. It is that Whedon is a rather funnier writer than either of them. Under Claremont, the team developed a nice line in dry banter that was used among themselves as much as to disconcert villains, but Whedon's dialogue is snappier. What is also noticeable about Whedon's comics dialogue is that it is closer to sounding like spoken dialogue, broken into parallel bubbles of short speech between breaths, than that of many others. He is perfectly capable of the rodomontade that is one of the besetting features of comics writing – some would say besetting sins, but I disagree – but in general his comics dialogue is laconic and anti-romantic. Again, he is not special in this, Brian Michael Bendis has made a trademark of something similar, but Whedon does what he does with great élan.

The storylines of the first two six-issue runs are full of Whedon trademarks. An alien – Ord of the Breakworld – is on Earth trying to destroy the X-Men or, failing them, humanity, because of a prophecy that one of them will destroy the Breakworld. He has funded a genetic 'cure' for mutation; he is in alliance with the more ruthless sections of the US government who regard the rights of mutants as nugatory beside the possibility of war with aliens. I have remarked above on the resonances of the 'cure' – *X-Men: The Last Stand* derived this storyline directly from Whedon, apparently; I will also comment on the extent to which fulfilling, averting and ironically outwitting prophecies is a Whedon trait.

The second storyline is equally resonant with Whedon's other work and with his skill in looking again at things we have come to take for granted. The X-Men have always trained in a computerized room of pistons and holograms called the Danger Room; it is as much part of their schtick as the costumes and the fast jet. Whedon comes up with a particularly intelligent 'what if?' – what if the computer that controls the Danger Room came to sentience? What would it feel about the young people it is supposed to test to near-destruction? And further, if you were Xavier and had to weigh the welfare of your team against that of a newly intelligent computer, which would you choose?

This is a storyline that enables Kitty to save the day through intelligence and empathy rather than relying on the brute strength of the men in the team. It is a chance for the team to quarrel, again, with their mentor, and among themselves. It is also the sort of intense powerful stuff for which we turn to Joss Whedon in whatever medium he chooses to write:

Xavier:	You made me so proud
Colossus:	You knew she told me in her head, right as I was about to crush her
Xavier:	Peter, I'm certainly not going to breach your mind right now. What did Danger say?
Colossus:	She spoke the moment you upgraded the danger room, the moment she was born, she called out to you.
	Professor, will you tell us what she said?
Xavier:	Where am I?
Colossus:	It took her a long time to know that you heard her, and ignored her. You knew that she was alive and you

kept her trapped for years so that you could run your experiments. You understand why that is a problem for me.

Xavier: I didn't ... By the time I realized what had happened. I saw no other course. My team needed to be prepared. Mutantkind needed to be protected. Whatever the cost.

Wolverine: What you been doin, Prof? Hanging with Magneto, cause that (expletive deleted) sounds just a little too much like him.

In the final arc of Whedon's run on *Astonishing X-Men*, still underway at time of writing, the inner struggle is largely done with and replaced by an external one again. The team, temporarily split by circumstance, but reunited in spirit, travel to the Breakworld, and whatever their good intentions, will doubtless fail to cheat prophecy. Ord and his peers, like most villains in comics, fail entirely to understand that to attack people in order to frustrate a prophecy is almost certainly to ensure its fulfilment. If this parallels all sorts of things in Whedon's television work – from 'Prophesy Girl' (*Buffy*, 1.12) to the 'father will kill the son' storyline in the third season of *Angel* – it is because he learned his plotting from comics in the first place, that he gives back to the form what he took from it to begin with.

7 Superherovision

From Comic to Blockbuster

Keeping Faith with the Original

When a story is uprooted from one art form – from the novel, say – into another, such as film, it is hardly germane to complain that the finer points of the novel have been lost in the film. A film may have subtleties of its own, but they will not, in general, be the same. Actors may use details of the writer's characterization as guides for how to inhabit the character, but equally may have their own ideas, while a designer's vision may be informed by a sense of period detail radically different from the author's. Many fine novels adapt into mediocre films, while some of the best films trust the strengths of books so forgettable that only scholars remember them. What is important is that the adaptor find in the material adapted some kind of truth, important to them and to audiences, both to an audience that carries over into the resulting film specific aspects of the original's plot and characters and to an audience that has no such close expectations.

The adaptation of various superhero continuities into blockbuster films has been characterized, at its best, by consideration of what Bryan Singer calls the essence of the material; the important thing is not to include every single detail of characters, but rather to discover the emotional truth of what the characters, and the major stories surrounding them, mean and then work with that material in an intelligent way. Superhero films have to find a large multiplex audience, but they have to do so without alienating the large body of fans of the comics, who will have certain expectations and whose goodwill is important to the word of mouth.

At the very end of Singer's second X-Men movie, *X-2* (2003), comes a moment that is entirely sublime to those of us who grew up on comics, most especially on the X-Men comic and the other productions of the Marvel group, and entirely mystifying to anyone else. Jean Grey, the telekinetic Marvel Girl, has given her life to save her friends, a group of young mutants, and the two men who love her have been seen stifling both their manly grief and their deep mutual dislike. On the face of the waters where she drowned there appears for a second what might be merely a flash of light, or might be the shape of a bird. In cinemas, one half of the audience sighs deeply; the other half doesn't.

This is because those who read comics know that continuity is being, in essentials, followed, and that the flash of light is a hint of Jean's eventual return as the Phoenix; the sigh is because all too soon, she drifts to become a force of amoral destruction as the Dark Phoenix. She dies heroically, but the power that brings her back is more than she can control. Even though later writers and artists tried to take it back, it is one of the authentic moments of tragedy in a popular art form in which the tragic only occasionally rings true. Singer, himself someone soaked deeply in this material, is at once too much an artist and too much a fan not to allude to the bittersweet inevitability that he at that point hoped to film.

The 40 years or so that most of the major Marvel titles have been appearing monthly on news-stands, the 60 years and more of DC, ensure that all of them have associated with them iconic moments that matter deeply to those of us who grew up with them. Perhaps they do not matter as much to us as Lear on the heath, or Emma snubbing Miss Bates, but they are as important as Holmes and Moriarty going together over the Reichenbach Falls. When they turn up as moments in big, blockbusting movies, it is a minimum requirement that the movies honour the emotional truth of those moments; movies and comics both trade in dreams and need to deal honestly with their audiences.

*   *   *

It is not always so, even when the film overtly copies specific images. The unsatisfactory Ben Affleck-starring *Daredevil* (2003) includes a moment important to anyone who followed the adventures of the blind vigilante lawyer during its finest hour – the period when Frank Miller was writing it. Elektra, played by Jennifer Garner (the disturbed father-obsessed woman assassin whom Daredevil loves), fights and is beaten and killed by the even more competent assassin Bullseye (Colin Farrell). He flicks a playing card that cuts her throat, and then impales her on her own trident. Her wounded lover crouches over her dying body as sirens wail in the distance. In the original, Elektra's death was a deliberately shocking image. Miller intended it to be read specifically as a sexualized killing of a kind that the heavily censored comics industry rarely allowed. By specifically copying the image and dialogue that were once shocking, director Mark Steven Johnson ends up weakening the moment's effect; it is perhaps the fact that he has copied it so precisely that we notice, not its power to shock.

The problem is Affleck; Garner has some of the right mad intensity and Farrell almost exactly the demon-king brutal deftness. Daredevil has always been the most interior of comic-book superheroes – in Miller's hands, each issue was an extended soliloquy of straining muscles and Catholic guilt – and Affleck and Johnson give us almost nothing of that inwardness. Having your hero repeat, with varying degrees of conviction, 'I'm not the bad guy' is so much less subtle than the best of the material they were drawing on as to be almost laughable.

This is a particular example of a more general issue about filmed comic books. It is almost too easy now to put on the screen what we saw on the garishly printed page, and only by making it difficult again is it ever going to work as well as it once did. Some of the best *Daredevil* artists – Romita and Colan, for example – were working for a writer, Stan Lee, Marvel's Ellington, who would give them a scenario and then add script to their drawings. At their best, the scenes, often using radical revisions of the standard comic-book grid, of Daredevil moving silently through the city he protects have a fluid grace that supersedes, rather than imitates, a sense of real elapsed time. Those still moments of motion, though, were the product of hours at a drawing board and the exercise of real skill.

To imitate that grace, but not the sense of effort that lies behind it, is always going to end up looking cheap. It is almost too easy to produce a CGI version of your hero and set him swinging from virtual building to virtual building. Significantly, one of the few really effective moments of *Daredevil* is the scene where hero and doomed heroine meet: a cute and brash pick-up, politely resisted, turns into a mutual display of martial arts skill as mating ritual; the stars fake it a bit, with wire work and stunt doubles, but there is actual flesh actually straining. Singer relies on CGI far more sparingly and less obviously in the X-movies. When, in *X-2* the teleporting midnight blue be-tailed Nightcrawler (Alan Cumming) raids the Oval Office, he flashes in and out of space so vigorously that the Secret Servicemen, and at least one eminent movie critic, Alexander Walker, think that there are several of him. Singer does not make the magic of superpowers look easy, and that is why his movies work. When Sir Ian McKellen, as the villainous Magneto, pulls the iron out of a victim's blood and uses it to smash holes in his prison, the actor makes it look difficult, and spends as much skill on portraying the strain of mental muscles as he does on the character's complex motivation.

It is not just that Singer loves the material, it is that he respects it and the processes of its production, and knows enough to let well alone. Marvel's were always the hip politically liberal comics; the material about mutants was always intended as a parable about the consequences of bigotry for us all. Magneto is an interesting villain because he is a terrorist responding in kind to the violence levelled at his people. (The comics often had as a subtext the possibility that he was right, the brief of the X-Men being very much that they defend people who hate and despise them and elect governments who periodically try to kill them.)

Ang Lee's *Hulk* (2003) is almost a fine film, though it failed at the American box office by comparison with, say, Singer's two films or Sam Raimi's *Spider-Man* (2002). Part of the problem is that the monstrous alter ego of his hero Bruce Banner is entirely CGI. The technology used – which draws on and distorts Eric Bana's features and the director's face-pulling – is inferior to that which mapped Gollum in Peter Jackson's *The Two Towers* (2002) on every last twitch of Andy Serkis' performance, and we are not yet ready for an entirely virtual protagonist. Oddly, the Hulk's galumphing leaps across the landscape are something that CGI can do well; that, and showing things being smashed. Yet, in the end, this can be done no more effectively than through a few lines on a page of a comic book.

In *Hulk* (2003) Ang Lee understands that the resonance of the Hulk comes from the fact that he is at once the werewolf, Frankenstein's monster and King Kong. He is the creature of violence that bursts from the id of an ordinary man; he is the creature made by science; he has as his main weakness his love for a woman. Jennifer Connolly does an admirable job of updating heroine Betty Ross – here Banner's fellow scientist – and Sam Elliott is extraordinary as her obsessed father, General 'Thunderbolt' Ross. For Lee, this is also a tale of fathers – an issue that obsesses him – and he rewrites the Hulk's back-story so that the creature is produced by a mixture of Banner and Betty's work on medical nanotechnology and ante-natal genetic manipulation of the young Bruce by his disturbed murderous father (Nick Nolte). Accordingly, the Hulk is not merely an expression of an average man's suppressed rage, but the instrument of his equally brilliant father's murderous spite.

This is interesting enough in itself as a revision of the comic's version of the origin story that it might have worked. The final confrontation, in which father and son have both become monstrous, lacks both that fine brutal madness that Stan Lee would have brought to it back in his heyday and that particular poetry that Ang Lee himself brought alike to the domestic drama of *The Ice Storm* (1997) and the aestheticized mayhem of *Crouching Tiger, Hidden Dragon* (2000). In the end, *The Hulk* does not work, but not for lack of skill or lack of intelligence or lack of love for the material, proving that it is as hard to adapt the textured resonances of 40 years of a comic book's continuity as it is any other literary source.

Stars in Their Class

Superman Films

The gold standard of superhero movies was set by the first Superman film – *Superman The Movie* (1978) – and by the first two Batman films, films that were dealing with characters so thoroughly embedded in popular culture that at some level audiences do not need to be told the crucial facts about them. Superman is, of course, one of the few figures in modern popular culture to have a life in our minds that no longer connects with the vast body of lore known as the continuity of the DC Comics Universe. He was born on another planet, carried to Kansas in his space-travelling cradle, reared humbly, and periodically dies to relieve the world's pain. In summary, his career sounds like a creed, which is why we feel, from time to time, the need to blaspheme. Some of us, come to that, do not clap hands to save Tinkerbell either.

Superman was invented by Jerry Siegel and Joe Shuster in the mid-1930s USA as at once the ultimate tough Jew on whom people did not pick and, in his guise as Clark Kent, the good-hearted greenhorn learning the big city from goyish sophisticates. At their best, Donner's original film and Bryan Singer's *Superman Returns* (2006) capture both those aspects of the character in a way that acknowledges 70 years of story – the utter implacable charming strength of Superman, the fussy competent clumsy charm of Clark and the amazing capacity of the characters around them to fail to realize that they are the same person.

Donner's original film starts off with pomp that was much mocked at the time but has worn surprisingly well: Jor-El (Marlon Brando in his most Shakespearian mould) helps despatch some miscreants to the Phantom Zone, and *Superman II* (1980), before deciding to send his son away just in time to escape the explosion of Krypton. The icy crystalline quality of Krypton's buildings and the austere asperity of Brando's tone are carefully contrasted with the home in Kansas where, in a second prelude, the future Superman grows up. Mario Puzo's intelligent screenplay is built around the realization that Superman is a man with two fathers, Jor-El, from whom he gets power and knowledge, and Jonathan Kent, from whom he learns to have a heart. This is less of a contradiction than it might have been, because Jor-El always intended him to be Earth's servant and saviour, but Jonathan and Martha are what makes that possible.

Superman retreats into the seclusion of the Fortress of Solitude and then arrives in Metropolis in a pair of fake eyeglasses to be about his fathers' business. Here he meets his soulmate Lois and his antagonist Luthor. One of the problems with the Donner film, let alone with the Dick Lester completion of Donner's second film and the subsequent inferior films with Christopher Reeve, is that too much of it is played for light comedy. This works, much of the time, with Lois – in spite of the reactionary implications of a plot that depends on an investigative reporter taking until the second film to notice the obvious – because Margot Kidder and Reeve manage to suggest sexual chemistry that sizzles, and because the comedy between them does not stand in the way of the darker side of their relationship, the lengths to which she is prepared to go for a story and the death from which he has to break his father's rules to save her.

It works far less well when Luthor is turned into an arrogant clown rather than a competent evil genius; Gene Hackman talks a lot about his brilliance, but his schemes are too vicious to be amusing, while being played in too broadly comic a tone to be upsetting or threatening. Nor does it help that he has the frenzied mugging of Ned Beatty at his side; in the first film, and the early parts of the second, he does have the entirely charming Valerie Perrine as his floozy. It is an interesting difference between the climate of the 1970s and the 2000s that in the earlier film, Perrine's Miss Teschmacher sneaks a kiss from the temporarily incapacitated Superman before saving him, on condition he divert the missile Luthor has sent winging towards her mother before saving

California, and Reeve is at some level flattered by her attention. There is no such moment of grace between Brandon Routh and Parker Posey in Bryan Singer's *Superman Returns*.

The strength of the first film, and what is good about *Superman II*, has in large part to do with the presence of Reeve, who manages to be knowing enough in both his personae that we are taken into the joke, while at the same time conveying a steely integrity that is no joke at all. It is a fascinating performance simply because it is an internally contradictory one. In the first film, Superman's adversary is Luthor, but his real enemy is time and chance and mortality; his home dies before he is old enough to affect it, and his adopted father dies of a heart attack. Luthor's attack on California jeopardizes thousands whom he does save, and kills Lois, whom he only rescues by turning back time. In the second film – Donner's cut of which was about to be released at time of writing, but was not yet available – his opponents are Zod and the other criminals that his father imprisoned, but his real enemy is his own desire for a normal life.

There is an incoherence here: the rule that he has to renounce his power to be happy with Lois, or renounce Lois to regain his power, is a completely arbitrary rule, imposed from beyond the grave by Jor-El, which only makes sense as plot convenience. There has to be a way for him apparently to lose his power in order for him to be able to defeat three equally powerful opponents, whom he tricks when he cannot defeat them. The other major incoherences in the second film are that Zod – impressively played by Terence Stamp – has no real agenda, bar dominance for its own sake, and that Luthor continues his alliance with the Kryptonian criminals, quite ludicrously, even after the third time they have betrayed him and decided to kill him. Good as the first and large parts of the second Superman films are, they do suffer from the belief by director and screenwriter that in important areas a comic book movie does not have to make sense.

After his work on the *X-Men* franchise, one had hoped that Bryan Singer would make more of the revived *Superman* franchise than he did, yet he ended up not merely repeating much of Donner and

Puzo's storyline, but much of the time recapitulating Lester's corny comedy. Returning to Metropolis as Clark, Superman struggles through the *Daily Planet* with enormous suitcases, not because he is feigning physical weakness but because they hold his life, are unwieldy as well as heavy. Yet there are moments where the comic has a darker tone that is rather more appealing: when a minor hood steps up and fires a bullet into Superman's eye, it flattens and falls to the ground; Superman looks at him with a glint in his eye that reminds us of what a man of such power could do, if he were not such a paragon.

At such moments Brandon Routh captures the magnetism and the strength of the character, as well as displaying a gift for physical comedy. Elsewhere – and elsewhere means far too many quarter hours of film – his performance is overly concerned with reverence, not merely to the religious parable, but to the legacy of the late Christopher Reeve. Routh has acknowledged that, much of the time, he did not so much act as imitate Reeve; however much one admired Reeve's patient fortitude in the face of humiliating illness, his knowing twinkle in the part was not something that should have been copied here.

Singer has, to a worrying extent, remade Richard Donner's 1978 movie, but in a darker key; his little bits of homage include recycling some of Marlon Brando's footage as Superman's Kryptonian father. As Lex Luthor, Gene Hackman wanted to break California from the mainland; reprising not only the part, but the scam, Kevin Spacey's sardonically murderous Luthor builds a new continent that will swamp the East Coast. Reminded by Kate Bosworth's Lois Lane that this will kill millions, he retorts, in the film's best line 'Millions? Billions . . . Yet again the press underestimates me.' There is a gutter viciousness to Spacey's Luthor as he stabs Superman with a deadly Kryptonite shiv that gels inadequately with light comedy touches copied from Donner.

We have, in so many respects, moved on since 1978. Parker Posey is as charming as Luthor's brainless floozy as was Valerie Perrine, but the joke was thin even then. What has worn less well is the assumption that Lois, most brilliant of investigative reporters, has never worked out that her hick colleague is the man of her dreams. This is a worn-out piece of 1940s sex war comedy, only made tolerable by the implied lubricity Kidder and Reeve brought to it, and both the comics and the TV show *Lois and Clark* dispensed with it long ago. It particularly does not work when we realize that Superman's absence on his homeworld has coincided with Lois' bearing his child, moving on to a more quietly heroic fiancé and writing articles of great bitterness on 'Why the world does not need Superman'.

There is nothing wrong with this sort of re-imagining – Mark Millar recently produced for DC an alternate universe in which Superman, reared in the Ukraine, became the heir to that other man of steel, Josef Stalin, and Grant Morrison's run revisits the charm of the 1950s Silver Age – but it needs to be more daring and less reverential. In the first two X-Men movies, Singer made good superhero movies because the Marvel characters lack that weight of significance held by, for example, Superman falling spent to Earth, after lifting Luthor's continent, in a posture of crucifixion.

Singer is at his best in, say, a flashback to the young Clark running exhilarated through cornfields and leaping into the sky. The film is intelligently designed; the clash of periods within the material is resolved by having the high tech of a modern newspaper office jammed into an art deco office no one likes to tamper with, which is not a bad metaphor for the film, come to that. Singer's vast special-effects budget makes us believe that a man can fly, all right, but the fatal uncertainty of tone that characterizes the screenplay and performances of *Superman Returns* leaves us uncertain that we need especially to care.

Batman Films

When fans heard that *Batman* (1989) had been placed in the hands of Tim Burton, they did not know what to think. After all, at that point in his career, Burton was as known for the quaint quirky camp of *Pee Wee's Big Adventure* (1985) as for the significantly darker *Beetlejuice* (1988). It was at least as plausible that he would pursue the jokey nonsense of the Adam West television series of the 1960s as that he would go with the dark tormented psychosis that was, in the mid-1980s, the cutting edge of the character as written by Frank Miller and Alan Moore. His decision to cast Michael Keaton, with whom he had worked on *Beetlejuice*, seemed like a pointer in that direction; Keaton has to be one of the least massive stars ever cast in the role of the Batman, or even considered.

Yet, in fact, there was a reason, apart from a good working relationship, why Burton had chosen him – he had already decided that part of his vision of the Batman was that the costume should be physically massive rather than the man inside it, that the sheer weight of the Batman's feelings of responsibility for the people of Gotham should have an objective correlative in the relationship between the suit and the man inside it. Burton argues that he needed an actor who could make it plausible that no one ever suspects Bruce Wayne of being the Batman; Keaton's comparative slightness made him a good choice here and also enabled him to play Wayne as a slightly Gatsbyish figure whom people do not recognize at his own parties. This is in contrast to the normal portrayal of him in the comics – Wayne is always a presence, even when he is pretending to be a social butterfly.

The production team had to experiment extensively with possible costumes in order to have a Batman suit that provided the necessary level of physical impressiveness while also being something inside which Keaton could act and move; even as it is, there are times when he is stiffer in his moves than is entirely appropriate to an action hero, and one may surmise that these were from early shoots, since his movements do become more fluid in some of the later sequences. What all of this loses is the sense of the Batman as someone who can move at great speed: the various set pieces, as when the Batman rescues Vicki Vale from the Joker and they abseil to safety, have ponderousness and weight where they should have had agility.

Of the serious actors cast as the Batman in film – I am omitting Adam West from consideration here since the film he starred in is so wholly and solely a spin-off from the television show – Keaton was vastly the best until Christian Bale, whom I somewhat prefer. Keaton gave the character vocal authority when it was needed and had a sense of the absurd, which meant that the long scene in which he tries to come out to Vicki Vale – as the Batman, but she assumes otherwise – is genuinely funny and ambiguous. He also gets the character's intelligence, the scenes where he and Alfred go through CCTV footage trying to work things out make us respect him, as well as the deep spiritual anguish: the scene where, spied on by Vale, he places flowers on the site of his parents' death is genuinely moving.

Much of the casting of the film is quite extraordinarily good – Pat Hingle plays Gordon as a man solidly in middle age, and at one point it was considered having him play Gordon as a young patrolman who consoles the young Bruce. Billy Dee Williams was an effective piece of colour-blind casting as Harvey Dent, and it is a matter for some regret that they did not stick with him when, in *Batman Forever* (1995), they got round to Dent in his later incarnation as Two-Face.

One of the things that characterize the Burton films for good and ill is that they avoid stupid decisions, but often come up with half-smart ones. Sam Hamm and Burton came up with the idea that the film should show the Batman as a man in love, as someone who has found one way of curing his psychic pain and is offered quite another in the shape of true love. The trouble with this is that they chose not to give him a heroine who was in all respects his equal; Kim Basinger is beautiful and shows signs of intelligence, but the character of Vicki Vale as written is a talented photographer with an alleged long history of war journalism (she has just returned from Corto Maltese, the war-torn island also referred to in Miller's *The Dark Knight Returns*), but who shows remarkably little capacity for taking care of herself in situations of physical danger.

The trouble with using Vicki Vale as the heroine is that she is a character from the 1940s and 1960s, whom Burton and Hamm failed to reinvent significantly in the feminist 1980s. There are reasons why she was largely dropped from the comic by Julie Schwartz in the 1960s; she was always a Lois Lane clone, more interested in finding out the truth of the Batman's identity than in pursuing Bruce Wayne. There are, in the vast sea of continuity, considerably more interesting female characters for the Batman to be involved with: Talia, the daughter of R'as Al Ghul, and the mother of the Batman's one known child, for one. Burton deliberately made a film that was set in several time periods simultaneously – the cars, the fashions and the buildings could be the 1930s, the 1950s or the near future – but in this particular respect, they went retro and it was not a good idea.

The other half-smart decision made was to cast Jack Nicholson as the Joker and to re-imagine the Joker as a character whom Jack Nicholson could play. The result is certainly magnificent in its way: Nicholson has a gift for the sinister and the demonic and for making a line as innocent as 'Haven't they heard of the healing power of laughter?' something wondrously appalling. Burton and Hamm made the entirely reasonable decision that the Joker is the Batman's shadow self and then pushed the point far too far. Not only did they have the Batman make the Joker what he is today, by precipitating his fall into a chemical bath that bleaches his skin and distorts his face – and in this they echoed Alan Moore's *The Killing Joke* – but they decided to over-egg the point by having Jack Napier, the Joker's earlier self, be the young thug who killed Bruce Wayne's parents.

This is too neat an idea to get away with unless with far more subtlety than Burton and Hamm bring to the table. As it is, when the Joker tries to kill Bruce Wayne – not having any idea of who else he is – he uses the line 'Have you ever danced with the devil in the pale moonlight?', a phrase he used 20 years earlier when threatening the child Bruce with his gun and which he likes to say before killing people, though we almost never see him do this apart from on these two occasions. To have the pair of them argue, during their final tussle, over which of them is responsible for the other's existence is to labour a point into the absurd.

The decision to make the Joker a man whose former identity as Jack Napier was already gratuitously murderous and occasionally whimsical, to have his defining characteristics previously present and merely pushed into extremity by his physical disfiguring, is too much of an explanation. The point of the Joker, as he evolved down the decades, was to be the evil Lord of Misrule, a figure who needs no reductive explanation because he is a principle of the universe. Moore's version – in which he is an innocent driven mad by tragedy and 'one bad day' – is already a revision of this, and not an unintelligent one, but it is not reductive so much as pushing the question to one remove. Sam Hamm's version is too pat and therefore too rational for a figure who embodies the casual cruelty of unreason. There was a further problem, which is that, by the time he came to play the Joker, Nicholson had already started to move from being stocky to being portly; he was too essentially solid a figure to play a quicksilver trickster with entire conviction. Powerful as his delivery of his lines is, it has a tendency to the portentous, which undermines their cruel flippancy. When he poses as a mime artist, or a ringmaster, it is always a matter of an earthbound presence playing with costume, rather than a devil-may-care figure playing another cruel game.

Hamm and Burton introduce an element of specifically sexual sadism to the character through Alice (Jerry Hall), the woman over whom the Joker quarrels with his gang overlord, and whom he disfigures with acid – announcing casually to Vicki Vale that Alice is the first sketch for the masterpiece he intends to make with her – and either kills or drives to suicide. This is not entirely alien to the things they admired in the comics: Alan Moore's Joker in *The Killing Joke* is less explicitly sexual in the scene in which he cripples Barbara Gordon, but there is a strong fetishist element in the scenes in which he tries to drive her father mad. Miller's Joker is almost explicitly in love with the Batman – 'Batman . . . *darling*' are the words with which he awakens from near-catatonia.

Alice loses her identity when she has her face cut and burned and has to hide what is left of herself behind a mask, a mask that, once she is dead, the Joker crushes like an eggshell. He does this in front of Vicki, indicating very clearly the sort of destruction he wishes to carry out on her, a destruction that is precisely parallel to his trashing of an art gallery in the name of his infantile ego.

Identity for men, in this film, is all bound up with the creation of a persona of strength; identity for women is bound up with their physical beauty. Comics have their own dark record of grotesque sexism, but the Burton film takes this to a new level.

Happily, in spite of all these mistakes and missteps, there are positive things to record about what was, and remains, one of the best films made from the general continuity of a comic book, if not from specific material. I have already referred to Keaton's performance and to the minor parts; Burton is surprisingly good at crowd scenes as well. What Burton did achieve, by hiring Anton Furst as designer, and through wonderfully gloomy cinematography – which fed back into the comic almost as much as the film took from it – was a sense of Gotham City as a concrete place and a state of mind. Bob Kane took Gotham's name from traditional representations of New York as a city of fools, but Burton, like others before him, saw that the Gotham of the comics was an essentially Gothic creation, and he went with what that gave him.

In its best sequences, the film is a wonderful blend of the action thriller of its own time and the expressionist gothic nightmares of earlier ones; there is no particularly good reason why the Joker should drag Vicki with him into a deserted cathedral except that it enables Burton to make the final fight between the Joker and the Batman into a distorted equivalent of a sacred marriage and do so on vertiginous heights with grinning gargoyles as witnesses and weapons. Much of the look of this sequence foreshadows Burton's later *The Corpse Bride* (2005) with its more explicit profanation. It is no small praise to say that one of its major strengths is just this – it *looks* like the idea of a Batman movie.

On the other hand, *Batman Returns* (1992) looks like the Platonic idea of a Tim Burton movie and is nonetheless splendid, and nonetheless a good Batman movie for that. The opening, after all, is pure Burton and might almost have been an out-take from *Edward Scissorhands* (1990) or one of Burton's stop-motion animation films: the hideously deformed child that will grow up to be the Penguin is abandoned by his upper crust parents, themselves no oil paintings, and dropped neatly in a cradle into one of Gotham's rivers, where he is swept away into an underground world of sewers and the concrete caves that serve as their meeting points. It is winter then, and it is winter 33 years later; *Batman Returns* is a film about justice and revenge and the coldness of heart that is necessary to go through with them, and it is also a film about Christmas and how the vengeful forget its meaning.

When people talk casually about *Batman Returns*, they often talk of it as a film with two villains, by which they mean that it is a film with two supervillains in it, forgetting that its real villain has nothing super about him except for his cheerful malice. There is never any pretence that Christopher Walken is anything other than bad; his name, Max Shreck, is almost that of Max Schreck, the little-known actor who played Nosferatu, and part of his grand scheme is to suck Gotham dry of its electricity under the pretext of giving it new supercharged life. This is a film in which the demented freaks have a certain amount of justice on their sides and the charismatic ordinary man is the stone killer who throws his inquisitive secretary out of a high window for knowing too much. He is a man who inhabits Bruce Wayne's world rather than the Batman's, and it is Bruce Wayne who sticks a major spoke in his wheels of intrigue by simply refusing to invest any money in his schemes.

Walken is extraordinary in this role, he was some years from the pretty boy psychopath he had been in *The Deer Hunter* (1978) and *Annie Hall* (1977) and had not yet matured into the demented paterfamilias role he plays in most of his later films, though that role is foreshadowed here. He has effortless charisma and is wonderfully patronizing; he plays the Penguin like a violin and is mercilessly condescending to the shorter, less gorgeous Wayne. Even before he decides to kill her, he treats Selina Kyle with an obnoxious sexism – 'We haven't yet housetrained her, but she makes a damn good cup of coffee' – that is a significant part of what will turn her into his nemesis.

Lest it sometimes seem that I am obsessed with comics continuity at the expense of things that are wonderful, let me clearly state here that Daniel Waters and Burton reinvent Catwoman and the Penguin

---

Heathers' Team

I have written elsewhere about Daniel Waters' script for *Heathers* (1989); it is worth pointing out that one of the strengths of *Batman Returns* is that it reunited the team of scriptwriter Waters and producer Denise De Novi and is visibly a product of their sensibility effectively melded with that of Tim Burton. Max Shreck is a more charming version of JD's satanic capitalist father, and Selina's persona as Catwoman is as much a revenant as Veronica in *Heather's* last scene. You become your real self by dying and being reborn – this is a Waters obsession (see also *Demolition Man* (1993)), though it is presented here in less religiose terms than it is in *Heathers*.

---

almost entirely, and that their versions are, if anything, superior to anything that comics have come up with, with the only partial exception of the silken smoothness of Jeph Loeb's Catwoman in *Hush!* and elsewhere. The Waters/Burton Catwoman is quite explicitly a reaction – not entirely a positive reaction – to feminism; at one point, rebuking a woman she has saved from muggers with the remark that 'you make it too easy', she goes on to say, 'I am Catwoman, hear me roar', echoing a well-known slogan.

Selina is almost a caricature of the good secretary with the hopeless life, saying, 'Hi honey, I'm home', like Lucy Ricardo every night she returns to a flat empty except for knick-knacks, mirrors, soft toys and clothes. Sanity has given her no identity, she is the daughter of a demanding mother and the secretary of a monstrous boss, and the only relationship she has is with her cat. When she is thrown to her death, it is the cats of Gotham who revive her, in a scene that makes no literal sense, but who cares? She is the spirit of female vengeance and the cat and she are also suddenly bizarrely sexual, whether in the leatherette costume she makes for herself, or in the identity of Selina, which has now become even more of a mask for the real her than Bruce Wayne is by now for the Batman.

Waters does not avoid the sexual comedy of Selina and Bruce's relationship: when Bruce dates Selina, they both have to make excuses and leave, and when they finally recognize each other's dual identity – after accidentally reprising, as Selina and Bruce, banter about mistletoe they exchanged in their masks – she says plaintively, 'Does this mean we have to start fighting?'. Their relationship is doomed, as opposed merely to not working out: she is the spirit of vengeance and he has sublimated his vengeance into a desire for justice. She wants to kill Shreck and he wants to have him sent to jail; as it happens, Shreck shoots her repeatedly, and she mocks him that all he is doing is taking away some of her nine lives, before frying him with one of his own power cables. She vanishes, seemingly dead. Bruce thinks he sees her from his car, but we cannot be sure of her survival until the last frames of the movie, when we see her on the rooftops of Gotham, looking up at the Batsignal.

What makes all of this work is not just Waters' script and Burton's direction, it is Michelle Pfeiffer whose performance here is quite extraordinary. After all, she has to make plausible several versions of the same woman – the oppressed secretary, the demented dominatrix and the slightly deranged possible girlfriend to name but the three most obvious poles she moves between – and to give all of them star quality and sexual charisma. There are many reasons for disapproving of Hollywood's sexism and this is one of them: that an actress as good as Pfeiffer got so few good roles by comparison with her male contemporaries and that those dried up when she got a little older.

Danny DeVito's performance as the Penguin is partly a matter of the prosthetics and the design, but he also brings a vengeful seediness to the part that makes what he does acting as well as a cartoon. He is an ugly little man, unsure in his humanity, but he is also a lecher and a glutton, both of them in an unappealing way. At one point Shreck tosses him a whole salmon and he chews it throughout the next scene, dribbling blood and guts onto his evening clothes. The Penguin is vain and unrealistic in his attempts to seduce Catwoman and a fool in his preparedness to be seduced from villainy to politics by Shreck. He is also, like all the best villains, an overreacher; he seizes control of the Batmobile and takes it on a rampage and makes the mistake of gloating at the seemingly helpless Batman, who almost casually records his words and uses them to discredit him in the middle of his political campaign. He is funny and horrid and murderous and disgusting; the thing that kills him, though, is that he betrays his own essence by trying to cast other first-born children into the sewers as he was cast, and then by using his own totemic birds as suicide bombers.

Up against three barnstorming performances like Pfeiffer's, Walken's and DeVito's, all that Keaton can do as Bruce or the Batman is hold his own as the straight man. In this film, the fact that he is the Batman is more or less a given and is only really examined by showing how good he is at it; there are many reasons why he is more accomplished and sane than his two shadow doubles here, and one of them is that he has put his energy into competence rather than demonic glee. This is in many ways the best Batman movie, simply because it gets what has always been the essence of the comics: that this is a man with problems, who has turned his anger into a fuel for justice and a joy in being good at things.

This is one of the aspects of the character largely lost in the next two films – *Batman Forever* (1995) and *Batman and Robin* (1997) – not least because when Joel Schumacher took over the franchise, he made some bad decisions about casting, including both the actors he hired as Batman. Notionally, at least, Tim Burton was the producer on *Batman Forever*, but it has never been clear how much input he had into it; it is significant that he makes no contribution to the extensive commentaries on the DVD release. Schumacher has talked at great length about the pop sensibility he wanted to impart; this was in large part the worst kind of music-video glitz, an over-miked sound-track and the use of a particularly garish palette in the design work. Generally speaking, the look and sound of Schumacher's films are inferior in look to the best of the Batman animated films – *Mask of the Phantasm* (1993) say, or some episodes of *Gotham Knights*.

Schumacher has also said that he cast Val Kilmer as Bruce Wayne in *Batman Forever* on the strength of his performance in *Tombstone* (1993); this is interesting because it helps to define what is peculiarly maladroit in his casting here. Kilmer was, indeed, extraordinary in *Tombstone*, playing, not the hero, but rather his eccentric doomed sidekick; Kilmer's Doc Holliday is a wonderful foil to Kurt Russell's deliberately stolid Wyatt Earp, a Southern gentleman-rogue who swaps Latin tags with the Ringo Kid and mocks the cult of the quick draw with a small silver tankard. But this does not qualify him to play either Bruce Wayne, whom he makes vaguely petulant and spoiled, or the Batman, for whom he lacks the authority. He is not helped by a dull Robin – Schumacher picked Chris O'Donnell after, he claims, considering both Ewan McGregor and Jude Law, a choice which, if true, is incomprehensible – and a vapid heroine. Nicole Kidman is a fine actress, but was given very little to do as a mildly depraved psychiatrist. The film is also weakened by its villains: Tommy Lee Jones never brought his considerable gifts to the part of Two-Face, preferring to mop, mow and grimace rather than to think out his performance; nor does it help that Jones is not the best-looking of men and that the unscarred side of his face is marked with lines, pocks and wens when the point is supposed to be that there is a contrast.

The performance by Jim Carrey as the Riddler is one that transcends consideration of good or bad acting into sheer weirdness; at a late stage, he says, 'Was that over the top? I can never tell', and a sighing audience reflects that his director should have been able to, even if he couldn't. There is a weird homoeroticism to the relationship between the villains here, as a progressively more sequinned Carrey twines himself around his partner in crime. Again, one should not fetishize continuity, but the point about the Riddler has always been that he was the astute trickster criminal, the auguste to the Joker's vicious pierrot, and Carrey plays the part as if he were auditioning to play the Joker.

It is such a cliché of discussions of superhero films that *Batman and Robin* represents some kind of nadir, certainly for that franchise, and arguably for the genre, that one is almost tempted to look for arguments for its rehabilitation. Certainly, there is a floridity to its badness that makes it more sheerly enjoyable than more boring bad superhero films like *Catwoman* (2004); a lot of money and even talent was expended on making a film that was this execrable. Several of the people who turn in quite remarkably dreadful performances have been good in other films: Uma Thurman, for example, whose Pamela Isley/Poison Ivy is a thin retread of the mousiness and demented sexiness of Michelle Pfeiffer's Catwoman, or Alicia Silverstone as Batgirl. Others, like Arnold Schwarzenegger as Mr Freeze, are just as bad as you would expect – which is interesting, given that Joel Schumacher appears to have considered getting Schwarzenegger on board as a dealbreaker for this movie.

Schumacher is certainly a significant part of the problem, here as in *Batman Forever*. He made the decision to opt for a light touch, in the name of making the franchise more 'family friendly', but his idea of a light touch is ill-timed and often tasteless jokes. Hardly has the film begun but Robin is bickering about having a motorcycle rather than a car and Batman is looking at the camera and saying 'This is why Superman works alone'; this is one of the very first lines George Clooney's Batman gets to speak and it seriously cuts into our chances of regarding the character as having the necessary gravitas and authority. Schwarzenegger's Freeze has joke after joke, most of them to do with the violent death of civilians; even James Bond's jokes – a schtick which has grown tired with the years – tend to be directed at people who have just paid the price of trying to kill him. *Batman and Robin* tries to recapture the campy archness of the 1960s television show, but has a catchpenny nastiness that deprives it of the innocence that went with that camp.

One problem is the designs for Gotham, which are Anton Furst re-imagined by a hyperactive child with a taste for Soviet posters and art nouveau; the beetling tower blocks of Gotham have been supplemented by monstrous concrete giants in contorted poses, holding up viaducts and the like. Gotham's Observatory, where much of the action takes place, is situated inside a giant sphere held up by a vast Atlas. One looks at the excess of this and wonders. Another issue is the new look of all the Batman's kit, from his car to his Batarangs to some handy individual heaters he pulls out of his utility belt when he needs to save Freeze's victims. These are constructed to be shiny, black and slightly fetishistic. Schumacher explains that he was told to redesign all of this in order to make them – his word – toyetic; we are used to films being hampered by the necessity of making a particular release date. *Batman and Robin* was produced to be coordinated with the release of toys.

For once, we cannot entirely complain that comics continuity has been neglected; Pamela Isley has Woodrue as her mentor, though he proceeds to betray her and attempt her death in a way that precisely parallels, and copies, Shreck's murderous attack on the future Catwoman. On the other hand, in a remarkable piece of telescoping of two parts of the DC Universe, Woodrue's major scientific enterprise is not plant-related, but the devising of Venom and the creation of Batman's steroid-fuelled nemesis, Bane. Or rather, it is a character who looks like Bane, but is almost entirely devoid of menace, being merely a heavy who does some of Poison Ivy's heavy lifting for her. I have written previously about the comics' strip-mining of their own continuity; it comes to something when a film franchise is allowed to pull all the teeth from a character that later episodes in the franchise might have wanted to do properly.

There are a very few things to relish in *Batman and Robin* other than for sheer kitsch value; Clooney is occasionally moving in his scenes with Michael Gough's dying Alfred, and Gough himself is unfailingly excellent in his last performance in this role. On the other hand, Pat Hingle is made to debase his role as Commissioner Gordon by having the old man lose all dignity under the influence of Poison Ivy's pheromones. The film is distinguished by some truly weak fight sequences, of which the one between Ivy and Batgirl is perhaps the most ineffectual; one young woman in black leather fights another who is wearing tight-fitting green leotards and brandishing a poisonous whip made of vines, and there is no charge to the scene whatever. What is the point of reducing the Batman franchise to the level of a cheap camp exploitation blockbuster and then not even delivering a good fetishist catfight?

*   *   *

One of the things that made the decision to revive the *Batman* franchise even remotely sensible was the sheer enthusiasm of Christopher Nolan to be involved with it. After the inventive psycho-thriller *Memento* (2000), he was a hot property, who got through the second-feature problem with reasonable success – *Insomnia* (2002) is not a great film, but it is not a disastrous failure either. He and his scriptwriter David S. Goyer on *Batman Begins* (2005) brought intelligent choices to the project. Nolan combined the early stages of Batman's career in Gotham, for which he had some particularly fine sources in continuity, Miller's *Batman: Year One* and Loeb's *The Long Halloween*. They also decided to spend a large part of the film not merely on the death of the Wayne parents but on the missing years during which Bruce acquired the skills that made him into the Batman.

The mechanism they chose for this was a villain who was added to the roster in the 1970s: R'as Al Ghul, the leader of a vast international conspiracy devoted to smashing modern civilization in order to put purifying barbarism in its place. They were true to the essence of the continuity's handling of this figure; he may never have been quite the father figure he is here, but he is, for example, the grandfather of the Batman's son. Casting Liam Neeson in the role was as intelligent a choice as using R'as in the first place, he has the accumulated authority of his mentor role in *Star Wars I – The Phantom Menace* (1999), not merely a mentor, but a mentor's mentor.

This is a film full of fathers, in fact: Nolan gives the young Bruce Wayne several to choose from, not least among them Michael Caine as Alfred. Given the charming effete world-weary Alfred that Michael Gough had sustained through four films, Caine had to provide something very different; he plays Alfred as a sergeant-major who is the source of much of Bruce's strength and all of his self-confidence. When Bruce asks if, during his absence, Alfred ever gave up on him, Caine gives his reply 'Never!' precisely the right combination of actorish resonance and parade-ground gravel.

Nolan had money to spend on his cast: Morgan Freeman makes Lucius Fox, the head of R&D at Wayne Enterprises, yet another father figure – the man who provides the Batman with his armour and his car and his grapple gun and who, after a boardroom coup, will run Wayne Enterprises so that Bruce does not have to. Gary Oldman, as Jim Gordon, manages to look quite stunningly like the drawings of the younger Gordon in *Year One*. Interestingly, Nolan picked up on the idea, mentioned by Burton as something he thought of, but did not do, of Gordon having been the patrolman who looked after the boy Bruce in the aftermath of his parents' death.

Nolan picks up on Loeb's idea that there used to be conventional gangsters in Gotham before the masked maniacs filled their ecological niche. Tom Wilkinson as Carmine Falcone, in a couple of very impressive scenes, demonstrates to the young Bruce that the city is run by powerful evil men. Wilkinson also demonstrates the utter powerlessness of ordinary criminals in the face of what is to replace them; it is the work of moments for Cillian Murphy's Doctor Crane – the Scarecrow – to reduce him to gibbering wreckage. In a movie full of great bulls of men, Murphy's silky slight villain is a useful contrast; he can be effortlessly sinister without raising his voice and manages to convey a sense of the doctor who is sick that imparts wonderful wrongness to his every scene.

The fact that the weapon R'as and Crane bring to bear against Gotham is fear usefully counterpoints the essence Nolan reads into Bruce's character, someone who is frightened of his own capacity for fear and has projected it outwards. Nolan's version of Bruce Wayne is a man who was scared by bats when he fell into the cave as a child, and who believes that his fear is what killed his parents by making them leave the opera early – he saw the demons in Gounod's *Faust* as more bats – and walk into the alley where they die. As he matures, Bruce learns to take that fear and project it outwards; his Batman decides that criminals are a cowardly and superstitious lot as a remedy for his own fear and his own irrational guilt.

Just as the hideously sane but amoral R'as comes to an accommodation with the merely criminal Falcone, whom he plans to betray and destroy, and the deranged criminal Crane, in order to pursue his agenda of destruction, so Bruce learns to make an alliance with what he hates and fears, to become what he hates and fears. Whereas when a child he was driven to distraction by bats, now, as the Batman, he summons them to distract his enemies. The performance of *Faust* that he gets his parents to leave is far from being an irrelevant decoration. He is aided in this quite subtle interpretation by an extraordinary performance by Christian Bale, who brought to the role the same steel-eyed intensity he had shown as Patrick Bateman in Mary Harron's *American Psycho* (2000). It is interesting that Nolan chose to cast neither an action hero nor a matinee idol like Clooney, but a young character actor; in this he made, in a very different way, the same sort of intelligent choice as Burton with Keaton. The only real weakness in Nolan's cast is Katie Holmes as the love interest, and even she has the odd excellent scene: when, at the end, she acknowledges that she has realized her childhood playmate is not the wastrel she thought, but a man of responsibility, and nonetheless walks away from him, she is quietly chilling.

Interestingly, Nolan only used CGI in *Batman Returns* to tidy up the stunt-work and miniatures on which the film largely depends; he believes that to make the incredible look real, it has to be as real as you can make it. His Gotham is less fantastic and baroque than the one Anton Furst built for Burton, partly because the additional decorations Schumacher had added to that look had spoiled it; the Gotham of *Batman Begins* is a combination of the golden city with its monorail and centralized services and the slums that exist in the shadows of its infrastructure as if they were in another decade.

Gotham is a character in Nolan's film far more even than in Burton's; its very modernity is the weakness that R'as planned to use to destroy it, by pumping Crane's fear gas through the high-pressure water-mains. When Bruce realized what R'as was about, he burned his remote monastery home about his ears; R'as replies by destroying the Wayne mansion, but fails to understand that

Gotham, far more than any mere house, is the habitation Bruce's father left to him. To save that city as a living organism, the Batman is prepared to destroy a significant part of it, the monorail.

The theme of fatherhood is tied up neatly in the last act: Lucius becomes head of Wayne Enterprises, Alfred pulls Bruce from the burning mansion, and Jim uses the weaponry Lucius provided to blow up the monorail. When Bruce leaves R'as to die, it is because he has found replacement fathers who will honour what his actual father left him, rather than trying to destroy it in the name of some utopian vision of destruction. In the ruins of the mansion, Bruce finds the fragments of his father's stethoscope; he has become the Batman, but he is also being acknowledged, by this legacy, as the physician and surgeon that Gotham needs.

Spider-Man Films

The temporary collapse of both the major DC-derived superhero franchises is part of the reason why Hollywood belatedly turned to Marvel as a source for material to adapt; another delaying factor here was that the major Marvel creator, Stan Lee, was still active and influential, and, after abortive Captain America and Nick Fury films, disinclined to cooperate with film projects that were not as good as they could be. Even so, some of the resulting Marvel-based films were more or less unsatisfactory: I have mentioned *Hulk* and the disappointing *Daredevil* and will pass over *The Fantastic Four* (2005), only pausing to mention that it was a film doomed by hopeless miscasting of most of its principals. The obvious exception, Michael Chiklis, had pretty much cast himself as Ben Grimm by walking up to people at parties and demanding the role; he was good, but casting directors are supposed to find the right person, not wait for them to turn up.

Sam Raimi's first *Spider-Man* adaptations are two of the very best superhero adaptations simply because they show a respect for the material that is rational and yet not slavish; they are free recensions of the origin story, the feuds with the Green Goblin and Doctor Octopus, and a version of the Mary Jane Watson love story. They are films neither of the original comics, nor of the *Ultimate Spider-Man* storyline, but draw freely but sensitively on both versions of the continuity. Without being flashily well-written (even though the sometimes-florid Michael Chabon worked on the screenplay of the second), they are solidly plotted; characters are given comprehensible motivations from the start that expand and become more complex in a way that draws on the complexity that years of comics make possible. They are a model of what films that draw on comics might be like.

The title sequence of *Spider-Man 2* (2004) – a sequence of images drawn by the hyper-realistic comics artist Alex Ross – does the double duty of reminding us of the events of the previous film and that we are to spend two hours in the world of Marvel Comics. When Steve Ditko and Stan Lee invented Spider-Man, the whole point of him was that he was young, vulnerable and made mistakes. Even more than the first film, *Spider-Man 2* inhabits not only the vehement acrobatics of the comic-book, but also its occasionally lachrymose emotional territory – rather more movingly because the corrosive effect of necessary secrets is a more common experience than the acquisition of vast power.

One of the major strengths of both films is the nearly profligate quality of the casting: a franchise that casts Cliff Robertson as Uncle Ben and Rosemary Harris as Aunt May is not stinting on the casting budget. Willem Dafoe has just the right level of insane glee to play Norman Osborne and the Green Goblin; he is also convincing in his scenes as Harry Osborne's disappointed bullying father – we believe that the Goblin's attempts to corrupt and co-opt Spider-Man are in large part a continuation of his earlier attempts to build a relationship with Peter Parker.

It might have been a repetition too much for Raimi to have built an element of paternal concern into the relationship between Parker and Doctor Octavius, before the latter becomes a monster – Alfred Molina has a chubby authority that is absolutely right and makes Octavius an appropriately tragic figure. 'I don't want to die a monster', he says as he sacrifices himself to save New York from what he has built, and it is one of the most moving lines Molina has ever delivered on screen. The fact that he is a man who, had an accident not robbed him of moral sense, might have been a mentor to Peter is present, but not over-stressed.

Rather than give us the complicated roster of Spider-Man's love interests, the films opt for the *Ultimate Spider-Man* strategy of having Mary Jane Watson be the girl of his dreams from the beginning; Betty Brant appears in her role as Jameson's invoice clerk, but there is never any clear reference to the brief liaison that existed between her and Parker in the comics. It is Mary Jane rather than Gwen Stacey that the Green Goblin hurls from the bridge, and she survives where Gwen Stacey died. The version of Gwen that appears in the third movie, played by Bryce Dallas Howard, is a thin shadow of the original who is essentially present so that Peter, during his brief period of contamination by an alien parasite, can demonstrate moral corruption by playing two women off against each other. It was pointless to introduce Gwen to so little ultimate effect.

One of the films' real strengths is the portrayal of Mary Jane by Kirsten Dunst, who has charm, vulnerability and emotional strength in equal measure. We believe in her as the woman as driven by dreams of a successful career as model and actress as Peter is by his sense of responsibility and his guilt; one of the most successful things in the first two films is the moment near the end of the second where he explains to her why they can never be together and she tells him that he is wrong, that she is strong enough to take the risks involved in being his love. And she proves it time and time again.

The first film has a moment of quite incomparable tenderness when, after Spider-Man has saved Mary Jane for the second time, he hangs upside down and she rolls down his mask to free his lips for a kiss. It is erotic precisely because he trusts her to roll it thus far and no further, and because she understands the game they are playing enough to comply with his wishes. It is a particularly intelligent piece of writing in the second film that it is when she starts to think again about that kiss that Mary Jane starts to realize that her friend Peter has never let her kiss him for fear that she will recognize the feel of his mouth. Kirsten Dunst understands the emotional good sense that makes Mary Jane Watson so much more than a Lois Lane clone; she walks out on her wedding to John Jameson and comes to Peter's apartment in her white floaty gown and is the girl of his dreams in his arms for a moment. A police siren screams past and he reacts; and she lets him go, knowing that the price of being with him is that he will always go off to his duty of being Spider-Man and leave her standing. The last thing we see of her in the second movie, though, is not the devastated sorrow when he left her at the end of the first; it is the resigned smile of a woman who knows that she has got what she wanted and is prepared to pay the price for it. Dunst has not been praised nearly enough for her work in these films.

Tobey Maguire's large eyes and hurt sensitive mouth make him ideal casting in the first film, where he has to start out as one of life's victims, a nerd bullied at school, and only gradually come to terms with his powers and the obligations they impose on him. He is, though, good at joy, at discovering he has become muscular overnight, at discovering that he can run around rooftops and swing down avenues, and is still as good when his face is covered by a mask and we cannot see those eyes.

In the second film his Peter Parker has had two years of having his life wrecked by his sense of obligation. Patrolling the streets cuts into his college course-work and his friendships; he has cut himself off from his sweetheart Mary Jane to prevent her being used as a hostage. The exhilaration of the highly coloured action sequences is set against the highly specified greyness of Parker's daily real life: a cheap flat, a greedy landlord, dishonest employers. When his powers appear to fade, it seems like a solution; the image of Parker walking away from a trashcan with his costume in it is one of many Raimi usefully copies from decades of the comic. Maguire is also good at mixed feelings: when it seems that he is losing his powers, he has to cope with the temptation of thinking that this is a good thing, and be called back to his duty by circumstance and by a pep-talk from Aunt May; unlike either of the comics version of the storyline, this Aunt May knows, even if she does not know that she knows. Maguire is perhaps a little prettier than one's ideal Spider-Man, but he has everything else that the role takes.

Where Raimi supplements the original material, it is occasionally with pregnant in-jokes; Spider-Man shares a lift with Hal Stark, the comics-obsessed Michael Novotny of the American version of the TV series *Queer as Folk*, implying a subtext to Peter's fraught relationship with his best friend Harry. More often, it is to undercut the daftest bit of the premise: Kirsten Dunst gives real authority to Mary Jane's fury at being left out of his decisions about their relationship, whereas in comics she always knew and resented not being told. When a wounded, mask-less Spider-Man is passed over the heads of Elevated-train passengers he has just saved, the convention of the secret identity is stretched close to breaking point, as it needs to be.

Raimi loves this material, but his attitude to it is never unthinking; he makes explicit in his films things that have often only been implicit in the comics on which they draw. Part of the tragedy of superhero and supervillain alike is that their roles are a seductive trap, an addiction whose name is endless repetition; this may be a feature of comics, but it is also an acute observation. Octavius' response to the disaster that killed his wife and warped him is to steal the equipment that will enable him to do it all over again, only more destructively. The difference between him and the younger Spider-Man is partly this – that he can only break the cycle by dying, whereas, by finally telling the truth, Parker can choose to change.

Spider-Man 3 suffers in general from an over-egging of the pudding and in particular from a failure to develop the themes of the second film seriously. In particular we simply have too many villains: we get the Sandman – a being made of sand in the Marvel Universe – who is reconfigured as the accomplice of the robber in the first film and as the man who actually shot Uncle Henry. The problem with this is partly that the Sandman is altogether too second-string a villain to carry the film and that the second thought that makes him Henry's killer brings the whole thing dangerously too close to make Spider-Man's back story identical to Batman's in general and movie-Batman's in particular.

We get the alien parasite and the rival photographer who it takes over and transforms into Venom, Spider-Man's evil twin, once Peter himself has rejected the corruption that goes with its power. One of the problems with this is that it is material from rather later in the comic's arc – the Venom storyline is darker than quite suits the tone of the films thus far. More importantly, neither of these villains can carry a movie by themselves, while together they are not an alliance that has any great resonance.

Lastly we have Harry, torn between his desire to avenge his father on Peter and his awareness that the Green Goblin is not a good thing to be. Having the trilogy culminate in Harry's redemptive death means that the focus on the trilogy is as much on Harry's arc as it is on Peter's or on Peter's relationship with Mary Jane. The reason this is a weakness is that it parallels both other arcs. True, it is about the valuable lessons Harry learns about power, responsibility and virtue, lessons which parallel those learned by Peter. On the other hand, though, inasmuch as it is about Harry and Peter losing friendship and then getting it back, and this up and down process parallels Peter's love affair, the homoerotic subtext between Harry and Peter becomes something that is not a radical interpretation of the text, but close to being text itself. Having Venom and Harry in the same film is at least one shadow double too many – the third film is the weakest of the series because it over-determines the material.

X-Men Films

The other successful Marvel franchise derives much of its strength from the fact that, though he rightly sees the X-Men as a free-floating signifier with whom a lot of groups can identify and from which they can take comfort, Bryan Singer made a lot of intelligent choices concerning their specific status as icons of the way membership of a subculture, the gay subculture for example, becomes a way of building a family of the heart. Families of the

---

The Gay Narrative of X-Men

If it seems fanciful to find in *X-Men* (2000) a specifically gay narrative, consider what happens in it. The first film is the story of how one character, discovering her outsider status but not knowing what it means, goes on a journey and eventually meets another person in a similar position of ignorance, who is as entirely different from her as it is possible to be, and yet somehow is exactly the same. And suddenly both of them find themselves in a new world, full of shiny people who are also like them, some of whom are bad and some good and all of whom want to make use of them. When you are alone, being of potential use to someone else, is, after all, not the worst thing that can happen to you. This is, in most respects, the standard narrative progression of a coming-out story.

---

heart, we are shown, can be a safe place in which characters can mature and grow. By the end of the second picture, Bobby Drake/ Iceman and Anna Paquin/Rogue have stepped up to be contributing members of the team.

X-Men fundamentally reconfigures the Rogue of continuity, a former criminal of mature years, into a waif who becomes the centre of everyone's attention. As written by David Hayter, and acted by Anna Paquin, Rogue becomes to some extent what is known in fannish circles as a Mary Sue, an idealized fan identification figure. To some degree, Singer chooses to do the same to Logan/ Wolverine, whose trademark berserker violence is distinctly toned down in this first film and is only occasionally unleashed even in the second; as played by the charismatic song-and-dance man Hugh Jackman, Wolverine becomes a matinee idol rather than a heavy.

Singer could not, dealing with a whole group, give us the sort of origin story that is the standard way of dealing with the first film of a superhero franchise; he had to treat the X-Men as an established group, of whose back-stories we are only vaguely aware, into whom our viewpoint characters are inserted and eventually treated as equals, or at least – in Rogue's case – equal foci of attention. By making this the story of how two members are inserted into the group, he provides a story that makes emotional sense.

His first film, *The Usual Suspects* (1995), had demonstrated how very good Singer is at creating an ensemble and working with actors; his second, *Apt Pupil* (1998), had given him a good working relationship with Ian McKellen, which meant that the question of whom he should cast as Magneto was solved pretty much from the outset. In a very real sense, that set the pattern for his casting as Charles Xavier of Patrick Stewart, another British Shakespearian gone Hollywood, and with both the acting skills and iconic quality to stand up to McKellen. The very few scenes across the franchise in which they are basically alone with each other are electric, which is why Singer, and Ratner after him, ration them.

The Auschwitz scene with which Singer inaugurates the franchise is here partly to show how Eric Lensherr's journey to becoming the monster Magneto started; it also reminds us of what the stakes are in something as seemingly innocuous as a Mutant Registration Act. One of the strengths of Singer's two films is that he raises, as the comic does only occasionally, the possibility that Magneto might be right; significantly, it is only at a late stage, when the life of Rogue, his quasi-sister, is threatened that Wolverine decides formally that he has found the right side in the X-Men and Xavier. This is not because they are the side that are going to win, but because they are the side that does not decide to murder adolescent girls for the greater good of mutantkind.

One of the subjects of Singer's two films is the moral decline of Magneto, who is not even loyal to his own, and terminates his alliance with the X-Men against Stryker at a moment's notice when given the chance to exterminate ordinary humanity – McKellen is a famous Macbeth and a famous Richard, and shows his Magneto learning to wade in blood, and be a king. One of the reasons why the fandom has so relentlessly eroticized the Xavier/Magneto relationship is that they are constantly trying to seduce each other politically; Xavier in particular is trying constantly to recreate the friendship and working relationship they once had.

The first film was made on a comparatively low budget as these things go, and accordingly had to ration both its effects and the extent of its ensemble work; it has a very good secondary cast in Famke Janssen, James Maynard, Ray Park and Rebecca Romijn-Stamos. One of the few weaknesses one can impute to it is the fact that we don't get enough of the byplay within the two groups, the heroes and the villains who are, in a sense, also part of their family – that is very much a matter of time and cost.

We get far more of this, as well as far more action and spectacular stunts, in the second film, *X2*, simply because Singer was given a far larger budget. The first film dealt with an attempt by Magneto to transform a large party of the great and good into mutants, powering a ray with the life force of the unfortunate Rogue, a plan which he continued after having it pointed out to him that his victims would only change briefly, and then die. The second deals with Stryker, a military scientist who abducts Xavier and intends to trick him with mind control into using the telepathic enhancer Cerebro to destroy all mutants; Magneto affects to assist the X-Men in preventing this, but is actually planning to have Xavier kill all humans instead.

Along the way, Magneto escapes captivity; Stryker's men attack the school; Storm and Jean Grey save the jet from air-to-air missiles by the power of their mind; Wolverine fights and kills Lady Deathstrike, one of Stryker's later experiments in building super-assassins, he being one of Stryker's earlier models. Jean sacrifices herself to save the group, thereby avoiding choosing between Scott, her long-term lover, and Wolverine, the bad boy to whom she is also attracted. In the first film, the limits imposed on him meant that Singer had to concentrate on comparatively few storylines; at the climax of the second, he is cutting between seven individuals and groups and managing to remain completely coherent. *X2* is an astonishingly assured suspense movie.

It is often also very funny – an early scene of young mutants loose in a museum, or the scene where the teleporting Nightcrawler demonstrates that the White House is not safe from him – these scenes are as entertaining as some of the others are deeply disturbing. In Brian Cox, Singer found a Stryker who could hold his own against McKellen and Stewart; this is a film about fanaticism and sacrifice. In the end, after all, the answer to the Strykers and the Magnetos is that they are keen to build a world, perfect to their specifications, with the deaths of other people; Jean Grey, on the other hand, is prepared to sacrifice herself.

Another point about Singer's films is the clear division he makes in his colour schemes, especially in the first film, between scenes where ordinary life, even the ordinary life of mutants, is going on, and scenes where superheroics and supervillainy are featured. Ordinary life is many-coloured and full of light, whereas superheroics take place in dark shadows with little illumination. Now, this is partly a matter of picking a lighting scheme that will show off special effects to their best, least cartoonish, advantage, but it is also a look that contrasts the dark deeds that are sometimes necessary with the bright day of Xavier's classes and the ordinary lives through which our heroes pass. A good example of this is the scene towards the end, when Xavier and his crew appear in the White House after freezing in time everyone save the President. He can go on with his broadcast and with ordinary life, but the mutants are out there, watching. He may not have known what he was endorsing when he empowered Stryker, but he does now. They tell him, and then they disappear, taking darkness away with them; the X-Men are benevolent, but they could choose to be a threat.

It is noticeable that most of the casual grace note references to continuity, the appearance of minor characters whom only the fans will spot, take place in these warmer scenes; when, in the second film, characters who had this role in the first film start to be relevant in the darker scenes, it is because they are seen as starting to step up to take on major roles. As one would expect, these are characters like Kitty Pryde and Colossus, who became major figures in the comic as it evolved.

The evolution of these two characters, and of Bobby Drake and Pyro, the Xavier pupil who defects to Magneto's Brotherhood, is one of the ways in which Brett Ratner's continuation of the franchise in *X-Men: The Last Stand* productively drew on the rules Singer had established for the franchise, just as the mad proliferation of grace notes was something where he allowed his co-writer Zak Penn, who had worked on the second movie, to talk him into fannish excess. My own feeling is that Ratner did not entirely understand Singer's possibly intuitive and unplanned use of light and shade – he copies the dark side of Singer's palette, but not systematically.

The real problem with his film, though, is that he, Penn and Simon Kinberg decided to combine two major X-Men plots, one of which, the potentially more powerful one, ends up being skimped as a result. It is widely rumoured that one of the reasons why Singer left the franchise to make *Superman Returns* is that he wanted to make the Dark Phoenix saga and saw it as a storyline that needed to stretch across two films; this may or may not be true, but it certainly reflects the fact that *The Last Stand* becomes unalloyedly the parable about women not being able to handle power that the comics version arguably to some extent avoided being.

In comics continuity, the resurrected Jean is fine for a while with her survival and increased powers and is then tormented by dark dreams of power, a gambit, a mental assault, by members of an organization of rich mutants, the Hellfire Club, who bring out Jean's dark side and find themselves with cause to regret it. Interestingly, though the *Ultimate X-Men* opted for the same solution as *The Last Stand*, that the Phoenix is a subconscious aspect of Jean that Xavier has repressed with his own mental powers, its creative team opted for the same solution as the original – that the Dark Phoenix is awakened by malignant tampering – whereas Ratner and his team have it be intrinsic to the resurrected Jean to the extent that the first thing she does on rising is kill Scott, off screen.

This, and Jean's subsequent murder of Xavier, are radical revisions of continuity, to put it mildly, and might have worked had they been stages in a consistent escalation; Jean wants to be free, this makes sense, and killing the more staid of her two suitors, and the mentor who trapped her power, are viable ways to this. What then happens is that she stands around for most of the rest of the film looking sulky and forms an alliance with Magneto more or less by default. It is, after all, not that Magneto does not want to control her, it is that he tries to do so with his usual rhetoric rather than by telepathy.

In order to give Magneto something else to do in this film, Ratner and his writers imported the Cure plot, which is ongoing in Joss Whedon's run on *Astonishing X-Men*. They make Rogue, rather than Hank McCoy (the casting of Kelsey Grammer in this role was surprisingly effective), the X-Man so unhappy with her lot that she takes the Cure, and make the Cure Magneto's pretext for a major mutant attack on a human centre of population. What makes no sense, even when given the superficial rationale of his preparedness to sacrifice foot-soldiers – 'Pawns go first' – is Magneto's unpreparedness simply to have Jean destroy the research facility with a pass of her hand.

When Jean eventually does let loose, she is out of control, killing as many of what is notionally by this point her own side as anyone else. Logan fights his way through the storm of debris she has created, taking terrible wounds that heal as we watch; the nascent love affair between them has, as its climax, his execution of her, and Jean, in a moment of briefly returning sanity, letting him. Given the extent to which the Dark Willow plotline in *Buffy the Vampire Slayer* drew on the original Dark Phoenix storyline, it was interesting to see an X-Men film draw on that sequence in its turn; the gashes on Logan's face were uncannily similar to those on Xander's as he tries to calm the mad Willow.

Ratner's film is full of moments that look good but add nothing past that; a crowd of mutants is moved in on by troops, only to prove to be manifestations of a single mutant man. Storm fights an equally photogenic female mutant who is supposedly Callisto, but the fight lacks the context that made that particular encounter so memorable. Ratner draws on the comic for imagery, but fails to do anything memorable with it apart from killing Scott; Magneto loses his powers, but gets them back at the end; Charles is killed, but is reborn in his brain-dead twin. Even Jean's death is qualified by the fact that she is, after all, the Phoenix. *X-Men: The Last Stand* is a long way from being a shameful mess, but it is, for reasons that should have been thought through, a huge disappointment after the Singer movies.

Elektra

It can be generally accepted that one of the good things about the deeply flawed *Daredevil* was Jennifer Garner's performance as Elektra, the ex-girlfriend turned tragic assassin; accordingly, we got an *Elektra* film in 2005, which is worth considering, even though Elektra is only marginally a superheroine, or supervillain. Garner had the right elongated ranginess and yet enough in the way of curves to wear one of the more bizarrely fetishist costumes even Frank Miller has ever designed. Director Rob Bowman has pointed to the paradox of that costume, which is that assassins wear black to hide in shadows, but Elektra goes around wearing pillar-box red or scarlet; she is so arrogant that she doesn't care if people see her.

The first problem with making *Elektra* was that the character's best story in comics continuity had already been told in *Daredevil*; she is a living embodiment of Matt Murdock's emotional pain as much as a character in her own right. The second is that the best single story she has ever been given in her own right, in the Miller/Sienkewicz *Elektra Assassin*, is a story that rehabilitates her by demonstrating that sometimes an amoral assassin is a necessary person, when, as for example, here, they are after a candidate for the US presidency who is a tool of an apocalyptic conspiracy. The combination of this storyline and the extreme bondage and domination relationship between Elektra and the agent who first tries to catch her, and then becomes her accomplice, made *Elektra Assassin* a dodgy proposition.

Intelligently enough, the film's makers then went to the contextualizing material of the comic: the ongoing feud between Elektra and Daredevil's blind *sensei*, Stick, and the mysterious Hand, a sort of ninja death cult force of ultimate evil, who do gangsterism and assassin work as a sideline to keep their hand in. Elektra was trained by the Hand when Stick rejected her, but could not follow them all the way into demonic treachery; another reason why she wears red is that these teams of good and evil are traditionally colour-coded, save for the chief villain, who wears a soiled cream.

Casting Terence Stamp as Stick had a positive side – he has the requisite authority – and a negative one – he played it with a posh English accent rather than a working class one, when the whole point of Stick as imagined by Miller is that he is a high-powered martial mystic who works as a janitor and acts like a working stiff. The central committee of the Hand, by contrast, are routine bureaucratic villains, save for their ambitious princeling Kirigi (Will Yun Lee), a charismatic martial artist rather than an especially talented actor. His team of specialists are a stylish array of freaks, most of them having some relationship with Marvel characters; they are one of the areas in which Bowman shows a capacity for fantastic visual poetry of which we could do with more in this mostly earthbound film.

Elektra is hired for a killing and asked to wait two days before being told her targets, a father and daughter with whom she has already bonded as neighbours. She protects them instead, and continues to do so when Stick refuses to help them. They are outmanoeuvred and outclassed by the Hand's team even when father and daughter prove to have skills of their own, but are rescued by Stick. The girl, Abi, is a martial arts prodigy whom the Hand wish to possess and corrupt; she brings out an apparently maternal instinct in Elektra that results in scenes that are mawkishly sentimental where they are not vaguely perverse. Years earlier, Kirigi assassinated Elektra's mother, starting Elektra on her rampage of vengeance and also afflicting her with obsessive-compulsive disorder. When this manifests itself in neat patterning of everything, from bathroom supplies to a fruit basket, it is a neat gag, but Bowman and his team of scriptwriters cannot resist having it spelled out as part of her psychic wound in an entirely over-determined and over-stated way. One of the reasons why this film has a worse reputation than it entirely deserves is its nervous underlining of every plot point. When Elektra says to Stick, 'You talk in riddles, old man', it is not merely a clunky line, it is a clunky line that restates the bleeding obvious.

The confrontation between Elektra and Abi on one side and Kirigi and his team on the other deserves to be in a better film. They meet in the abandoned house and garden maze of Elektra's parents – handily close to Stick's camp in one of the script's many infelicitous coincidences – and Kirigi twirls through the air at his victims in a storm of dustsheets, among which he hides and which he manipulates with his mental powers. He defeats Elektra, who is rescued by Abi, who in turn is trapped by snakes – which have crawled out of the tattoos of one Kirigi's team – and killed by Kirigi's female minion Typhoid. Elektra summons her resources of strength and kills Kirigi and his servants, then raises Abi from death, as Stick had done for her. This latter scene is a colossal letdown; the fights, and most especially the scene with the dustsheets, are remarkably impressive up to that point.

Elektra is a long way from being a good film, but it has touches of visual invention that make it entirely superior to the execrable *Catwoman* with which it is often compared. Its strength is that, much of the time, it trusts the continuity vision of the ethically challenged heroine, and it notably falls apart whenever it shows the softer side that the character does not really have. From Miller onwards, Elektra was one of the areas of the Marvel Universe that drew on the creepily mystic side of martial arts movies, and the film uses this interplay effectively. It is sentimentality that is its principal undoing.

What is remarkable is how much Hollywood has made use of existing comics material rather than using its own. The reasons for this are essentially that the track record of invented material is even worse than that of bad adaptations of less-than-stellar comics. As another example, we have the rather good Guillermo del Toro film *Hellboy* (2004), adapted from Mike Mignola's comic books about a son of Satan turned supernatural crime fighter. We have the far less good *Blade* films, with *Blade 2* (2002), also by del Toro, adapted from a minor Marvel title about a half-vampire who kills his father's kind. There is also the entirely disastrous *Van Helsing* (2004), which draws vaguely on the Universal creature features of the 1940s, but is essentially a continuity created for the occasion, and only intermittently entertaining in its derangement.

One of the things that comics continuity gives a film about superheroes is an overarching sense of what all of this stuff is for. There are points in M. Night Shyamalan's *Unbreakable* (2000) where you simply long for the characters to reference the comics they are shown as reading, simply in order to provide short-cuts for explanations that become long-winded as Bruce Willis' hero discovers from a series of accidents, and beatings, that he is invulnerable, and Samuel L. Jackson's character persuades him to start fighting crime. At the point when Willis realizes that the physically fragile Jackson engineered the train crash that he survived and others did not – and has as his motivation the desire to be a villain since he is not a hero – you feel an almost physical need for him to say, 'so you want to be my Lex Luthor?', just to stop the string of circumlocutions with which direct reference is avoided.

Comedies tend simply to take the content of continuity for granted; the weak comedy *My Super Ex-Girlfriend* (2006) assumes audience familiarity with a vocabulary of superpowers, supervillains and mysterious meteors. The teen comedy *Sky High* (2005) does the same: a teenage son of heroes who appears to have no powers trains as a sidekick and stays true to his friends even when his powers develop; together they defeat a villain who underrates them. Even the one good superhero comedy – the Pixar-animated *The Incredibles* (2004) – draws on the whole post-*Watchmen* discourse about the role of superheroes in society, with its set-up of superheroes forced to withdraw into civilian life because of the endless litigiousness of the people they rescue, and its fanboy turned supervillain. Part of the point is that its central family's powers are inevitably ones we relate to similar powers elsewhere – great strength, great speed, invisibility and force fields, endless tensile strength. At the end, after defeating their would-be nemesis, the Incredibles find themselves up against the troglodytic Undermayor. Not only are they a mixture of the Justice League and the Fantastic Four, but they find themselves fighting a villain who is more or less the Fantastic Four's Mole Man with the serial numbers filed off.

*   *   *

Examples could be multiplied – the point, however, is clear. Superpowers are a useful metaphor for thinking about talent and the role of the talented in society, whether from the Incredibles' quite right-wing standpoint – 'if everyone's special, then no one is' – or from Spider-Man's more liberal one – 'With great power comes great responsibility'. We need to think about political power and personal autonomy and good citizenship and gender equality and the treatment of minorities, and the superhero comic has been, over the years, one of the places within popular culture where these issues were considered and given useful metaphors as tools for thinking about them. Marvel's *Civil War* storyline is only the most recent and extreme example of this. The fact that these discussions have taken place for the most part in the superhero comics of DC and Marvel, and the films adapted from them over the last decades, means that the vocabulary in which we discuss these issues has become one in which, for convenience, we use analogies drawn from those continuities. Superhero comics and films are not merely a vast narrative construct, but a way of thinking about the issues they regularly discuss. They are not about just men and women with bulging muscles and fetishist costumes; they are about the real meaning of truth and justice, and ways of living in the world.

Index

A —actor
AR — artist
D — director
DC — DC and Vertigo character etc.
E — event

F — film
M — Marvel character etc.
R — run
T —TV show, character from TV show etc.
W — writer

A title in italics without a code indicate a comic published independently or semi-independently